INDIA AND REGIONAL INTEGRATION IN ASIA

BY THE SAME AUTHOR

India's Relations with Pakistan, 1954-57

India and Regional Integration in Asia

Sisir Gupta

ASIA PUBLISHING HOUSE

BOMBAY   CALCUTTA   NEW DELHI   MADRAS
LUCKNOW   LONDON   NEW YORK

COPYRIGHT © SISIR GUPTA 1964

PRINTED IN INDIA

BY SURESH JAIN AT THE HINDUSTAN SCIENTIFIC
PRESS, DELHI, AND PUBLISHED BY P. S. JAYASINGHE,
ASIA PUBLISHING HOUSE, BOMBAY-1

Foreword

SINCE THE end of the Second World War the newly-emergent countries of Asia have been faced with the task of developing new relationships with each other, as well as with other countries of the world. Confronted by many similar problems, and with a common interest in preserving and consolidating their newly-won freedom, these countries have a common stake in regional cooperation for common ends. Yet thus far little progress has been made in regional integration in Asia.

As the major nation of South and South-East Asia, India's attitude toward regional integration is particularly important. This subject should be considered in the light of India's overall objectives and policies in foreign affairs, the role which India has played in various conferences of Asian States and in various efforts toward regional integration, and the impact of domestic policies and the attitude of Indian elite groups. It should also be considered in the light of the attitudes of other Asian States and of trends in Asian and international affairs.

All of these developments and considerations are discussed in this brief volume which is a significant contribution to the study of Asian and international affairs, as well as of Indian foreign policy. The author calls attention to the "serious impediments in the way of India playing a major role in Asian integration." He believes that these impediments are less formidable in the sphere of economics, although he recognizes that economic cooperation between the countries of Asia has as yet been quite limited, and that India's attitude toward this kind of cooperation has been a rather hesitant one. He feels that the process of integration should start in the Indo-Pakistan subcontinent, and he is convinced that "India and Pakistan have between them the most fertile ground for attempted integration in Asia"; but he realizes that many impediments stand in the way of Indo-Pakistan cooperation.

Some of the author's most challenging suggestions fall within the sphere of international rather than regional affairs, although they obviously affect India's approach to regional integration. He finds that India, in spite of its policy of nonalignment, has been a factor in the "international conflict of the Communist world" and also in "the politics of the Western bloc." Like Prime Minister Nehru, he sees many "signs of the inevitable Soviet stake in the containment of China in the region," and he points out that "the China-India problem is not a problem between the entire Communist world and India." Like Nehru, too, he hopes that India may become "an area of agreement" between the United States and the Soviet Union. If India could be a meeting ground between the two super Powers, it would indeed make a major contribution to the cause of international cooperation and peace.

The author has discussed a large and important subject with a commendable breadth of approach and perception, and he has opened up a fruitful field for further investigation. For this, all students of Asian and international affairs, as well as of Indian foreign policy, will be grateful.

Philadelphia   NORMAN D. PALMER
25 March 1963

Preface

IT IS necessary to state what this book does not pretend to do; it neither assesses non-official Indian attitudes to the question of regional integration nor does it attempt to discuss the attitude of other Asian countries to integration. It is an attempt primarily to discuss Indian official policies in this regard and also to analyze the problems as viewed in India. Since India is a key factor in political developments of the Southern Asian region, it is hoped that the book does throw some light on the general nature of the problems of regional integration in Asia.

The book is divided into three sections: the first is a brief analysis of the assumptions, motivations and style of India's foreign policy, based mainly on the foreign policy speeches of the Prime Minister of India; the second, a discussion of the various attempts made at different levels for progress in the direction of integration and India's experiences with them; the third, a somewhat analytical interpretation of the problems and prospects of Indian participation in regional integration in South Asia.

It is imperative for any adequate research on this problem to explore the attitudes of neighbouring countries to this question and also to deal at greater depth with the structure of the elites in the various South Asian societies. For, in the ultimate analysis, regional integration is a function of elite attitudes. Integration based on racial or religious solidarity, for example, may be contemplated in a future Asia where the Westernized elite has been displaced from power; but of what relevance or use would such integration be is a question which needs to be answered.

This book was written during my stay in the United States in 1961-63; a few Indian friends in Philadelphia and Boston helped me in many ways to complete it. I am particularly grateful to two friends, Dr C. N. Satyapalan of the S. N. College, Quilon, for going through the manuscript and Dr Vishal Singh of the Indian School of International Studies for making a few valuable suggestions. I am also indebted to Professor Norman J. Padelford, of the Massachussets Institute of Technology, for some very useful discussions on the theories of regional integration. My wife prepared the manuscript for the press. None of them, however, has any responsibility for the views expressed in the book.

New Delhi   Sisir Gupta
15 January 1964

Contents

CHAPTER ONE

India's Foreign Policy: Assumptions, Motivations and Style

THE INDIAN attitude to regional integration in Asia and adjacent regions is derived from its overall foreign policy objectives, as indeed it is of any other country. In understanding and evaluating this attitude as well as its possible trends in the future, it is therefore essential to broadly take into account the foreign policy of India, its assumptions, motivations and style. An attempt is made in this chapter to analyze this policy with emphasis on those aspects which have a direct bearing on the question of regional integration.

Changing Concepts of National Interests

India's foreign policy has been the product of the interaction of many and varied factors—the traditional values of Indian society, the commitments of the Indian national movement during the struggle for freedom, the nature and structure of elite opinion in India, the geopolitical realities of the State as it emerged after partition, the economic needs of a society urgently in need of a take-off, and the internal political pressures and pulls generated by a democratic system.[1] Subject to the influences exerted by these factors, the foreign policy has sought

[1]For a comprehensive account *see:* J. C. Kundra, *Indian Foreign Policy, 1947-54*, Groningen, J. B. Wolters, 1955; K. P. Karunakaran, *India in World Affairs, 1947-50*, Oxford, 1952; N. V. Rajkumar *The Background of India's Foreign Policy*, New Delhi, 1953; and Bimla Prasad, *The Origins of Indian Foreign Policy*, Calcutta, 1960.

primarily to pursue India's national interests as conceived by the governing elite. It is in terms of this primary motivation that the enunciation and evolution of India's foreign policy has to be viewed.

In one of his early speeches in the Indian Parliament, the Prime Minister stated: "Whatever policy you may lay down, the art of conducting the foreign affairs of a country lies in finding out what is most advantageous to the country. We may talk about international goodwill and mean what we say. We may talk about peace and mean what we say. But in the ultimate analysis, a government functions for the good of the country it governs and no government dare do anything which in the short or long run is manifestly to the disadvantage of the country ... whether a country is imperialistic or Socialist or Communist, its Foreign Minister thinks primarily of that country."[2] This platitude was important to reiterate in the early years of India's freedom, as for long the freedom struggle of India, conducted on idealistic lines, had in its foreign policy attitudes largely ignored some of the important considerations of a strategic and political nature.[3]

Paradoxically, the British statesmen, who decided the external posture of India in the pre-Independence years, had a greater concern for India's needs; as it happened, India was the heartland of the British Empire in the East, around which the rimlands of West and South-East Asia were built up. In one of his oft-quoted statements, the Viceroy of India and British statesman, Lord Curzon, said at the turn of the century: "India is like a fortress, with the vast moat of the sea on two of her faces and with mountains for her walls on the remainder; but beyond these walls, which are sometimes by no means of insuperable height and admit of being easily penetrated, extends a glacis of varying breadth and dimension. We do not want to occupy it, but we also cannot afford to see it occupied by our foes. We are quite content to let it remain in the hands of our allies and friends, but if rival and unfriendly

[2]*Jawaharlal Nehru's Speeches, 1947-49*, New Delhi, 1949, p. 207.
[3]For a detailed review of these attitudes *see:* N. V. Rajkumar, *op. cit.*

influences creep up to it and lodge themselves right under our walls, we are compelled to intervene because a danger would thereby grow up that would one day menace our security. That is the secret of the whole position in Arabia, Persia, Afghanistan, Tibet, and as far eastwards as Siam. He would be a short-sighted commander who merely manned his ramparts in India and did not look beyond."[4]

These aspects of the foreign interests of India escaped the thinking of relevant leaders of the freedom struggle; what is more, the understandable need to align with the adversaries of the British Empire often provoked Indian statements disowning and criticizing such concepts as imperialistic. The Indian National Congress found itself totally against the use of India as the base for the protection and promotion of the British Empire in the East. As early as 1904, for example, the Congress had opposed the British expedition to Tibet: "Tibetan expedition was but part of a general forward policy which, with the missions to Afghanistan and Persia, threatens to involve India in foreign entanglements which cannot fail to place an intolerable burden on the Indian revenues and prove in the end disastrous to the best interests of the country."[5]

It was not possible for the new Government of India, however, to define India's national interests in the way of the outgoing raj. On the contrary, they were bound by their past commitments as well as the present realities to totally re-evaluate these concepts. In the first place, the succeeding Government of India was not as powerful as the previous one. Secondly, India's partition had considerably reduced the geographical extant of the Indian State. Thirdly, the very upsurge of national sentiments which led to the freedom of India was bound to be felt elsewhere and expressed in the form of resentment to any new approach of domination. Fourthly, India's emergence in the world coincided with the emergence of a vast ideological confrontation in the world, which was backed by the

---

[4]Cited by J. C. Kundra, *op. cit.*, pp. 32-3.
[5]N. V. Rajkumar, *op. cit.*, p. 37.

changed power realities of the European and American continents. Lastly, much of the old strategic concepts were ruled out by the development of nuclear arms and the emergence of air power as the major weapon of war.

Functioning within these limitations, India had to evolve a foreign policy which would advance not only her own security but, what was immensely more urgent for her, the status of the country in international politics. It was through the advancement of this status that India sought to attract attention and sympathy for her and similarly-placed countries and also to underline the significance of the new countries in the context of global politics. One might indeed say that in the early years of her foreign policy India was pursuing the understandable search for a short cut to international status.

The Consciousness of India's Weakness

Speaking in the Indian Parliament on 8 March 1948, Nehru said: "... our responsibility is very little. We may have acted well or badly on the international stage, but we are not, frankly speaking, influential enough to affect international events very much."[6] A year later, speaking at a public meeting in New Delhi, the Prime Minister said: "We are as an independent country, a fairly young country at present ... and therefore our foreign policy is gradually developing and there is no particular reason why we should rush in all over the place and do something that comes in the way of this gradual development."[7] Speaking in the Parliament on 6 December 1950, Nehru said: "The fate of the world depends more on the USA, the United Kingdom, the Soviet Union and China than on the rest of the world put together."[8]

In a penetrating analysis of the ultimate needs of India's functioning in world affairs the veteran Indian Civil Servant, G. S. Bajpai, then the Secretary General of India's External Affairs Ministry, wrote in 1952: "India then has to develop

[6]*Jawaharlal Nehru's Speeches, 1947-49*, p. 213.   [7]*Ibid.*, p. 260.
[8]*Jawaharlal Nehru's Speeches, 1949-53*, New Delhi, 1954, p. 178.

her strength to support foreign her policy. The inherent goodness of that policy is insufficient to sustain or further it. On this view the inference that politics cannot be divorced from power holds true also for India. . . . Today, India is the major stabilizing factor for peace in Asia; the measure of stability that she can impart to this part of the world is not a matter of good intentions but of power. . . . It is not power but its misuse or abuse which is morally reprehensible. . . . Thus viewed the ideal of balance of power is nothing evil or incompatible with India's highest ideals."[9]

It is this consciousness of the inability of India to play any significant role in the traditional sense of diplomacy backed by power that governed much of the foreign policy thinking and behaviour of the country.

The Consciousness of India's Strength

It is not, however, the prospects of an inevitable reconciliation with the status of insignificance that the Indian leaders faced. Much as the country was militarily insignificant, it represented an entirely new element in world politics, of which the potential strength was of great importance. Two factors made India strong in her foreign policy functioning: in the first place, as virtually the first and the biggest of the newly-freed countries of Asia and Africa, her voice was bound to count for something in a world where decolonialization was on the agenda; and, secondly, by itself, India represented a vast country with a huge population, the future of which was bound to affect the course of an important section of mankind.

This consciousness of India's strength was particularly apparent to the Indian Prime Minister who had been known for his capacity to view events in the canvas of history. In one of his early speeches, he said: "The fact of the matter is that in spite of our weakness in a military sense . . . India even today counts in world affairs. . . . If we had been some odd

[9]G. S. Bajpai, "India and the Balance of Power," *Indian Year Book of International Affairs,* Madras, 1952.

little nation somewhere in Europe or Asia it would not have mattered much. But because we count and because we are going to count more and more in the future, every thing we do becomes a matter for comment."[10] Dwelling on the positional importance of India, Nehru said in another speech: "Now that period and epoch (of European domination) has ended and India now comes, I think, into the forefront in national events and world affairs."[11]

It is the announcement of this arrival of India in the international arena which was evidently the major preoccupation of the Prime Minister in so far as his early speeches are concerned. In carrying out this immediate post-Independence task, the Prime Minister of India stressed two aspects: the crucial role of Asia in world affairs of the impending decades; and, the pivotal position of India in Asia.

The Resurgence of Asia

Declaring the need for recognizing that a revolution was under way in Asia, Nehru carefully emphasized the nature of this revolution and the differences between the problems of Asia and the relatively more-developed regions of the world. In fact, much of the essence of India's foreign policy outlook is contained in the early speeches of Jawaharlal Nehru proclaiming the emergence of Asia.

Inaugurating the Asian Relations Conference in New Delhi on 23 March 1947, the Prime Minister of India said: "We stand at the end of an era and on the threshold of a new period of history. Standing on the watershed which divides two epochs of human history and endeavour, we can look back on our long past and look forward to the future that is taking shape before our eyes. Asia after a long period of quiescence has suddenly become important again in world affairs."[12] The theme continued to dominate his speeches throughout the early years of Indian freedom; he took particular care to stress it before his Western

[10]*Jawaharlal Nehru's Speeches, 1947-49*, p. 222.
[11]*Ibid.*, p. 235. [12]*Ibid.*, p. 299.

audiences.[13] Speaking at the eleventh session of the Institute of Pacific Relations on 3 October 1950, Nehru said: "While people readily agree that Asia has, to a certain extent, become the focal point of world tension, they relegate the Asian problems to the positions of relative insignificance and tend exclusively to emphasize the importance of European and other world problems. . . . In the perspective of things to come they were wrong in not devoting the requisite attention to the problems of developing Asia."[14]

This complaint was made earlier. "Even in the councils of the United Nations, the problems of Asia, the outlook of Asia, the approach of Asia, have failed to evoke the enthusiasm that they should."[15]

The need to underline the problems that the Asian situation posed was one of the first tasks of Indian foreign policy. The problems of Asia were not the problems of Europe and any attempt at the identification of the two was bound to understate the Asian case in the world. As Nehru put it: "There are many ways of distinguishing between what may be called the approach of Asia and the approach of Europe. Asia today is primarily concerned with what may be called the immediate human problems. In each country of Asia—underdeveloped countries, more or less—the main problem is the problem of food, of clothing, of education, of health. We are concerned with these problems. We are not directly concerned with problems of power politics."[16] Again: "Asia compels attention in many ways. . . . But what is most needed is an understanding that Asia is going through a process of change and that it is in ferment."[17] The problems of Asia were primarily social and economic, and as the political domination by Europe was

---

[13]This need for emphasis on Asia constituted the central theme of the Indian Prime Minister's speeches during his visit to the United States and Canada in 1949. Of special significance was his speech at the University of Columbia (*see* text of speech, *Jawaharlal Nehru's Speeches, 1949-53*, pp. 398-405).

[14]*Ibid.*, pp. 158-9.

[15]*Jawaharlal Nehru's Speeches, 1947-49*, p. 236.

[16]*Ibid.*, 236.

[17]*Jawaharlal Nehru's Speeches, 1949-53*, p. 159.

ending, long-term problems were being thrown up by the revolutionary ferment.

India's Position in Asia

If Asia was in ferment, India had a special status and a responsibility in regard to Asia. Various factors contributed to this phenomenon. "It is fitting that India should play her role in this new phase of Asian development. Apart from the fact that India herself is emerging into freedom and independence, she is the natural centre and focal point of the many forces at work in Asia. Geography is a compelling factor, and geographically she is so situated as to be the meeting point of western and northern and eastern and South-East Asia. Because of this, the history of India is a long history of her relations with the other countries of Asia."[18] Again: "India is very curiously placed in Asia and her history has been governed a great deal by the geographical factor plus other factors. Whichever problem in Asia you may take up, somehow or other India comes into the picture. Whether you think in terms of China or the Middle East or South-East Asia, India immediately comes into the picture.... She cannot be ignored also because of her actual or potential power and resources."[19]

It would perhaps be a legitimate conclusion to arrive at that the stress laid on India's pivotal position in Asia was meant not for Asian countries or audiences. For, every such statement had an inevitable effect of generating suspicion of India's ambition for Asian leadership. In fact, in almost all the speeches, the Prime Minister of India took special care to deny India's claim or aspiration for leadership. "People vaguely talk of India's leadership in Asia. I deprecate such talk."[20] Obviously, the Indian attempt was to underline her own potential role in Asia to the Western countries, of Europe and America, that were at this stage struggling to evolve an

---

[18]*Jawaharlal Nehru's Speeches, 1947-49*, p. 302.
[19]*Ibid.*, p. 254.　　　　[20]*Ibid.*, p. 316.

Asian policy which would be able to cope with the vastly changed political map of the continent.

The Foreign Policy of India

It is in the light of this attempt of India to draw attention to herself and the problems of the continent to which she belonged that the evolution of Indian attitude to other aspects of foreign policy has to be noted. The basic tenets of India's foreign policy were stated by Nehru in these words in a speech at the University of Columbia: "The main objectives of that policy are: the pursuit of peace, not through alignment with any major group of Power but through an independent approach to each controversial or disputed issue, the liberation of subjected peoples, the maintenance of freedom, both national and individual, the elimination of racial discrimination and the elimination of want, disease and ignorance, which afflict the greater part of the world's population."[21]

It is the policy of nonalignment in the cold war which lent to Indian policy the distinctive characteristics which have at once made it controversial and complex. It is not relevant here to describe the foreign policy in details or to indicate the specific Indian views on major world problems dividing the great Powers.[22] What needs to be emphasized in connection with the subject-matter under review, however, is that the policy of nonalignment was basically an instrument of pursuing the goals of India's national interests; it is, therefore, not the negative aspect of this policy of remaining aloof from the cold-war alignments but the more positive attempt implicit in this policy of emerging as the area of agreement between the great Powers of the world, which should be considered the core of India's foreign policy.

The national needs of India were well stated by Nehru himself: ". . . in the long run, it is to the advantage of India

---

[21]*Jawaharlal Nehru's Speeches, 1949-53*, p. 401.
[22]For a factual survey, *see* the series entitled *India in World Affairs*, I.C.W.A., New Delhi.

to try to attract to itself the sympathy and the hope of millions of people in the world without offending others."[23] Nonalignment, as such, was relevant to the extent that any Indian decision to line up in the cold war might tend to freeze that part of the world. India's primary interest was not in arresting the revolution that was inevitably unfolding itself in the area but to so mould it as to be consistent with the needs of world peace and freedom. In this sense, India's foreign policy is inextricably bound up with the internal approach to her problems. The three basic planks of India's State policies—nonalignment in world affairs, a democratic and liberal political system, and an increasing governmental participation in the economic life of the community in order to force the pace of economic growth—are all meant to serve the twin objectives of unleashing the revolution and phasing it, objectives which could become the basis for her friendly posture to both the great Powers of the world.

Most of these objectives were well stated by Nehru himself, although the burden of his office increasingly made him circumspect in his speech. Referring to the initial disadvantages of a policy of nonalignment, he said: ". . . there was suspicion in the mind of one group that we were really allied to other group . . . and the other group thought we were really allied to the other group in secret though we were trying to hide the fact."[24] Nehru said in a tone of apparent confidence on 4 December 1947: "Nonetheless, that is the only honourable and right position for us to take and I am quite sure that by adopting that position, we shall ultimately gain in national and international prestige, that is to say, when we take a long view of the situation, not a short view of immediately getting a vote here or there. . . . I have no doubt that fairly soon, in the course of two or three years, the world will find this attitude justified and India will not only be respected by the major protagonists in the struggle for power, but a large number of smaller nations which today are rather helpless will probably look to India more than to other countries for a lead in such matters."[25] In the same speech, he

[23]*Jawaharlal Nehru's Speeches, 1947-49*, p. 219.
[24]*Ibid.*, p. 204.   [25]*Ibid.*, p. 206.

said: "We propose to keep on the closest term of friendship with other countries unless they themselves create difficulties. We shall be friends with America. We intend cooperating with the United States of America and we intend cooperating fully with the Soviet Union." Speaking on 8 March 1948 in the Indian Parliament, he said: "We want the help of other countries; we are going to have it and we are going to get it too in a large measure. I am not aware of this having been denied to us by any large extent. Even in accepting economic help or in getting political help, it is not a wise policy to put all our eggs in one basket."[26] Again: "Our policy will continue to be not only to keep aloof from power alignment, but to try to make friendly cooperation possible. Fortunately, we enter upon our independence as a country with no hostile background in regard to any country. We are friendly to all countries ... we approach the whole world on a friendly basis and there is no reason why we should put ourselves at a disadvantage, if I may say so, by becoming unfriendly to any group."[27]

The Nature of the Communist Challenge

Underlying this policy is an assumption which was not shared by many other countries in the world: the nature of the Communist bloc is neither monolithic nor is there any inevitable expansionist tendency of the Communist bloc as a whole. What is more, to the extent that communism poses a social, economic, and political challenge internally in all these countries, it has to be answered in social, economic, and political terms. An undue emphasis on the military challenge might not only detract attention from these spheres of policy but prove self-defeating by eroding the flexibility and vitality of the democracies in Asia. A posture of status quo for any Asian (or African) country would isolate it from the main historical trends in the region and leave communism as the only ideology seeking radical solutions for difficult situations.

[26]*Ibid.*, p. 220.   [27]*Ibid.*, p. 246.

Professor Hans Morgentheau has very well summarized the essence of the difference between the predominant Western view and the Indian in this regard: "The foreign policy of India has also been one of containment. India is also interested, albeit not in the same way as the United States, in the preservation of the status quo vis-a-vis the expansionism of both the Communist notions and the Communist revolution.... India looks at the world from the vantage point of Asia and not of Europe and America.... To look at the world from the vantage point of Asia signifies to look at it from the perspective of the Asian revolution as an autonomous historic force. Being an autonomous force, it owes as such nothing to communism. Being a historic force, the circumstances of its growth compel it to assert itself primarily against the West. Everywhere in Asia, Communist or non-Communist, that revolution has had two goals: national independence and social reform. India has achieved the first of these goals and has embarked upon the experiment of a five-year Plan to realize the second. And so has Communist China. As India sees it, in Asia at least the issue between communism and democracy has been joined and will be decided on the plane of social reform. If the Indian experiment succeeds it will at the very least have stopped communism at the frontiers of India. And India deems it quite conceivable that this success will establish democratic India rather than Communist China as the model and the leader of the Asian revolution. It stands to reason that such a policy which thinks of the struggle with communism in terms of competition between different social systems is not only unable to take an interest in military measures, but must also regard Western emphasis upon them as a pernicious interference with that competitive struggle."[28]

What Morgentheau might have added is that for India the resistance to communism is as important a goal of national policies as to achieve a social and economic revolution by

[28]Hans J. Morgentheau, "The United States, India and Asia," *India's Role in Asia*, Ed. by Robert I. Crane, Chicago University, 1955 (mimeographed), pp. 195-6.

itself. It is interesting to note that in a speech in the Parliament on 22 May 1952, Nehru said: "So long as this Government or the party which forms the Government acts as a liberating force in this country, it will function effectively. Once it becomes what Hon'ble Members (the Communists who had by then won about thirty seats in the Indian Parliament and were sitting as the major Opposition group) think it has become, it will have ceased to be a liberating force and become a restrictive, repressive force. Then it will fade away in the process of history."[29]

Earlier, speaking in the Canadian Parliament on 24 October 1949, Nehru said: "To regard the present unsettled state of South-East Asia as a result or as a part of an ideological conflict would be a dangerous error. The trouble and discontent of this part of the world and indeed of the greater part of Asia are the result of obstructed freedom and dire poverty. The remedy is to accelerate the advent of freedom and to remove them. If this is achieved, Asia will become a powerful factor for stability and peace."[30] He told his audience at the Institute of Pacific Relations: "I am often asked: what is communism doing in this country? How does it affect us? We have to think about deeper questions.... We have to deal with deeper problems of every country... more difficult questions than questions of communism and anticommunism and fighting communism, as if that is the only question left in the world."[31] In 1953, he said in the Indian Parliament: "But between us (China and India) there is a very big difference, the effects of which it remains for history to show. The difference is that we are trying to function in a democratic set-up.... Ultimately, it is a question of which set-up and which structure of government—political or economic—pays the highest dividends. When I say highest dividends I do not merely mean material dividends, though they are important, but cultural and spiritual dividends also.... We have deliberately chosen a

[29] *Jawaharlal Nehru's Speeches, 1949-53*, p. 36.   [30] *Ibid.*, p. 127.
[31] Cited by J. C. Kundra, *op. cit.*, p. 66.

democratic set-up, and we feel it is good for our people and our country in the ultimate analysis."[32]

From these and other statements made by the Indian Prime Minister, it is clear that in the Indian conception of the Communist problem, the military aspects of the challenge of communism were relatively unimportant; what is important, however, is to establish the superiority of the democratic system, even for Asian and other backward countries. In this sense the rise of Communist China, though posing a problem for India in many fields, was not entirely an evil. Between them, communism and nonalignment performed the very necessary function of underlining the nature of the basic problems faced by Asia in its phase of resurgent revolution. The divergence between the Indian and American outlook in the matter of China emanated from this basic evaluation of the nature of the new State.

It must be added, however, that it would not be entirely correct to say that India did not take into account the military problem that China posed for her security; as early as December 1950, the Indian Government made it clear that it recognized the threat when it unilaterally extended guarantee to the northern neighbour, Nepal. The Himalayas involved India's security and none would be allowed to cross it (into Nepal) without confronting India. Also significant was the initiative that India took in arranging Commonwealth economic and military aid to Burma to stave off the Communist threat. It was a tactics therefore—vital in the context of the overall requirements of India's national interests—to understate this aspect of the problem in order to be able to meet with international support the more challenging task of competing with China in other spheres.

In the internal sphere there was little softness demonstrated in the treatment of the Communists, although they were allowed to function freely after 1951, when they gave up their aim of immediate revolution in India. In fact, the Prime

[32]*Jawaharlal Nehru's Speeches, 1949-53*, p. 259.

Minister of India has in his speeches and statements maintained a constant offensive against the local Communist party as well as the Communist doctrines as a whole. Speaking shortly after the Bulganin-Khrushchov visit to India, Nehru said: "Let us come to the Communists—these brave revolutionaries whose revolution consists not in application of intelligence but in trying to find out what is happening 5000 miles away, and trying to copy it, whether it fits in or not with the present state of India. ... Unfortunately, our friends of the Communist Party of India have so shut their minds and have so spent all their time and energy in learning a few slogans of the past that they are quite unable to appreciate what is happening in India. In fact, these great revolutionaries of the Communist Party of India have become great reactionaries."[33] Talking in 1960 to an Indian journalist, Nehru said in a reference to Marxism: "There is no proletariat of the Marxist conception in America ... although the logical reasoning of Marx was correct, other factors have intervened. The sum of them ... that is these new factors and particularly the two features I have mentioned of political democracy and technological advance ... have produced a new set of conditions and Marxism must be reviewed in this new context."[34] Earlier, Nehru had made a cogent criticism of the Marxist philosophical system and the irrelevance of it in the new situation while enunciating his "basic approach" to politics;[35] the publication of this brought a sharp retort from the Communist world, accusing Nehru in classical Marxist terms of practising violence on the proletariat while professing nonviolence, etc.[36] In fact, the publication of these Nehru-Yudin exchanges made it clear that a section of the Communist world was preparing for a decisive onslaught on the Nehru position in politics. It may be difficult to separate the subse-

[33]*Jawaharlal Nehru's Speeches, 1953-57*, New Delhi, 1957, p. 137.

[34]R. K. Karanjia, *The Mind of Mr Nehru*, London, George Allen and Unwin, 1960, p. 31.

[35]Jawaharlal Nehru, "The Basic Approach," *World Marxist Review* (reprinted from the *AICC Economic Review*), Vol. 1, No. 4, December 1958.

[36]Academician Yudin, "Can we accept Pandit Nehru's 'Basic Approach'?" *Ibid.*

quent India-China problem from this growing inconvenience that Nehru caused for the Communist leaders of China in the context of the Afro-Asian situation.

The Nature of the Communist World

One of the basic assumptions of India's foreign policy on which much of its validity rests is that the Communist world is not only not monolithic but that hopes must be placed on its ultimate disintegration and the rise of liberal forces inside the Communist world. One of the possible reasons for India's initial enthusiasm for China was the fact that Soviet Communism under Stalin had described India as the lackey of imperialism and attempted to foment revolts within India. The fact that Mao's revolution was self-propelled in nature meant a possible breakthrough in Communist solidarity and rigidity. In spite of the obvious difficulty for any official statement to mention it, Nehru said in the Indian Parliament in December 1950: "China is in a position to shape her own destiny and that is a great thing. It is true that she is controlled by the Communists as Russia is. It would be interesting to know whether or not their type of communism is the same as Russia's, how she will develop, and how close the association between China and Russia will be."[37] The Indian Press went further than this in explaining this. *The Tribune* wrote that the U.S. position in regard to China "only serves to promote the interest of the Soviet Union," and added: "Few Americans seem yet to grasp the obvious fact that Mr Nehru's China policy is not designed to strengthen Communist imperialism but to weaken it by demonstrating to the people of China that their friends are to be found not among the Communist States alone but everywhere."[38]

This initial hope in China was replaced by a hope in the prospect of liberalization in the Communist Party of the Soviet

[37]*Jawaharlal Nehru's Speeches, 1949-53*, p. 186.
[38]Cited by Satish K. Arora, *American Foreign Policy Towards India*, New Delhi, 1954, p. 84.

Union, after the process of destalinization had been started by the Twentieth Congress of the party. Welcoming the change, Nehru made a statement in the Indian Parliament: "I should like to take this opportunity of drawing the attention of the House to a very important event in recent weeks. I refer to the Twentieth Congress of the Communist Party of the Soviet Union which met recently in Moscow. There can be no doubt that this Congress has adopted a new line and a new policy. This new line, both in political thinking and practical policy, appears to be based upon a more realistic appreciation of the present world situation and represents a significant process of adaptation and adjustment. . . . We feel that the decisions of the Twentieth Congress of the Soviet Union are likely to have far-reaching effects. I hope that this development will lead to a further relaxation of tension in the world."[39] It is during the subsequent years of the growing China-India rivalry and conflicts that this approach was further underlined in Indian policy statements. During his last visit to the United States, the Indian Prime Minister was reported to have remarked in his off-the-record conversations that "Mr Khrushchov sees India as a future bulwark against China and that it is in the Soviet interest to help restrain Peking."[40] Naturally, much of this hope remains unstated publicly; but there have been enough official statements to show the extent to which the USSR is depended upon in the conflict with China.

The basic Indian assumption would seem to be that as the Soviet society is transforming itself from a backward to an advanced economy and the pent-up consumption urge of the Soviet people is seeking satisfaction, there is bound to be an increasing stake felt by the Soviet Union in the peaceful resolution of world problems. Also, in an age of declining colonialism, it is difficult for any great Power to view with equanimity the prospect of adding to its empire, specially when Communist theory, on which such an empire is based,

[39]*Jawaharlal Nehru's Speeches*, 1953-57, p. 318.
[40]Selig S. Harrison, "South Asia and U.S. Policy," *New Republic*, 11 December 1961.

implies the impossible task of underwriting allied economies. As the potential expansion of the Communist world can only be in Asia and as Asian problems in general are similar to the Chinese, there is an inevitable likelihood of new Communist States ideologically lining up with the Chinese. To put it differently, if the famous Communist maxim of "from each according to his ability to each according to his need" is substituted by the maxim of "from each Communist *nation* according to its ability to each Communist *nation* according to its need" there can well occur serious Soviet rethinking in regard to the expansion of communism in Asia.

India and Inner-Bloc Politics

Apart from this assumption in regard to the politics in the Communist world, India has emerged as a factor in that politics and it is obviously one of the objectives of its foreign policy to continue to be so. It is the least publicly talked of aspect of the motivations of Indian policy; for, obviously, public expression of this can become self-defeating. But pieces of evidence suggest that India regards it as of tremendous consequence to be able to remain an item of controversy inside the Communist bloc.

It has been noted by analysts of Indian foreign policy that Tito is one of the world statesmen who exerts a considerable influence on India's foreign policy, particularly in relation to the Communist bloc. The biographer of Nehru, Michael Brecher, noted in his discussion of the decision-making process of Indian policy: "One other personal influence deserves recognition. During the past few years Nehru's assessment of events in the Soviet Union and Eastern Europe appears to have been affected by the views of Marshal Tito with whom lengthy visits were exchanged in 1955 and 1956."[41]

The noted Soviet expert, Isaac Deutscher, wrote in the *Reporter* in early 1960 in an article on the internal politics of

[41]Michael Brecher, *Nehru: A Political Biography*, Oxford, 1959, p. 575.

the Communist world: "The gesture of Soviet neutrality in a conflict between a Communist government and a bourgeois one must have shocked not only Peking but even some people in Moscow, who hold that the frontier dispute has been artificially concocted not by Mao but by India's Congress Party.... Khrushchov has evidently refused to endorse the view and to some extent has deliberately strengthened Nehru's position vis-a-vis both Chinese and Indian Communists. Uncommitted opinion in Asia is bound to conclude that if even the Soviet leader refuses to declare his solidarity with Mao Tse-tung on this occasion, then Mao must be in the wrong. ... The Maoists view India as the next great battlefield of the class struggle; and recent developments in India with which they are more closely concerned than the Russians give them no cause for satisfaction.... They see the surrender of their Indian comrades as part of Moscow's design to appease Nehru."[42]

It may be said with some justification that in the whole debate in the Communist world over the nature and role of what has been officially described in recent Communist documents as the "national democracies," India has been the focal point of conflict. The Chinese decision to make a direct assault on relations with India cannot be separated from the fact that it was necessary for her struggles within the Communist bloc to prove that the neutral nations like India were not in reality neutral and posed a long-term problem for the Communists. It may be noted here that in an article reviewing the Belgrade Conference, Walter Laqueur had said: "... it is highly likely that the neutrals rather than the West may clash with the Communists in the years ahead."[43]

The fact that India has joined issue with the left-wing Communists in the inner debate of the Communist world is clearly illustrated from the following extract from a speech by Nehru in the Indian Parliament in late 1959: "China is very very far

---

[42]Isaac Deutscher, "Khrushchov Plays the Waiting Game," *Reporter*, 21 January 1960.

[43]Walter Laqueur and Alfred Sherman, "The Meaning of Belgrade," *New Republic*, 25 September 1960.

from normality, and that is our misfortune and the world's misfortune. ... That is, strength, considerable strength, coming in an abnormal state of mind. ... That is why you find a marked difference between the broad approach of the Soviet Union and the Chinese approach. I do not think there is any country in the world which is more anxious for peace than the Soviet Union. ... But I doubt if there is any country in the world ... which cares less for peace than China today. ... The world is changing and I can conceive of the two great colossuses today, the Soviet Union and the United States, coming very near to each other, as they are slightly coming. ... This talk about international capitalism and international communism, reflecting an old slogan, merely prevents us from thinking straight and understanding the changed world."[44]

It is also to be noted here that the nature of the Soviet and Chinese advice to the Indian Communist Party has been different;[45] also different has been the official Indian attitude in the matter of the Communist Party's links with Moscow and Peking. In the last Congress of the Indian Communist Party at Vijayawada, held in April 1961, the Chinese could not attend the conference but the chief Soviet guest at the Conference, Suslov, was accorded welcome by officials of the Indian Government.

Just as India has not remained nonaligned in the internal conflict of the Communist world, she has found herself involved in the politics of the Western bloc. It is now known that both in the Indo-Chinese and the Korean conflicts, India was regarded as a friend by the British Government, while she was sometimes regarded as an unwanted intruder by the United States.[46]

In the Geneva Conference on Indo-China, Sir Anthony Eden found India as an ally. "I had to describe the situation

---

[44]*Lok Sabha Debates,* 27 November 1959, Cols. 2203-7.

[45]*See* review of the Communist Party Congress at Vijayawada in *Statesman Overseas Weekly,* 27 April 1961.

[46]This is not to suggest that the differences within the two blocs were qualitatively similar but only to indicate India's role in the inner bloc controversy in both cases. Apparently, India should have a greater stake in the disintegration of the Communist bloc, which will inevitably loosen the Western alliance.

somberly and try to convince the Communist nations of the sincerity of my convictions. In this I had an ally, India. That country also had a concern in limiting the onward rush of Communist forces."[47] Again: "Nobody could tell what the future would hold, but it was essential not to alienate India by our actions in a part of the world which concerned her closely. For these reasons I was disturbed to hear from our High Commissioner in Delhi that Mr Dulles' recent speeches had created the worst possible impression there."[48] Earlier, during the Korean War and the MacArthur crisis, Nehru said in the Indian Parliament: "We welcomed the decision of the Prime Minister of England to go to the United States to meet President Truman and wished him godspeed in his endeavours to prevent war and to find a peaceful way out of this tangle. We found that there was a good deal in common between the British Prime Minister's view of the present situation and ours."[49]

Even when the crisis in Egypt began, India attempted to understate the British role in fomenting the crisis; but as the crisis advanced and ultimately resulted in the invasion, Indo-British relations suffered a setback. It is of interest to note that it is in this period that, following the Indian Prime Minister's visit to the United States in December 1956, the relations between India and the United States began to improve.[50]

It is this aspect of India's foreign policy—the attempt to remain a factor in inner-bloc politics while remaining generally nonaligned in the cold war—which needs to be emphasized. For, no policy evolved for a closer association of nations of the region or the nonaligned in general which would tend to take the unity of the rival cold-war blocs and their inclination to wage this cold war for granted would be consistent with the

[47]Anthony Eden, *The Full Circle*, Boston, 1960, pp. 139-40.
[48]*Ibid.*, p. 105.
[49]*Jawaharlal Nehru's Speeches, 1949-53*, pp. 171-2.
[50]Commenting on the Nehru-Eisenhower meeting, the weekly *Thought* wrote on 22 December 1956: "That the leaders of the two largest democracies of the world should have found themselves so close to each other is a measure not only of goodwill and understanding between two men but of the essential identity of interests and aims of India and America in these anxious times."

needs of India, or her conception of the needs of the neutral or the nonaligned world.

The Importance of International Cooperation

These needs as conceived by India are of paving the way for greater international cooperation through the mitigation of cold war and the underlining of those issues in world politics which should be able to transcend the cold war. The hopes of backward regions of delivering the goods internally depended largely on their capacity to utilize the growing surplus of the advanced countries generated by a vastly improved technology and the constant technological revolution under way. The need for these countries was not so much to exert the strength that they potentially possessed but to invoke international cooperation in the solution of their vital problems. In this respect India's approach was distinguishable from that of some other countries which would defy both the great Powers and regard them as monsters rather than attempting to devise possible bases for their cooperation, at least in the field of the problems of the underdeveloped world.

Speaking before the United Nations on 3 November 1948, Nehru drew attention to some of the long-term problems which the world faced, and said: "The effects of this inequality in the past have made themselves felt in Asia, Africa and other parts of the world much more than in Europe, leading towards a conflict in the future, and it is a problem which if it is not properly understood will not be solved. It is a strange thing that when the world lacks so many things, food and other necessities in many parts of the world and people are dying of hunger, the attention of this Assembly of nations is concentrated only on a number of political problems. There are economic problems also. I wonder if it would be possible for this Assembly to take a holiday for a while from some of the acute political problems which face it and allow men's mind to settle down and look at the vital and urgent economic problems, and look at places in the world where food is lacking."[51]

It is from this viewpoint of the possible expansion of the scope and potentialities of international cooperation that India has stressed not only the need for avoiding war and maintaining peace but also for mitigating the cold war, specially through arms control. In a conversation with the French journalist, Tibor Mende, in 1956, Nehru was asked about the growing world consciousness of the need to lift the backward regions; the Prime Minister replied: ". . . we are going (towards international cooperation) but not fast enough. I think all this is tied up with the present context of the cold war. If that was removed, if the present tensions were lessened in the world, if fears and apprehensions were less, then I think it would advance much more rapidly. . . . If they could supply ten or twenty per cent of that money now spent on armaments that would be a big sum."[52] Talking to an Indian journalist four years later, Nehru said: "It is generally understood now that it is as imperative for richer countries to help raise the standards of the underdeveloped nations as it is for the latter to speed up this process. The large sums of money presently spent on armaments can suitably be utilized for advancing the cause of advance in the world. The problem is one of social and economic balance on a global plane."[53]

The Stake in U.S.-USSR Rapprochement

This assumption that any mitigation of the cold war and the arms race was bound to throw up areas like India as the problem areas of the world demanding cooperation from all developed regions, irrespective of their ideology, led to the Indian emphasis both on the possibility and desirability of U.S.-USSR rapprochement. There was an obvious area of agreement between the two great Powers, according to India, and a

[51]*Jawaharlal Nehru's Speeches, 1947-49*, pp. 320-1.
[52]Tibor Mende, *Nehru: Conversation on Indian and World Affairs*, New York, 1956, pp. 66-7.
[53]R. K. Karanjia, *op. cit.*, p. 44.

common stake in certain spheres of world developments. Nehru said in 1960: "I have always maintained that there is so much in common between these two great Powers that all this business of the cold war is altogether unrealistic and artificial. Once they begin talking, as they have, despite occasional breakdowns and frustrations, the ground will be cleared of all the wreckage of ten years of suspicion and fear and what might be called areas of agreement might become visible."[54]

The Indian interest in U.S.-USSR rapprochement was heightened by the feeling that among the visible areas of agreement between the Power blocs, particularly the great Powers, India was a major item. In his reply to a question whether the big Powers could make India the laboratory of the next phase of Soviet-American economic coexistence on the basis of helping to reconstruct the underdeveloped world, Nehru said in 1960: "... both are cooperating with us in a big way. There is Bhilai and there are American projects, British projects, Canadian projects, German projects in our development plans. ... The important fact is that there is realization of what you called economic coexistence, although at present it is developing more on a competitive than cooperative basis. But the latter is bound to follow."[55] Again, towards the end of the conversation, the Prime Minister said: "... today there is an almost universal understanding and appreciation of what we are trying to do on the economic plane ... that is planning under a democratic pattern of socialism. This has set a new pattern for Asian and African development and it is significant that economists and other experts from both the worlds, particularly the West to which economic planning is something foreign, are extremely interested in development plans and progress. ... This makes India itself a kind of an area of agreement between the opposing ideological forces. Without boasting about it we can claim to be the only underdeveloped country trying to do it in a big way."[56] This aspect of the position of India was earlier noted by the American economist, Malenbaum: "India seems

---

[54]*Ibid.*, p. 88.　　　[55]*Ibid.*, p. 44.　　　[56]*Ibid.*, pp. 100-1.

to be one of the few underdeveloped countries where both the United States and the USSR maintain aid programmes significant in terms of the country's requirements. These evidences of the coexistence of the East and West in Indian economic and political life bear testimony to the skill with which leaders of India have conducted its domestic policy and international relations in the past four or five years. This ability to remain on friendly terms with the great conflicting Powers has in itself enhanced India's world status. Indeed, both American and Russian involvement in Indian economic affairs has tended to grow."[57] Writing in March 1961, the Indian Deputy Minister for External Affairs, Mrs Lakshmi Menon said: ". . . nations, small and big, should come together to bring about the much needed rapprochement between the USA and the USSR."[58]

One of the specific assumptions of Nehru in this regard is that in the politics of the modern world, ideology is of little relevance or consequence, except as a propaganda weapon. "Although there is a great deal of talk about ideologies, I doubt if they come into the picture at all except as weapons."[59]

It may be pertinent to sum up the Indian view of the world in the following terms: apart from the generally recognized line dividing the world, that between the Communist and the non-Communist world, there is another and a more formidable, albeit subdued, dividing line at work. This is the line dividing the developed and the underdeveloped world. What makes this line more pernicious and explosive in the long run is that it broadly coincides with two other lines dividing the peoples of the world; it so happens that the developed world is in the main the white and the underpopulated part of the world and the underdeveloped the coloured and the over-populated. If this line is taken into account, it cuts across the line dividing the Communist and the non-Communist world. From the viewpoint of this division, the Indian and the Chinese pattern of develop-

[57] Wilfred Malenbaum, *East and West in India's Economic Development*, Washington, National Planning Association, 1959, p. 3.
[58] Lakshmi N. Menon, "Our Policy," *Seminar*, March 1961.
[59] *Jawaharlal Nehru's Speeches, 1949-53*, p. 186.

ment have different connotations; it is inherent in the nature of Chinese development, based on the mobilization of manpower by whipping up an entire sleeping population and putting them to spartan discipline to build up State power, that where conflicts exist they will be sharpened. It is the dynamic of the Indian approach to development, based on the cooperative utilization of the surplus of the developed regions, that it will stress international cooperation and peaceful resolution of conflicts. To the extent that the Chinese approach is bound ultimately to challenge the structure of world politics, there is a common stake of the great Powers to promote the Indian experiment. Her proximity to China, the size of her population and the inevitable influence that she exerts on other peoples of the region make India somewhat like the developed nations' model farm in the underdeveloped world. The basic objectives of India are to remain in this position and demonstrate the possibility of solving the problems of similarly-placed countries with the cooperation and sympathy of the great Powers of the world.

The Style of Indian Foreign Policy

It is out of these basic objectives that the distinctive style of Indian policy emanates. A distinguished British journalist has said that India does not have a foreign policy; she only conducts a vigorous foreign commentary.[60] To a large extent this is illustrative of the style. Even without the means to implement a foreign policy of any great positive content, India has chosen to continue this commentary in the hope that her urgent need of attracting attention would thus be served. What is distinctive in this style is the way India has stressed the need to avoid offending any great Power. It has been often repeated by Nehru that it was not India's way to shout from the housetops or to use strong language; also, that friendship with one country should not be sought in terms which were hostile to another.

[60]W. D. Clarke, "The Asian Revolution," *International Affairs*, London, July 1958.

Speaking in Moscow on 22 June 1955, Nehru said: "Let our coming together be because we like each other and we wish to cooperate and not because we dislike others and wish to do them injury."[61] Chastizing the Indian Communists later, Nehru said: "... Our friends, the Communists, have the idea that friendship with one country inevitably means hostility to another country, that is, to be friends you must not only be friends with me but you must be enemies to my enemy, or those whom I consider my enemy. This surely is a remarkable attitude to take...."[62]

After the Suez nationalization, Nehru said in a public speech, indicating the style of India's foreign policy: "... the way Egypt took hold of the Suez Canal was not our way ... our way is a little different.... If they had followed a different way, so many difficulties would not have arisen."[63]

It is in the backdrop of this discussion of some aspects of Indian foreign policy that the question of Indian attitude to regional integration in South and South-East Asia has to be viewed.

[61]*Jawaharlal Nehru's Speeches, 1953-57*, pp. 304-5.   [62]*Ibid.*, p. 136.

[63]*Indian Affairs Record*, Vol. 2, No. 9, October 1956. Goa may be regarded as an aberration from the Indian foreign policy style; also it did not involve any great Powers directly. (*See* Nehru's interview with Karanjia, *Blitz*, 30 December 1961.)

CHAPTER TWO

Attempts at Regional Integration

REGIONAL INTEGRATION has been defined as "an association of
States based upon location in a given geographical area, for
the safeguarding or promotion of the participants," an association whose terms are "fixed by a treaty or other arrangements."[1]
Apparently, such an association can only be the product of a
long gestation period of regional cooperation with less formalized and institutionalized bases for it; and regional integration
could also, in this broader sense, mean any tendency on the
part of any group of nations belonging to some region or
adjacent regions to cooperate in the fields of their national and
international policies or coordinate their efforts in order to
promote an ever increasing mutual relationship, as distinct from
the relationship with other parts of the world. However
defined, the region of Asia has witnessed in the postwar period
several attempts at closer integration of the various countries
of the vast continent—sometime as a whole, sometime on the
basis of a more specific region of it. An attempt will be made
in the following pages to review some of these efforts from the
viewpoint of India and India's experiences with them.

Early Indian Attitudes

During the Indian struggle for freedom, closer collaboration
with fellow Asians became one of the basic objectives of the
movement; the antipathy to European imperialism often led

[1]Norman J. Padelford, "Regional Organization and the United Nations,"
International Organization, May 1954, p. 203-16.

to an uncritical glorification of the role of other Asian countries in the world. For example, one of the great anti-British movements in India—the Khilafat—was built around the Indian Muslims' dissatisfaction with the disintegration of the Ottoman Empire. That the Arabs were struggling against the Ottoman Empire or that within Turkey itself great political changes were under way were not factors immediately taken into account. In this case, the potentialities of generating a mass upsurge in India on the basis of a slogan which was intelligible—the onslaught of European Britain on Muslim Turkey—were far more important than the actual merits of the cases involved.[2]

While the Khilafat agitation in the years following the First World War indicated a large measure of concern among the Muslim minority of India for the Middle Eastern countries, the national movement as a whole was mainly looking to Japan in the early years of the twentieth century for emotional sustenance and strength in the struggle against Britain. The victory of Japan over Russia in 1905 was regarded by many in India as the demonstration of the fact that there was nothing inherently superior about the British. One of the Indian periodicals of that time, the *Indian Review*, wrote in apparent elation that at least an Oriental country had defeated and "humbled a huge European Power, a by no means mean representative of all that is haughty and arrogant among the nations of the West!" Japan could become the model for India: "There can be no surer road to a final success than that which Japan has trodden!"[3] Earlier in 1893, the great Indian religious and social reformer of that time, Vivekananda, had been deeply impressed by Japan and exhorted all Indian young men to go to Japan and see what was happening, take a look at the army and the navy and follow her example.[4] Between 1898 and 1906, the

---

[2]Writing about the Khilafat agitation Nehru said later: "The influence and prestige of the Moulvies, which had been gradually declining owing to new ideas and a progressive Westernization, began to grow again and dominate the Muslim community. . . . I used to be troubled sometimes by this growth of the religious element in our politics." (*Autobiography*, London, 1936, p. 72.)

[3]Quoted in: Werner Levi, *Free India in Asia*, Minneapolis, University of Minnesota, 1952, p. 23. [4]*Ibid.*, p. 22.

number of Indian students in Japan rose from two to sixty and a general sense of gratitude to Japan persisted. The gradual change in Japan's international posture and her militaristic conduct was being noticed later with some disappointment; the Indian poet, Tagore, was disturbed by the nature of Japan's nationalism and its manifestations on the mainland when he visited Japan in 1924. But the sympathy for her continued, and Tagore criticized the American Seclusion Bill as much an insult to India as to Japan! The fund of goodwill for Japan was almost exhausted by the time she attacked China; a positive disaffection took the place of the earlier enthusiasm hereafter in many minds. There were still many, however, who would welcome Japan's victory in any war because of its anti-European character. But, by and large, Japan had forfeited her credit in India by her policies in relation to China and Korea.[5]

While the Japanese lost their position by the middle of the thirties, in India there was no lack of sympathy for Asia as a whole. In fact, China replaced Japan in Indian minds, not so much as a source of hope and strength, as a similarly-placed country, potentially great and struggling to assert herself against heavy odds. In this gradual replacement of Japan by China as the great Asian compatriot, there was reflected a change in the composition and character of the leadership of the Indian national movement. With the emergence of Gandhi on the Indian scene in the postwar years, there was a marked shift of emphasis in the outlook of the Indian National Congress from a mere nationalistic organization to one committed to structural reforms of Indian society. By the beginning of the thirties, Socialists and left-wing intellectuals began to occupy an important role in the politics of the Congress. This role of the left became almost one of predominance in the sphere of foreign

[5]When Japan reached the borders of India during the Second World War, Nehru said in a statement: "I consider it my duty to oppose any foreign invasion of India. . . . The news of Japanese bombing of the coastal areas of India must stir the heart of every Indian. The Japanese assertion that they are coming to India to set us free is absurd and totally false. That was clear from Japan's misdeeds in China and Korea." (Quoted in: J. C. Kundra, *Indian Foreign Policy, 1947-54*, p. 40.)

policy; the foreign outlook of the Indian national movement ever since 1927 was largely determined by Jawaharlal Nehru. This change was reflected in two ways: a gradual shift of emphasis from purely Asian to world affairs in general; and the application of ideological criteria in the assessment of the Asian States. China and the Kuomintang appeared to India at this time as the major source of inspiration. Writing in 1940, Nehru said: "I spent less than two weeks in China and these two weeks were memorable for me. . . . I found to my joy that my desire that China and India should draw closer to each other was fully reciprocated by China's leaders, and more especially by that great man who has become the symbol of China's unity and her determination to be free. . . . I returned to India an even greater admirer of China and the Chinese people than I had been previously. . . ."[6] It is largely under Nehru's guidance that the Indian National Congress sent a medical mission to China during her war with Japan as a token of India's sympathy with the Chinese people. In 1940, Nehru proposed the formation of an eastern federation of India and China and other eastern countries as a constituent of a world federation of the future.[7]

In fact, the Congress had expressed such vague ideas even before. In 1920, Gandhi wrote of the growing solidarity of Asian countries. In 1922, C. R. Das, presiding over the Indian National Congress, urged Indian participation in an Asian federation which he regarded as inevitable. Next year the great Muslim leader, Mohammed Ali, presiding over the Congress, asked for an eastern federation. The need for an Asian federation was again stressed in the Congress session of 1926. A resolution to this effect was adopted by the organization in 1928.[8]

Two countries which were propagating ideas of Asian unity and cooperation at this time were Japan and the Soviet Union. In fact, it may be noted that the first congress of Asian peoples

---

[6]Jawaharlal Nehru, *Autobiography*, p. 608.   [7]*Ibid.*
[8]B. G. Gokhale, "India's Role in Asia," *India's Role in Asia*, Chicago, p. 16; Bimla Prasad, *Origins of Indian Foreign Policy*, p. 72-7.

to be held anywhere was at Baku in 1920. The Indian movement had no direct link or relation with either and there were among the nationalists those who looked to the Soviet Union and those who looked to Japan for emotional links. Among the former was Jawaharlal Nehru; among the latter the extreme nationalist, Subhash Bose. While Nehru attended the Communist-dominated League against Imperialism in 1927, Bose left India for Japan during the early phases of the war and organized the Indian National Army to fight with the support of the Japanese Army. A third trend grew among the Indian Muslims, as noted earlier, which looked to cooperation with the West Asian countries for anti-British struggle.

These general expressions of sympathy and expectations of support from other Asian countries apart, there was a degree of exchange of ideas and opinions among the nationalists of Asia; the sessions of the Indian National Congress regularly received messages from other Asian movements like the Wafd Party of Egypt, the Kuomintang of China and the Burmese national leaders.[9]

Notwithstanding these contacts based on a common struggle against imperial rule, the fact must be noted that the Indian elite was largely Western oriented and drew their ideas and inspiration from the countries of Western Europe. Among the foreign groups which moulded Indian opinion to a great extent, the most influential and significant were the left wingers of the British Labour Party and the friends of India in Britain.

Nehru on Regional Integration

The inevitable postwar trend towards regional integration was foreseen by Indian leadership. Writing during his prison days in 1944, Nehru said in course of his references to impending changes in the structure of world politics: "It is possible, of course, that large federations or groups of nations may emerge in Europe or elsewhere in the Pacific and form huge multi-

[9]*Ibid.*

national States."[10] G. D. H. Cole had earlier called India itself a supranational State and held that ultimately it would be the centre of a bigger suprantional State lying between the Soviet Union in the north, a Sino-Japanese Soviet Republic in the northeast and a new State based on Egypt, Turkey and Arabia in the west. And Walter Lippmann had visualized three or four orbits encompassing the globe—the Atlantic Community, the Russian, the Chinese and the South Asian. Nehru's reaction to these visions of the future was characteristically undogmatic: "For my part, I have no liking for a division of the world into a few huge supranational areas unless those are tied together by some strong world bond. But if the people are foolish enough to avoid world unity and some world organization, then these vast supranational organizations, each functioning as one huge State, but with local autonomy, are very likely to take shape. For, the small national State is doomed. It may survive as a culturally autonomous area but not as an independent political unit."[11] About the Lippmann idea he said: ". . . (this) is a continuation of power politics on a vaster scale and it is difficult to understand how he can see any world peace or cooperation coming out of it."[12]

While these passages indicate an uncertainty of approach, after his release he made at least one statement which indicated a greater enthusiasm about the idea. Speaking in Kashmir in August 1945, he said: "Small States of the world of tomorrow have no future in store and they are sure to be reduced to the status of satellite States. . . . I stand for a South Asia Federation of India, Iraq, Iran, Afghanistan, and Burma."[13]

The Asian Relations Conference

Even before India became formally free, the leaders of the Indian national movement took steps to convene the Asian Relations Conference in New Delhi. Although organized by

---

[10]Jawaharlal Nehru, *Discovery of India*, Calcutta, Signet Press, 1945, p. 569.
[11]*Ibid.*, p. 570.   [12]*Ibid.*, p. 572.
[13]J. S. Bright (ed.), *Before and After Independence*, New Delhi, 1950, p. 279.

the nonofficial Indian Council of World Affairs, the conference was directly inspired by Nehru who was the guiding spirit behind it. It met in Delhi from 23 March to 2 April 1947 and was attended by 25 Asian countries, including Egypt.[14] Japan was invited to the conference but was not allowed to attend by the occupation authorities. The conference agenda included: (*i*) National Freedom Movements in Asia; (*ii*) Racial Problems and Inter-racial Migration; (*iii*) Cultural Affairs; and (*iv*) Agriculture and Industry.[15]

The tone for the conference was set by Nehru in his inaugural address. Four major elements in his speech were: the proclamation of Asia's arrival on the world scene; the stress on the need for Asian unity; the need to avoid the expression of anti-Western sentiments; and the need for greater regional cooperation. The statement of the Indian leader contained the following passage: "It so happened that we in India convened this conference, but the idea of such a conference arose simultaneously in many minds and in many countries in Asia. There was a widespread urge and an awareness that the time had come for us, peoples of Asia, to meet together, hold together and advance together. It was not only a vague desire but the compulsion of events which forced all of us to think along these lines."[16] Other specific features of the speech were: a special welcome to observers from Australia and New Zealand "because we have many problems in common especially in the Pacific, and in the South East region of Asia, and we have to cooperate together to find solutions"; "in this conference there are no leaders and no followers"; "this was not some kind of pan-Asian movement directed against Europe or America"; the ideal was One World

---

[14]Afghanistan, Bhutan, Burma, Ceylon, China, India, Indonesia, Korea, Malaya, Nepal, Mongolia, Iran, the Philippines, Siam, Tibet, Turkey, Vietnam, Georgia, Armenia, Azerbaijan, Kazhakistan, Kirgizia, Tajikistan, Ujbekistan, Egypt, Palestinian Arabs and Jews. There were observers from Australia and New Zealand; among the leaders who could not attend due to pressing business at home was Ho Chi-minh.

[15]*Keesing's Contemporary Archives*, 1947, p. 8862.

[16]*Jawaharlal Nehru's Speeches, 1946-49*, p. 300.

and "we should work for that ideal and not for any group which comes in the way of the larger group"; Asia had a special responsibility in regard to Africa, to "help them to their rightful place in the human family." Among the specific suggestions made by Nehru was the setting up of an Asian institute for the study of common problems and a school of Asian studies; beyond this there "is much more that we can do but I shall not venture to enumerate all these subjects for it is for you to discuss them and arrive at some decisions."

While cautious in his prescriptions for the future, Nehru nevertheless attempted to lay down an ideological basis for Asian cooperation when he said: "The freedom we envisage is not to be confined to this nation or that or to a particular people but must spread out over the whole human race. That universal freedom also cannot be based on the supremacy of any particular class. It must be the freedom of the common man everywhere...."[17] It is this latter part of the proposition on which there could be no easy agreement among the rulers of the Asian countries.

However, the conference started with a great deal of initial expression of enthusiasm: Ceylon's Bandaranaike saw in it the beginning of an Asian federation, while Burma's Aung San in his message urged the Asian countries to stand together in weal or woe.[18] Most other delegates expressed their great satisfaction at this sign of Asian resurgence and unity. The conference also ended on a hopeful note; the Asian Relations Organization was to be created with the objectives of promoting Asian studies and greater cooperation among Asian countries and "between them and the rest of the world."[19] There was also agreement on the issues of freedom for the colonial areas, the need for uplifting the status of women in Asia, the importance of inter-Asian communications and the urgency of supple-

---

[17]*Ibid.*, p. 305.

[18]For a description of the conference proceedings and resolutions, *see: Report of the First Asian Relations Conference*, New Delhi, Indian Council of World Affairs, 1948.

[19]*Keesing's Contemporary Archives*, 1947, p. 8862.

menting political freedom by economic progress. The delegates also agreed to hold another conference of this type in China in 1949.

Behind this apparent success of the conference were hidden the grim conclusions to which the conference drove all objective students of the subject: "One merit of the conference was to show what cannot yet be done in Asia."[20] According to Werner Levi: "The conference marked the apex of Asian solidarity and the beginning of its decline. The reasons for this were many and varied; the two major sources of discord were the intense rivalry between India and China in the conference and the common distrust of the two Asian giants among the smaller countries of the region. The Chinese began by protesting against a map displayed at the conference dias which showed Tibet as a separate State; throughout the conference they were found to be more interested in pressing claims for leadership than helping to build up common decisions."[21] Levi wrote: "The Chinese had no wish to be tied to an organization in which India was predominant. Their tactics at the conference was to keep India's status within bounds. No more did the Indians wish to surrender any power to the Chinese. They were altogether doubtful of the possibility of close political bonds with a China whose political colour and foreign political orientation were uncertain."[22]

A more important political factor inhibiting this success of the conference was the distrust among smaller Asian countries of their more powerful neighbours. Even before the conference began, the Indian Muslim League dissociated themselves from it on the ground that it was a "thinly disguised attempt on the part of the Hindu Congress to boost itself politically as the prospective leader of Asiatic peoples."[23] The party was to lead Pakistan five months later. During the conference, a Burmese delegate was reported to have said: "It was terrible to be ruled by a Western Power, but it was even more so to be ruled by an

[20]Levi, *op. cit.*, p. 39.   [21]*Ibid.*   [22]*Ibid.*, p. 37-8.
[23]*New York Times*, 20 March 1947.

Asian Power." Malayans strongly supported this view: a Ceylonese delegate feared not only domination but "ultimate submergence."[24] One of the issues on which the smaller countries of South Asia made common cause was migration; it was their attempt to resist any idea of freer population movements in the region.[25]

Summing up the difficulties faced by the conference, an American author wrote in November 1955: "Neither the Indians nor the Chinese were prepared to concede leadership to the other, the Arabs were uninterested and the South-East Asians frankly afraid that such an arrangement would mean the end of their freedom, almost before it had been won."[26]

The conference has been viewed as a success by most Indian writers. "Within the limited context of its aims and objective conditions in Asia at that time, the conference may be said to have been a success."[27] As Nehru said: "The most important thing about the conference is that it was held."[28] There were grave difficulties in the way of concrete attempts to forge Asian unity; nor was it the objective to promote a pan-Asian movement. The conference succeeded, however, in proclaiming Asia's rebirth, so to say, in the family of nations. Viewed this way, the conference might well be called a landmark in Asian history, as the Indian Prime Minister had asserted in his inaugural address.

On the other hand, viewed from the angle of regional integration, the conference was evidently more important for exposing the problems involved in any such attempt than in achieving concrete results. The conference scheduled to be held in 1949 in China was not held for obvious difficulties in making China the venue of any international conference of this kind. The Asian Relations Organization continued a precarious existence as a nonofficial organization for about ten years; it was quietly wound up in 1957.

---

[24]Levi, *op. cit.*, p. 39.   [25]*Ibid.*

[26]William Henderson, "Regionalism in South-East Asia," *International Organization*, November 1955.

[27]B. G. Gokhale, "India's Role in Asia," *op. cit.*, p. 19.

[28]Quoted in: K. P. Karunakaran, *India in World Affairs, 1947-50*, p. 85.

It should be noted here that at this stage the cold war had not become an important factor in the politics of the Asian region and much of the difficulty was of internal origin. However, there was, as Nehru pointed out, some apprehension in the West that any Asian solidarity would have an anti-Western slant; it is only after the conference was over that the *New York Times* reported with relief: "It has striven to sidestep any discussion that might suggest that this conference was the beginning of a pan-Asiatic bloc against white imperialism or whites generally. It has thereby avoided unfavourable attention from the Western world."[29] As against this, the Soviet reaction was intensely critical, in spite of the fact that the conference invited seven Central Asian Republics of the USSR and gave it the status of an Asian Power. The India expert, Zhukhov, wrote after the conference: "The fact is that the conference in Delhi was financed among other things by certain Indian capitalists who as a rule are not interested in the gifts of culture.... Certain circles had set as one of the secret rules of the conference to try on a new basis the idea of pan-Asianism and further to make precisely India as the centre of the pan-Asiatic movements. As is well known, the imperialist Japan had formerly declared herself as the centre of pan-Asianism. She exploited it in order to justify Japanese expansion. Now someone is dreaming of exploiting the Japanese heritage in his own interest."[30]

The New Delhi Conference on Indonesia

The next important step towards Asian cooperation was also initiated by India, following the Dutch invasion of Indonesia on 18 December 1948. This thinly-disguised attempt of a European Power to re-enter Asia and impose colonial rule was regarded by most Asians as an affront to the whole of Asia: India convened a conference of interested countries to consider the Indonesian situation, apart from steps taken by her to help the

29*New York Times*, 2 April 1947.
30Quoted in: Karunakaran, *op. cit.*, p. 90-1.

Indonesian cause in the form of denial of refuelling and landing facilities to Dutch planes in Indian airports.

The conference on Indonesia, unlike the earlier Asian Conference, was a conference of Asian governments and had official character; it was also specifically political in nature.

The conference invitees were this time less in number than in the earlier Asian Conference;[31] the Soviet Central Asian Republics were omitted and Australia and New Zealand were included. China, Nepal and Thailand were represented by observers only. The main item on the conference agenda was Dutch "Police Action" and possible assistance to Indonesian Republic. The conference, however, was meeting in the context of such a heavy emotional upsurge that many feared it would lead to the emergence of an anti-colonial Asian bloc. The United States and the United Kingdom in particular feared such a consummation and expressed their anxieties to India through their ambassadors.[32] It became apparent that any Asian bloc created solely on the basis of the prevailing anti-colonial sentiment would hinder the all-important task of cooperation with the developed nations of the world.

The conference met in New Delhi on 20 January 1949; it was apparent from the Indian Prime Minister's inaugural address at the conference that more than Indonesia was on the conference agenda: the need was to demonstrate that "Asia, too long submissive and dependent and a plaything of other countries, will no longer brook any interference with her freedom."[33] Nehru enunciated a three-fold task for the conference: (*i*) to frame and submit reasonable proposals for the settlement of the Indonesian question; (*ii*) to suggest lines of action to the Security Council in case either party fails to act according to its recommendations; and (*iii*) to devise machinery and procedure for the assembled governments to keep in touch

[31]Afghanistan, Australia, Burma, Ceylon, Egypt, Ethiopia, India, Iraq, Iran, the Philippines, Saudi Arabia, Syria, and Yemen.

[32]For a detailed account, *see:* Lawrence K. Rosinger, *India and the United States*, New York, Macmillan, 1950, pp. 86-100.

[33]*Jawaharlal Nehru's Speeches, 1946-49*, p. 327.

with each other. Nehru also made an open appeal for regional integration: "We see creative and cooperative impulses seeking a new integration and new unity. New problems arise from day to day which, in their implications, concern all of us or many of us. The Americans have already recognized a certain community of interest and have created machinery for the protection and promotion of common interests. A similar movement is in progress in Europe. Is it not natural that the free countries of Asia should begin to think of some more permanent arrangement than this conference for effective mutual consultation and concerted effort in the pursuit of common aims—not in a spirit of selfishness or hostility to any other nation or group of nations, but in order to strengthen and bring nearer fulfilment the aims and ideals of the Charter of the United Nations?"[34] Interestingly, on the next day of the conference, Nehru opposed the formation of such a bloc, obviously in view of the expression of Western misgivings on this account.[35] There was also the Arab urge to create an anti-Israeli bloc from which India wanted to dissociate itself.

The conference adopted three resolutions: one, strongly criticizing Dutch action and urging effective UN action; second, agreeing that the representatives of the attending countries in the United Nations should consult among themselves on the issue of Indonesia; and third, asking the participating governments to "consult among themselves in order to explore ways and means of establishing suitable machinery ... for promoting consultation and cooperation within the framework of the United Nations."[36]

It is the third resolution which was relevant for the future of regional integration in the area; there was now a specific declaration of the willingness of the countries of the region to devise an institutional base for cooperation. Interestingly, more than Nehru, it was now Carlos Romulo of the Philippines, who was interested in promoting the regional idea. During the con-

---

[34]*Ibid.*, p. 329.   [35]Levi, *op. cit.*, p. 40.

[36]Quoted by Harris Wofford, "An American Interpretation of India's Asia Policy," *India's Role in Asia*, p. 131.

ference, Romulo urged the establishment of "a continuing machinery ... including a small permanent secretariat in New Delhi, or may be Manila, to serve as a clearing house of information essential to concerted action by our various governments. ...."[37] He hoped that out of such methods of co-operation in nuclear form, they would be able to evolve a permanent organization of Asian States, functioning as a regional body alongside other associations of its kind, as contemplated by Article 52 of the Charter. By such methods of self-help, he said, they could strengthen "the forces of democracy and prevent other ideologies from capturing the faith of Asia by default!"[38] The question was, however, left over for the future to decide.

Among the non-Asian Powers there was no immediate reaction to the conference, except a general sense of satisfaction that the conference was moderate in its resolution and did not give vent to extreme anti-Western feelings prevalent at the time in Asia. The *New York Times* published an assessment of the conference by Robert Trumbull which said, *inter alia:* "...Asia is feeling its muscles. However, the record indicates that statesmen like Pandit Nehru and General Romulo can be counted upon to shy away from fostering racial or geographical antagonisms. India particularly is anxious to avoid the ideological cleavage that now separates the democracies from the Soviet sphere.... The New Delhi conference served notice that the Asian nations though individually of weak voice can and will speak together to make themselves heard by the other half of the world."[39]

Earlier, a report from New Delhi said: "The deep concern shown by the United States and the European colonial Powers over the possible development through this conference of the atmosphere for the growth of regionalism and racialism reacted powerfully upon the Indian Prime Minister, Pandit Jawaharlal

---

[37]*Ibid.*, p. 131.

[38]H. Venkatasubbiah, "Prospects of an Asian Union," *India Quarterly*, July-September 1949. [39]*New York Times*, 30 January 1949.

Nehru. When the possibility of his inadvertently fostering potential cleavages was impressed upon him by foreign diplomats here, he immediately made it clear in public that his intention was to act within the UN agencies alone and that no 'Asian bloc' or 'brown bloc' would come from this conference. Other nations quickly followed Pandit Nehru's lead."[40] Interestingly, on 4 April 1949, the *Pravda* also attacked Nehru for being anti-Soviet and interpreted the Asian Conference on Indonesia as an attempt to establish an anti-Soviet bloc.[41]

In India, the period following the Indonesia Conference was one of great hopes about such developments as would pave the way for an Asian integration. The Prime Minister, speaking in the Indian Parliament on 8 March 1949, said: ". . . one of the resolutions passed at that conference was that we should explore methods of close cooperation. We are pursuing that line of enquiry and perhaps in the course of a month or two or perhaps more we may have some more definite results to consider; possibly we might have another conference to consider possible lines of cooperation. Again that cooperation can only be the cooperation of independent nations without the least commitment of one to the other. . . . We have not yet decided what the region of cooperation might be, because, as I said a little while ago, India is interested in several regions of Asia. Whether all should be grouped together or separately we do not know. That is for us to consider together and to decide what is more feasible; but in any case two things have to be kept in mind. One is that whatever structure of cooperation we may build up will be entirely within the scope of the Charter of the United Nations. Secondly, there will be no binding covenant in it, and this will be largely an organization for the consultation and cooperation that naturally flow from common interests."[42]

The Indian Council of World Affairs, the organizers of the earlier Asian Conference and the organization linked intimately

[40]*Ibid.*, 23 January 1949.
[41]J. Frankel, "The Pacific Pact," *World Affairs*, October 1951.
[42]*Jawaharlal Nehru's Speeches*, p. 246.

with the Asian Relations Organization, published a long article at this time laying down the blueprint of the Organization of Asian States on a less formal basis than the Organization of American States.[43] The author of the article concluded: "For the structure of the permanent Asian Organization, that of the Organization of the American States is far too elaborate a model. The organs of the OAS have grown over several decades and their integration has come over gradually. An Asian union would find so many organs at the very start unmanageable and overlapping. Organs may grow in number as the organization develops and needs increase. ...."[44]

The Rise of China and the Changed Context

By the end of the year, however, Indian opinion became totally sceptical of the possibility of such developments and there was now a positive aversion to such attempts. Of course, among some nonofficial circles the idea still had its appeal; writing in 1951, an Indian student of world affairs considered the formation of an eastern federation of urgent necessity for India.[45] But official and responsible opinion had undergone a total change by the end of the year. In the India-America conference held in New Delhi in late 1949, the question was raised but it was stated by most Indian delegates to this nonofficial conference that they did not visualize any such development in the near future. The published report of the conference stated in a section entitled "Indian Opinion About the Possibility or Desirability of Regional Groupings in Asia": "A brief canvas of this question, at the suggestion of an American delegate, revealed general agreement among the Indians who spoke that there was no likelihood of regional groupings in the years immediately ahead."[46]

The change of Indian opinion illustrated by these developments within the span of a year reflected a vast change that

[43]H. Venkatasubbiah, "Prospects of an Asian Union," *op. cit.*
[44]*Ibid.*
[45]Shantilal Kothari, *India's Emerging Foreign Policies*, Bombay, Vora, 1959.
[46]*Indian-American Relations*, New Delhi, ICWA, 1950, p. 6.

had in the meantime taken place in the Asian political scene. Even as the Asian delegates at the Indonesia Conference were deliberating, news from China indicated that Chiang Kai-shek had virtually abdicated and his successor was seeking peace with the Communists; by the end of the year Communist revolution in China was complete. It was now futile to expect any regional movement in the Asian region which could be made to grow in isolation from this development. It was impossible to think of accepting China in any regional arrangement for Asia without making it a hotbed for Communist intrigues; likewise, any association formed to counter the Chinese situation would mean a definite lining up of Asia with the West and behind some of the regimes of the continent which felt threatened by China due to their internal weaknesses. In short, Asia was now face to face with communism and the urgent task for all the countries was to devise a policy towards the cold war which had entered the continent and threatened to engulf it. It is here that India and some other Asian countries faced the difficulty in aligning with elements whose approach to the cold war was radically different from India's.

It should also be noted that the rise of Communist China had secured for India what she had sought to secure through determined efforts earlier—a recognition of her importance by the rest of the world. With or without Asian integration, the emergence of Asia on the world scene was now bound to be accepted, so also the status of India. Writing in the *New York Herald Tribune* on 10 January 1949, Walter Lippmann had said: "Where then shall we look for allies now that nationalist China, the Netherlands, and France are so manifestly unable to play the role in Asia which we had supposed they would play? That, it seems to me, is the fundamental problem which has to be solved in order to form an American policy in Asia.... We would be well advised to enter into immediate consultations with Nehru about our whole course in Indonesia and China."[47] The War in Korea in June 1950 had further augmented the process initiated by

[47]Quoted in: J. C. Kundra, *op. cit.*, p. 117.

China—the rise of Asian communism and the inevitable status for the other nations of Asia in the changed context. Two consequences followed out of this situation: an erosion of Indian urgency for regional integration and an immense difficulty in conceiving any association in Asia which would be consistent with the need of avoiding alignment and invoking the potential sympathy of the two blocs in the solution of the Asian problems.

It should be noted here that when the Korean War broke out some Indians asked for another Asian Conference; Nehru rejected the suggestion on the ground that Korea was a world question and an Asian conference could be of no use in this regard.

The Baguio Conference

Thus, when the Philippines took the initiative next in convening a conference of Asian countries to consider matters of regional concern, India's response was at least half-hearted and unenthusiastic. India had earlier rejected an Australian attempt to form a Pacific pact; while Australia was ready to go it alone with the United States (she eventually did), Britain insisted that India should be included in such a conference and India insisted that the conference should concern itself with only non-military aspects of cooperation.[48] The solution was ultimately found in the Colombo Plan on the one hand and the ANZUS on the other. The problem with the Philippines initiative was that it was almost clear from the beginning that any such regional effort would be anti-Communist in nature. For the two men who displayed great enthusiasm for it and virtually held all the preliminary discussion among themselves were Syngman Rhee and Chiang Kai-shek. According to Werner Levi, the idea appealed to only those who "had everything to gain and nothing to contribute—Chiang and Rhee."[49] On 1 April 1949, Rhee had stressed the need for collective

[48]Levi, *op. cit.*, p. 41.
[49]Dutt, *India's Foreign Policy*, New Delhi, ICWA, 1950, p. 43-4.

security in Asia; on 11 July Chiang met Quirino in Manila and decided to "start the ball rolling for a Pacific pact, with the Philippines taking the first step."[50] This parentage of the proposal ended whatever interest India might have had in it: "Nehru cooled to the idea as soon as Quirino included Chiang Kai-shek and Syngman Rhee."[51] On 14 July 1949, Mrs Pandit told a meeting in Los Angeles: "It is not possible to form a Pacific pact. With whom is one to deal?"[52] As a Professor of the Columbia University noted in writing on the subject of Asian integration in 1954: "Both Chiang and Rhee are looked on as satellites of the United States and the peoples of the area want no satellitehood even by association."[53] In rejecting the proposed Pacific Pact, India stated that such alliances would retard the chances of reducing world tension, that an anti-Communist bloc by itself was no answer to Asia's problems, that Asian countries were to frame economic and political polices to face the challenge and that the emphasis would have to be on economic rather than the military solution of the problems.[54] The sponsors of the idea did not ask or expect India to be a member immediately but hoped that ultimately she would come in; apart from the three sponsoring countries, there would be Burma, Indonesia and Thailand. The weaknesses and futility of such an attempt, however, was soon evident to the leaders of the Philippines. Romulo, who was entrusted by his government to arrange the conference, gradually dropped both Chiang and Rhee from among the invitees and pressed on India to attend. Speaking in New York on 2 September 1949, Romulo said: "I want India to realize that the proposed Union is only a continuation of the Asian Conference and nothing more." The Philippines was taking up where India had left off and the Asian Union would, according to Romulo, undoubtedly function under India's

---

[50]Levi, *op. cit.*, p. 57.   [51]Dutt, *op. cit.*, p. 48.

[52]Wofford, "An American Interpretation of India's Asia Policy," *op. cit.*

[53]Dutt, *op. cit.*, p. 45.

[54]Nathaniel Peffer, "Regional Security in South-East Asia," *International Organization*, May 1954.

leadership, "for, India was the strongest and most enlightened nation of Asia today."[55] The explanations given by Romulo did not change India's attitude to the proposal; it was after it was made clear that the conference would not discuss political matters and would essentially concern itself with cultural affairs that India agreed to attend. The composition of the Indian delegation was itself an indication of India's lack of enthusiasm for it; and at least one author has implied that India not only hoped that nothing would come out of the conference but worked towards that end.[56]

The conference, held in May 1950, was attended by India, Pakistan, Australia, Indonesia, Thailand and Ceylon. Its resolutions recommended general cooperation in cultural fields.

It should be noted here that at this stage the United States agreed with India about the general nature of Asian problems and was not wholeheartedly favouring an anti-Communist alliance in the region. According to an Indian writer: "On account of the peculiarly fluid conditions in Asia, she (U.S.) was reluctant to take steps which might deeply offend popular sentiments and which might create an impression on the minds of the Asian peoples that an unpopular move was being forced on them. U.S. Secretary of State, Dean Acheson, agreed with Prime Minister Nehru that time was not yet ripe for a pact on the lines of the North Atlantic Pact."[57] A Pakistani author charged in 1960: "U.S. Secretary of State Dean Acheson almost killed the idea by remarking in a speech on 12 January 1950 that the real need of Asia was improvement of economic conditions...."[58] A British author noted in 1951: "It (the United States) employed Nehru's argument that the Pact was not feasible until the conflicts in Indonesia and Indo-China and elsewhere had been settled. The initiative for a Pacific pact received support only from the militarily and economically

[55]Dutt, *op. cit.*, p. 45.
[56]Levi, *op. cit.*, p. 58.
[57]Dutt, *op. cit.*, p. 44.
[58]Aslam Siddiqui, *Pakistan Seeks Security*, Karachi, Longmans. 1960, p. 138.

weak regimes of Chiang Kai-shek and Syngman Rhee, and from the President of the Philippines."[59]

Peace Area and the Afro-Asian Bloc

Under the impact of Asian developments, India's attitude to the question of integration took a distinct shape from the beginning of 1951. It was no longer any machinery for cooperation or any specific regional institution which India favoured. Nehru propounded at this time his doctrine of the *peace area*— an area free from the cold war and military alignments. Apparently, it was no longer feasible to treat a region as such as an entity; more important was the foreign policy outlook of the countries concerned. Without a basic minimum of agreement in this regard, there could be no meaningful arrangement for cooperation.

It is also at this time after the victory of the Chinese Communists and the beginning of the Korean War that the foreign policy of India found a new level of stability. Several factors could be cited as paving the way for this new self-confidence gained by India at this time. In the first place, it was demonstrated that while an intense cold war might often lead to local wars, neither of the Power blocs was ready to fight a general war: the needs of this peculiar situation of waging the cold war without starting a hot war enhanced tremendously the role and significance of countries which might serve as mediators, at the most, or as international post-offices, at the least. Secondly, the Western world was proved to be disunited in its techniques, if not basic aims, of conducting foreign policy: the policy of recognizing China in early 1950 was in fact a Commonwealth policy. Likewise the British and the U.S. attitudes to Korea diverged considerably. Thirdly, with the acquisition of China, the Communist world had become too big to be monolithic. Fourthly, the spotlight had at last been turned on Asia. Lastly, the expansion of the cold war arena had converted the policy of nonalignment into a positive policy, which had to be

[59]J. Frankel, "The Pacific Pact," *op. cit.*

cautiously guarded and not by any means taken for granted. The combined effect of all these developments was to secure for India without any regional integration what may have been the primary motivation of her foreign policy—a short cut to a status to which she was only potentially entitled.

This success of India and the new difficulties in any plan of Asian regionalism together brought about the next stage in India's policy regarding similarly-placed Asian nations—viz. a preference for what has been called the emergence of a peace area or a third area of peace. Speaking in the Indian Parliament on 12 June 1952, Nehru said: "I want to be perfectly frank with this House. I should like an ever-increasing number of countries in the world to decide that they will not have another war, whatever happens. I should like the countries in Asia— I speak about our neighbours—and other countries also to make it clear to those warring factions and those great countries that are explosively bitter against each other that they themselves will remain cool and not enter the arena of warfare whatever happens and that they will try at least to restrict the area of conflict. ...."[60] A year later, on 17 February 1953, he further elaborated this approach: "Mention has been made of a third force; I have not been able to understand quite what it means. If by the term is meant a Power bloc, military or other, I am afraid I do not consider it desirable, apart from the fact that it is not feasible either. The biggest countries today are small compared with the two giants. It would be absurd for a number of countries in Asia to come together and call themselves a third force or a third Power in a military sense. It may, however, have a meaning in another sense. Instead of calling it a third force or the third bloc, it can be called a third area, an area which—let us put it negatively first—does not want war, works for peace in a positive way and believes in cooperation. I should like my country to work for that. Indeed, we have tried to do so, but the idea of a third bloc or a third force inevitably hinders our work."[61]

[60]*Jawaharlal Nehru's Speeches, 1949-53*, p. 220.   [61]*Ibid.*, p. 236-7.

The peculiar needs of the creation of a third area of peace while avoiding the creation of a third world bloc had led to the emphasis by India on the nebulous but meaningful Asian-African group in the United Nations. It is during Nehru's visit to the United Nations that the Indian delegation arranged a meeting of the Arab and Asian delegates in Paris in 1948. From that time onwards, there was an Arab-Asian group functioning in the United Nations. With the growth in the number of African members of the United Nations, the group became known as the Afro-Asian group or the Asian-African group. While much of the group's solidarity was based on colonial issues, it had also a relevance in terms of the gradual emergence of what may be called a world public opinion. Also, the group had constantly forced attention from the United Nations on the problems of poverty and backwardness which these countries faced in common and which deserved to be tackled internationally. As an Indian writer commented: "Although these were the questions which usually produced the Asian-African alignment, they were not the only ones on which these States displayed a certain unity of approach. On some occasions, even on questions of war and peace, the members of the Asian-African group consulted one another and tried with some success to evolve a common policy."[62] Again: "The peace area was only a vague concept and the Afro-Asian group was only a lobby during the period 1950-53. But even in this period this concept and this group clearly emerged as a significant factor in the international field. Many observers felt that in the postwar world this development was next in importance only to the existence of the cold war between the major Powers."[63]

While there was an element of integration involved in the formation and growth of the Afro-Asian bloc in the UN, it should be noted that it was an amorphous institution and also that it lacked a clear regional base. Writing in 1961, the Indian Deputy Minister for External Affairs, Lakshmi Menon, implied that the

[62]K. P. Karunakaran, *India in World Affairs*, Bombay, Oxford, 1957, p. 47.
[63]*Ibid.*, p. 253.

Asian-African group in the United Nations was not so united as it appeared; for example on Algeria, "eleven French speaking African delegations stood opposed to any UN intervention in an Algerian referendum and are in favour of recommending immediate talks between the French and Algerian rebels, while the other countries are committed to a referendum under UN auspices."[64] In a report on the growth of an African Power bloc by Allan A. Michie, published in the *Reporter* in March 1960, the author had stated: "During the session the African members quarrelled regularly with the Asians. . . . One of the most spectacular quarrels centred on the attitutde of India as leader of the Asians and the prickly personality of the head of the Indian delegation, V. K. Krishna Menon. India's influence in the Afro-Asian alliance has repeatedly been thrown on the side of moderation and last October Menon personally failed to support the African bloc's demand that South Africa be hauled before the International Court of Justice for its adminis-tration of South-West Africa. Again the Asians, led by India, overruled the African members of the joint bloc and substituted milder language in the African resolution condemning France's nuclear test plans. India, charged the Africans, was simply playing up to the colonial Powers. The Africans took reprisals against India by failing to back its candidacy for election to the Economic and Social Council, enabling Japan to win."[65]

The Colombo Powers' Conference

An attempt to lend a geographical connotation to the peace area concept was contained in the conference of the Colombo Powers—Ceylon, Burma, India, Indonesia, and Pakistan—in Colombo in April 1954. Convened by the Prime Minister of Ceylon, the conference had on its agenda the Indo-China situa-tion, the question of the H-bomb, the question of Tunisia and Morocco, and the question of communism in general. Al-

---

[64]Lakshmi Menon, "Our Policy," *Seminar*, March 1961.
[65]Allan A. Michie, "The Growth of an African Power Bloc," *Reporter*, 17 March 1960.

though, as is the rule with such conferences, agreed resolutions on all these problems were adopted and released in the form of a communique, the discussions revealed that the cold war had already driven a wedge among the Asian Powers. In the opening statement itself the difference in emphasis was evident: Ceylon stressed the Communist danger and asked for greater cooperation among the members from this viewpoint; Pakistan thought that the major issue for the conference should be Kashmir; Burma emphasized mutual cooperation in the economic field; Indonesia urged for an Afro-Asian conference; and Nehru wanted the emphasis on the question of the H-bomb and Indo-China.[66] At the conference, Ceylon, supported by Pakistan, submitted a resolution declaring communism as the region's major problem. India, supported by Indonesia, opposed the resolution as one inconsistent with their policies. The compromise resolution condemned interference by Communist, anti-Communist and other agencies. The differences were concealed in a vague statement: "The Prime Ministers made known to each other their respective views on and attitude towards Communist ideologies. The Prime Ministers affirmed their faith in democracy and democratic institutions and being resolved to preserve in their countries the freedoms inherent in the democratic system, declared their unshakable determination to resist interference in the affairs of their countries by external Communist, anti-Communist or other agencies."[67]

While the conference undoubtedly served a vital role in the context of the Indo-China situation and the Geneva Conference,[68] as a regional effort its value was limited because of the inability of the countries to arrive at any kind of agreement on the cold war questions. The communique nevertheless mentioned several hopeful items: the Indonesians were asked to go ahead with the idea of an Afro-Asian Conference, the possi-

---

[66]*Keesing's Contemporary Archives*, 1954, p. 13576. [67]*Ibid.*

[68]Sir Anthony Eden had written to the Commonwealth Prime Ministers during the conference on Indo-China and much of the conference discussions was based on this note. In fact Eden made a special effort to remain in constant touch with the conference.

bility of future conferences was noted and a paragraph on economic cooperation talked generally of economic cooperation. The paragraph, however, also revealed the caution with which such problems were approached by the Prime Ministers: "The Prime Ministers considered certain proposals relating to economic cooperation and mutual aid and decided that they should be referred to the governments represented at the conference for their consideration. In their relations with one another the Prime Ministers affirmed their adherence to the principles of respecting the sovereignty of each country, and non-interference in the domestic affairs of the others."[69]

The last time that the Colombo Powers met was in New Delhi in November 1956 to consider the Egyptian and Hungarian crises. The Pakistan Prime Minister did not attend the Conference "due to other pre-occupations," and even a request to depute a Cabinet colleague of his was not complied with. The Prime Ministers condemned Britain and France on the one hand and the Soviet Union on the other for their aggression and intervention against weaker countries. Even at this conference, the Prime Ministers agreed to have joint and cooperative action, and set up a machinery for this purpose.[70] Nothing, however, has happened since to revive the concept of a Colombo Powers' group or bloc.

U.S. Aid to Pakistan

Behind the policy differences at the first Colombo Conference loomed large the fact that one of the governments of the region had by this time given up its policy of nonalignment. The development, however, had more significance than the mere decision of one of the South Asian countries to tread a different path in foreign policy; the extension of U.S. aid to Pakistan meant to India a definite attitude on the part of the United States to regard India as lost. Much has been written

[69]*Keesing's Contemporary Archives*, p. 13576.
[70]*Indian Affairs Record*, December 1956.

on this subject;[71] but what is of relevance here is the impact of this decision of the United States Government on the prospects of regional integration in the Asian region.

As Michael Brecher has noted: "Nothing has done more harm to the friendship between them (India and America) than the American arms aid to Pakistan since 1954."[72] India had made her concern clear about the involvement of Pakistan in any cold war alliance or in any military build-up in the region as early as in late 1952, when rumours circulated regarding the formation of MEDO with Pakistan as its keystone. Speaking at the annual session of the Congress Party in January 1953, Nehru said: "Obviously if any such development takes place it means the region of the cold war comes right up to our borders. We have to be concerned with any matter which directly or indirectly affects us."[73] While the idea of MEDO seemed to have been dropped at this stage, a year later, definite reports emanated from Washington that a U.S.-Pakistan military agreement was in the offing. Nehru stated in a Press conference: "This is a matter on which constitutionally or otherwise it is none of our concern what Pakistan and the USA are doing. But practically it is a matter of the most intense concern to us and something which will have very far-reaching consequences on the whole structure of things in South Asia and especially in India and Pakistan."[74]

In the following months both official and non-official opinion in India was greatly exercised over this issue and, without exception, the political parties, newspapers, journals and distinguished public men expressed their concern at these develop-

[71]A very able criticism from the American point of view is contained in three articles written in 1959 by Selig S. Harrison in the *New Republic*. "The Case History of a Mistake," "The Cost of a Mistake," and "The United States, India and Pakistan," *New Republic*, 10 August, 24 August, and 2 September 1949. Also *see:* James W. Spain, "Military Assistance for Pakistan," *American Political Science Review*, September 1954.

[72]Brecher, *Nehru: A Political Biography*, p. 579.

[73]For other statement *see:* Sisir Gupta, *India's Relations wih Pakistan*, New Delhi, ICWA, 1957.

[74]*Times of India*, 16 November 1953.

ments. Even such vehement critics of Nehru's foreign policy and advocates of India's greater alignment with the West as A.D. Gorwala wrote that India, which was "the greatest democracy of the East," had every right to expect "better understanding and treatment" from the United States.[75] In fact, "the whole country was emotionally charged in its opposition to the U.S. move to aid Pakistan militarily."[76]

The official announcement of the U.S. decision to extend military assistance to Pakistan was made by President Eisenhower on 25 February 1954.[77] The President reassured India that in case arms given to Pakistan were used for aggression against any country, he would immediately undertake appropriate action both within and without the UN to thwart such aggression. He also offered arms to India if she would accept it! On 1 March 1954, the Prime Minister of India made in the Parliament what may be regarded as the angriest of his statements about the United States,[78] and wanted US citizens of the UN observers' group in Kashmir to leave, as the USA was now no longer regarded as an impartial observer of Indo-Pakistan relations.

Two factors made the Indian reaction to the U.S. decision violent and its expression couched in strong terms. In the first place, the leaders of Pakistan had made no secret that they were accepting U.S. aid not to fight communism but to advance their interests *vis-a-vis* India; and secondly, too often U.S. leaders of this period gave the impression of having been in an urgent need to precisely promote this—an antidote to India and neutralism. As Nehru said in a subsequent statement, "the Pakistan newspapers and statements of responsible people in Pakistan make it perfectly clear that they have joined this pact because of India."[79] A year later the Prime Minister of Pakistan said while speaking on foreign affairs in his Parliament: "I may tell you that most of our foreign policy is depend-

[75]*Indian Daily Mail*, 26 December 1953.
[76]Kundra, *op. cit.*   [77]*Department of State Bulletin*, 15 March 1954.
[78]Text in: *Indiagram*, 3 March 1954.
[79]*Jawaharlal Nehru's Speeches, 1953-57*, p. 319.

ent on the Kashmir question, and if they are with us on Kashmir, they are with us in our foreign policy." A few minutes later the Prime Minister said: "I seek the friendship of China. I am not isolated. I feel perfectly certain that when the crucial time comes, China will come to our assistance. It has already done so."[80] Also, it was frankly stated by the Prime Minister that her alliance with the USA was designed to advance Pakistan's interests in relation to India.[81]

As for the U.S. motivation, while the Indian Prime Minister officially stated in the Parliament that he did not doubt them, it has been subsequently brought out by American analysts that there was an implicit anti-neutralist element in the U.S. decision. Selig Harrison, in one of the most incisive analyses of U.S. policy in South Asia published in the *New Republic* in 1959, wrote that the biographer of Nixon, Ralph Toledano, "leaves little doubt that Nixon urged this alliance not for its purported defense value against Soviet aggression but for the very reason Pakistan has sought aid—as a counterforce to the confirmed neutralism of Jawaharlal Nehru's India."[82] The decision, it should be noted, was not unanimously approved in the United States; Senator Fulbright voiced a strong note of dissent in the Senate: "I disapprove of this move and I wish the record to show very clearly my disapproval because in the future when the results of this policy are evident to all I want to be clear where the responsibility rests."[83] It was, therefore, with some justification that Brecher noted: "American assistance to Pakistan has deepened the Indian mistrust of U.S. motive in creating military blocs in South-East Asia and Middle East."[84]

One implicit effect of the step taken by the United States was to impede regional cooperation efforts in the one area

[80]*Dawn*, 26 February 1957.

[81]Foreign Minister Feroz Khan Noon said earlier that India was Pakistan's "only enemy" (*Dawn*, 22 October 1956).

[82]Selig S. Harrison, "Case History of a Mistake," *New Republic*, 10 August 1959.

[83]*Ibid.*   [84]Brecher, *op. cit.*, p. 579.

where it appeared logical—the Indo-Pakistan subcontinent. Selig Harrison noted in 1959: ". . . as matters stand the U.S. is seriously and perhaps critically disabled in any efforts to support a stable India and Pakistan by its attachment to a policy which arose out of calculated indifference to their geographic and historic interdependence. . . ."

The South-East Asia Treaty Organization

It is in this background of a general deterioration in Indo-American relations and an increasing lack of confidence in each other's bona fides that the SEATO proposals were mooted. Just as the decision to extend military aid to Pakistan was based on a certain distrust of India's capacity and inclination to function as any kind of a bulwark against communism, in India the American moves paved the way for a sudden upsurge of pro-Chinese sentiments and an overly enthusiastic response to China's diplomatic moves in the region. Within two months of the U.S. decision, India and China signed the Agreement on Tibet, proclaiming also in its preamble the Five Principles of peace and coexistence.[85] In June 1954, Chou En-lai visited New Delhi and signed a joint declaration with Nehru reaffirming these principles and envisaging Sino-Indian cooperation and consultation in the cause of peace.[86] In mentioning the sequence of events it must be noted also that even before the aid to Pakistan was announced there was positive evidence of U.S. aversion to allotting India any significant role in the area. In 1953, the United States, backed by the Latin American countries, opposed India's inclusion in a Far Eastern Political Conference. In 1951, before signing the Japanese Peace Treaty, Dulles undertook a fact-finding tour of Asia and omitted India from the list of countries to be visited. Writing on the foreign policy of India in 1955, an American author noted: "Dulles undoubtedly blundered in not visiting India, as

[85]INDIA (Lok Sabha). *Foreign Policy of India: Texts of Documents, 1957-59*, New Delhi, 1959, pp. 101-9.
[86]*Ibid.*, pp. 111-4.

he did other interested capitals to discuss the Japanese Peace Treaty."[87] And Nehru said, after the U.S. vote against India in the United Nations in 1953: ". . . of the twenty-one countries who voted against India, eighteen were from the Americas, seventeen from what is called Latin America. . . . Nearly the whole of Europe and nearly the whole of Asia wanted one thing in this political conference while a number of countries, all from the Americas, did not want it . . . (it) is not realized by many great Powers of the world that the countries of Asia, however weak they might be, do not propose to be ignored, bypassed and sat upon."[88]

Interestingly, the SEATO's spade work also reflected this tendency. In his memoirs, Sir Anthony Eden has written: "I repeatedly emphasized that although India and other Asian countries might well choose to remain outside such an arrangement, they should nevertheless be given every opportunity to participate and should be kept fully informed. If they could not be with us, we must not put them against us . . . (Mr Dulles) suggested that the controversial issue of India on the one hand and Formosa on the other should be avoided, and that the discussions should be limited in the first instance to South-East Asia proper. I did not like this balancing of India against Formosa. The two did not seem to be comparable. . . . It appeared that Mr Dulles had taken steps to settle the question of membership in advance, on his own terms. . . . Not only had India been given no opportunity to express her views, but Burma, too, was closely concerned and there had been no time for proper consultation with either the Indian or the Burmese Governments."[89]

Ultimately, an invitation was extended to India to attend the Manila Conference; as was expected, India declined it. The reasons as explained by Nehru were: (*i*) "Apart from every reason, big or small, it is obvious that our participation in the Manila Conference would have meant our giving up our basic

---

[87]Harris Wofford, *op. cit.*, p. 137.
[88]*Jawaharlal Nehru's Speeches, 1953-57*, p. 241.
[89]Anthony Eden, *Full Circle*, Boston, 1960, p. 109-11.

policy of nonalignment. We were not going to give up that basic policy, which we have followed for so many years, merely to participate in that conference"; and (*ii*) "our going there would obviously have affected our position as chairman of the three commissions in Indo-China. We were chosen for these responsible posts because we were thought to follow a certain policy."[90]

India not only declined to attend the conference but found herself positively opposed to the concept. The various reasons stated may be summarized as follows:

(*i*) It did not lead to any advance towards lessening of tension and towards peace. Soon after the Asian situation had improved, after the successful conclusion of the Geneva Conference,[91] "it has definitely added to the tensions and fears of the situation."[92]

(*ii*) The treaty could be extended to countries which did not want its protection; it "had established a roving commission to protect people who did not want to be protected, affecting the sovereignty of the nations of this region."[93]

(*iii*) The treaty would tend to be dangerously inclined in the direction of spheres of influence to be exercised by powerful countries. "After all, it is the big and powerful countries which will decide matters and not the two or three weak and small Asian countries that may be allied to them."[94]

(*iv*) The treaty not only concerned itself with outside aggression but was meant to invoke intervention by powerful nations in any internal development in these countries which might be regarded as untoward;[95] "does this not affect the whole conception of integrity, sovereignty and independence

[90]*Jawaharlal Nehru's Speeches, 1953-57*, p. 265.

[91]Nehru had described the success at Geneva as "one of the outstanding achievements of the postwar era . . . a great step forward" (*Times of India*, 22 July 1954).

[92]*Jawaharlal Nehru's Speeches, 1953-57*, p. 266.

[93]Speech by Krishna Menon in the General Assembly, 6 October 1954, quoted by Kundra, *op. cit.*, p. 97.

[94]*Jawaharlal Nehru's Speeches, 1953-57*, p. 267.

[95]*See* Article 4 of the Treaty.

of this area?"[96]

(*v*) The treaty engulfed a potential "area of peace": "We have thought that one of the major areas of peace might be South-East Asia. The Manila Treaty rather comes in the way of that area of peace . . . and converts it almost into an area of potential war."[97]

(*vi*) The treaty might extend to colonial possessions in the area.

(*vii*) The treaty appeared to ignore the views of Asian countries. It was not denied that what happens in South-East Asia is also the concern of the rest of the world, not only of South-East Asia. But, "when decisions of vital significance are made for an area excluding the views of the vital part of that very area, then there is something wrong in the procedure."[98]

(*viii*) Lastly, "they tend to encircle us."[99]

To Nehru, the treaty's "whole approach was wrong from the point of view of any Asian country."[100]

The Indian Press and platform were near unanimous in the criticism of the SEATO proposal. Only a small section of the extreme anti-Communist groups seemed to favour it and lent implied support to this concept. In their public statements, however, they also refrained from directly supporting the SEATO; all they wanted was the development of the Asian nations' capacity to fight communism, with or without Western backing. By and large, however, Indian opinion considered the SEATO proposal as inopportune, futile, harmful and one directed against the peace area concept.[101]

Baghdad Pact

India's general opposition to military pacts in the region was also expressed in regard to the Baghdad Pact.[102] Speaking in

---

[96] *Jawaharlal Nehru's Speeches, 1953-57*, p. 268.   [97] *Ibid.*, p. 268.
[98] *Ibid.*, p. 20.   [99] *Ibid.*, p. 268.   [100] *Ibid.*, p. 319.
[101] For a survey of Indian opinion *see:* V. P. Dutt and Vishal Singh, *Indian Policy and Attitudes Towards Indo-China and SEATO*, New York, Institute of Pacific Relations, 1954.
[102] Now called the Central Treaty Organization.

the Indian Parliament on the Commonwealth on 5 December 1955, Nehru referred to the pact and called it "a most unfortunate and deplorable action on the part of the countries who have joined it, deplorable not only from our point of view, but from the point of view of peace and security."[103]

Once again, India's opposition was stated both in general and specific terms. In the first place, the pact had "created in Western Asia far greater tension and conflict than ever before"; it had put one country against another.[104] Secondly, ". . . surely, nobody here imagines that the Pakistan Government entered into this pact because it expected some imminent or distant invasion or aggression from the Soviet Union! The Pakistan newspapers and the statements of responsible people in Pakistan make it perfectly clear that they have joined this pact because of India." Thirdly, these pacts were almost like international trusts or combines; "we do not quite know who is pulling where."[105]

India's fears about these pacts were partly justified when both the SEATO and the Baghdad Pact adopted statements on the necessity of resolving the Kashmir question. In March 1956, the SEATO in its Karachi meeting noted that the UN resolutions were in force and affirmed the need for an early settlement of the Kashmir issue. The Baghdad Pact followed suit.

Behind these objections of India was also a general feeling that the military approach to the problems posed by communism was not only inadequate but self-defeating. It was India's view that communism posed a political and economic challenge; it is on these planes that the challenge had to be met by the new

---

[103]*Jawaharlal Nehru's Speeches, 1955-57*, p. 312.

[104]*Ibid.*, p. 319. Writing in 1960, a Pakistani author confirmed the validity of this criticism: "By destroying Arab unity and by making the Arabs more suspicious of Western intentions, the Baghdad Pact increased instability in the region. If the intention of the Western Powers was to keep out, through the pact, instability and Soviet influence from the Middle East, they have succeeded in achieving just the opposite." (K. Sarwar Hasan, *Pakistan and the United Nations*, New York, Manhattan, 1960, p. 76.)

[105]*Jawaharlal Nehru's Speeches, 1953-57*, p. 319-20.

and emerging nations of Asia. This involved the evolution of a social and economic system which could deliver as much of the goods as communism and be of greater relevance for the common people of these countries. An equitable social structure, implementation of reform measures and a vigorous promotion of the institutions of freedom were the surest answers to the Communist challenge. It was imperative for these countries to respond to these challenges; because, the problem for these countries was not merely communism but economic decay and political autocracy which bred it. The danger of military alliances was that it might shift the focus to other tasks, perpetuate outdated regimes, prevent social reforms, impede economic programmes and thus defeat the very purpose for which they were apparently formed. Moreover, the direct involvement of these countries with the cold war might hinder the all-important need of these countries to underline the issues in world politics which transcended the cold war and communism—the problems created by the growing gap between the developed and underdeveloped countries of the world, the explosive situation created in areas like Africa by racial discrimination and colonial rule, in short, the need for Asians and Africans to be taken into account in world affairs. From these viewpoints, these pacts would reverse the process of history!

This approach was not fundamentally different from that accepted by the great Powers in some of their activities; the difference was great, however, in so far as the Western nations emphasized the military threat of communism and nations like India emphasized the other aspects of it. This has been well summed up by Hans Morgenthau, as quoted earlier.

Some of these Indian objections were shared by many American experts and analysts on Asia. The following two quotations, one from a former U.S. Ambassador to India, and the other from an American adviser to the Prime Ministers of Pakistan for five years, are of great relevance in evaluating the merits of the Indian attitude to military pacts unbacked by other considerations.

Chester Bowles: "Some nations who agree with us ... do not

really agree with us. They are so very close to the margin of survival that they have wrapped their arms around our neck in a desperate effort to be saved. They are ready to pay a price for it. Other nations, more proud, perhaps, but more sure of themselves, more confident of what they have, are less likely to do that."[106]

Charles Burton Marshall: "When we enter into contractual relations with a government which is really a clique, an in-group, inevitably the tendency is to commit the prestige of the United States ... to the fortunes and tenure of such an in-group. ... Moreover, the commitment to an in-group in the guise of a government in the usual sense tends to foreclose the U.S. from interchange with rival in-groups."[107]

In a fluid situation like the Asian, commitment to an in-group might indeed be tantamount to underwriting regimes which are the least capable of executing tasks which they are expected to execute to meet the many pronged challenge of communism. The SEATO, unlike NATO, was the extension of U.S. guarantee to a region without any real commitment by the other parties concerned, either in political, ideological, or economic terms.

In a searching analysis of the military alliances in Asia entitled "Military Illusions," Hans Morgentheau wrote in the *New Republic* of 19 March 1956: "The absurdity of these military alignments is surpassed only by the absurdity of their political consequences. ... In every respect our military policy in Asia is a failure. It is a failure in its own military terms, and it is a failure in the political consequences it has had for the relations with our potential friends and actual allies."[108]

The Bandung Conference

The attempts at regional cooperation, however, continued at other levels and the Bandung Conference is usually regarded

[106]Quoted in: Selig Harrison, "The Case History of a Mistake," *New Republic*, 24 August 1959.   [107]*Ibid.*

[108]Hans J. Morgentheau, "Military Illusions," *New Republic*, 19 March 1956.

as the high point of an Afro-Asian attempt to develop agreed bases of policy and a common approach to their problems.

The conference arose out of a suggestion made by the Indonesian Prime Minister during the Colombo Powers Conference of April 1954; a second meeting of the Colombo Powers held at Bogota, Indonesia, on 29 December 1954, considered the proposal in details and decided to hold the conference with the following purposes: (*a*) to promote goodwill and cooperation among the nations of Asia and Africa, to explore and advance their mutual as well as common interests, and to establish and further friendly relations; (*b*) to consider social, economic, and cultural problems and relations of the countries represented; (*c*) to consider problems of special interest to Asian and African peoples, e.g. problems affecting national sovereignty and racialism and colonialism; and (*d*) to view the position of Asia and Africa in the world today and the contribution they can make to the promotion of world peace and cooperation.[109] The conference also decided the list of invitees to the conference; Israel was excluded in an obvious attempt to make it possible for the Arabs to participate. What is important for us here is that the conference also declared unequivocally that in convening the Asian-African conference "they had no desire . . . that the participating countries should build themselves into a regional bloc."[110]

The conference met in Bandung from the 18th to the 24th April 1955; all the invitees with the exception of the Central African Federation joined the conference. The conference released an agreed communique at the end of their labours; the communique dealt with economic cooperation, cultural cooperation, human rights and self-determination, problems of dependent peoples, and problems of world peace and cooperation. The most significant part of the communique was the last section containing a declaration on the promotion of world peace and cooperation. The major declarations relevant

[109]INDIA. *Foreign Policy of India: Texts of Documents*, pp. 149-54.
[110]*Ibid.*

for the subject of regional integration were as follows:

(*i*) In the economic sphere the conference agreed to the general need for economic cooperation in the region, of providing mutual technical assistance, of exchange of know-how, of the establishment of regional training institutes, if possible, of collective action to stabilize raw material prices, of intra-regional trade fairs, collective bargaining with shipping lines, establishment of regional banks, etc.; but the most emphasized part of the communique was the demand that the UN should create the Special United Nations Fund for Economic Development and divert more resources to the region. What was left unmentioned was that such assistance was to come bilaterally.

(*ii*) In the cultural sphere also the communique emphasized the need for improving the communications between them and of reviving contacts which had been cut-off during the past centuries; specific mention was made of three items: the acquisition of knowledge of each other's country, the promotion of mutual cultural exchange, and the exchange of information.[111]

These positive aspects, however, were more or less unimportant compared to the major lesson that the conference discussions held out: that there was not one but at least three main trends of political opinion in the Afro-Asian world. As an Indian observer summed it up in 1961: "Bandung has passed into history as a broadly successful conference. So it was in the sense that it brought together a large number of Asian nations that had recently become free, and in that it gave notice to the world that Asia had arrived. But behind its agreed resolutions Bandung served to show that the varying pattern of conflicts between the great Powers had more to do with the mutual relations of Asian nations than any geographical contiguity and mutuality of interest."[112] From the viewpoint of

---

[111]Text of communique in *ibid.*, p. 171-81.

[112]G. N. Acharya, "India's Role in South-East Asia," *Far Eastern Economic Review*, 21 September 1961.

India, the major difficulty at this time arose out of the studied attempts made by the pro-Western nations at the conference to belittle the role of the nonaligned. It is of great interest that although these delegations sought to discredit nonalignment by painting a grim picture of the Communist threat, their relations at the conference with Chou En-lai were cordial while the leaders like Nehru were the main targets of attack. And the delegations succeeded in this objective; it has been the general opinion that at the conference, Chou outshone Nehru and the only elements to fade out of the conference were the Nehru-type neutralists who had little sabre-rattling to undertake and few polemics to indulge in.

Interestingly, the British and American reactions to this phenomenon were different. The *Times* of London noted in one of its despatches on Bandung: "Thus at Bandung it was not Mr Chou who felt the force of continual sniping, and sometimes heavy shelling from Turkey, Iraq, the Philippines, Siam, Pakistan, and Ceylon . . . it was Mr Nehru and his friends whose hopes were dashed and whose plans were wrecked by this anti-Communist assault, and two of the attackers were among the five sponsors. . . . The corollary of this *move directed against Mr Nehru and his friends* (italics mine) was that he was hardly called upon to act as mediator between China and the rest. At times one almost felt that it was Mr Chou who was playing such a part on behalf of Mr Nehru . . . yet . . . if Asia as a concept and political entity is to survive, Mr Nehru is its embodiment. . . ."[113] As against this the *New York Times* despatches almost noted the same fact with apparent satisfaction: "One of the most surprising developments at Bandung, it was agreed, was Premier Nehru's inability to keep the conference on the course he had charted for it. He was described by reporters as increasingly irritable and snappish as he was frustrated in his effort to prevent ideological conflict at the open sessions, and second, to prevent discussion of specific issues such as Palestine."[114] It is only the *Washington Post* which

[113]*Times* (London), 26 April 1955.
[114]*New York Times*, 24 April 1955.

commented later: "... the most significant development at Bandung was the relative eclipse of India. This could be a bad thing whatever the momentary satisfaction on the part of those who dislike Mr Nehru's self-righteousness. For, India and China are essentially rivals in the allegiance of free Asia. Anything that diminishes Indian leadership tends to strengthen the Chinese magnetism."[115]

It is Ceylon, backed by Pakistan, which again brought the cold war issues right into the front of the conference stage by demanding condemnation of Communist colonialism: interestingly, Pakistan assured China that it had nothing against it and Kotelawala of Ceylon was personally on the best of terms with Chou En-lai. There was little doubt left at the time of the conference that the real purpose of these nations was to assert that nonalignment in the cold war was meaningless. The result was to lend the status to Chou which he had hardly expected when the conference started; he was at the beginning almost living on the nonaligned nations' sufferance.

It should also be noted in discussing the Bandung Conference that there was a difference between Nehru and other neutralists in regard to the general tone of the conference. In his closing statement at the conference, Nehru said: "We want to be friends with the West and friends with the East and friends with everybody ... we mean ill to nobody ... we send our greetings to Europe and America. We send our greetings to Australia and New Zealand ... they are next to us and I would like Australia and New Zealand to come nearer to Asia. I would welcome them because I do not want what we say or do to be based on racial prejudices. We have enough of this racialism elsewhere."[116] Also of some embarrassment for Nehru was the Arab insistence to discuss the Palestine issue which he hoped initially to avoid in the conference.

It is not surprising, therefore, that the Indian reaction to Bandung was not enthusiastic. While the historical importance

---

[115]Quoted by Harris Wofford, "An American Interpretation of India's Asia Policy," *op. cit.*, p. 145.

[116]*Jawaharlal Nehru's Speeches, 1953-57*, p. 290-1.

of the very occurrence of the conference was noted, the decision to avoid any regionalism at the conference was regarded as wise. Reporting on Bandung in the Indian Parliament, Nehru said: "These recommendations (for cooperation) wisely avoided any provision for setting up additional machinery of internation cooperation, but on the other hand sought to rely on the existing international machinery in part and for the rest on such decisions, as individual governments might by contact and negotiation find it possible to make."[117] At Bandung itself, while Iraq asked India to lead the smaller nations of region, Nehru spurned the idea: "There is no friendship when nations are not equal, when one has to obey the other and one dominates the other."[118] There was an obvious element of tragicomedy involved in the whole suggestion after the role that the then friends of Iraq had played at the conference.

While the Bandung Conference vaguely mentioned the possibility of holding another conference, and later the Communist countries, particularly China, favoured the holding of such a conference, India declined to support the idea. In fact, the Indonesian leaders as well as the Egyptians are known to have favoured the idea and attempted to persuade Nehru. The Government of India, however, took the stand that there was no particular value in a geographical concept; the need for Asia and Africa was cooperation with also the other countries of the world and not merely to stress their common problems. Behind this abhorrence was the Indian inability to adjust with the nations of the region who came to such conferences merely to make their presence felt and who had little areas of agreement in regard to either foreign or domestic policies.

The Conference at Brioni

From India's viewpoint more meaningful was the conference at Brioni a year later (18-19 July 1956) among the leaders of the three nonaligned nations with any degree of similarity of

---

[117]*Ibid.*, p. 294.   [118]*Ibid.*, p. 2.0.

approach—India, Yugoslavia and Egypt. Even here, however, the difficulties of saving the Indian foreign policy style and content after adjusting it with other neutralists became obvious. The conference came out again with an agreed communique whose emphasis was on the crucial importance of international development efforts to lift the less-developed countries through UN machineries. One of the special references to the communique was to the Middle East: "In the Middle East the conflicting interests of great Powers have added to the difficulties of the situation. These problems should be considered on their merits and safeguarding legitimate economic interests but basing the solution on the freedom of the people concerned."[119]

All the reports on the conference agreed that Nehru had played the moderating role. It is noted in the *Facts on File:* "The conference . . . produced no formalized neutralist bloc which Nehru was said to have opposed."[120] The *New York Times* brought out an interesting aspect of the conference in an editorial: "Aside from their neutralist attitude, the three statesmen have little in common . . . and each has separate and individual problems to meet. Tito is a Communist, Nehru is a democratic Socialist and Nasser is a military dictator. To Tito and Nasser the meeting with Nehru, head of one of the most populous countries of the world, meant undoubtedly an accretion of prestige and was exploited as such. It served to emphasize their independence of both East and West and to minimize the isolation into which they were isolating themselves. But to Nehru the meeting could mean neither prestige nor profit, and it was he, therefore, who put the brakes on whatever larger ambitions the other two might have had. . . ."[121]

What heightened India's suspicion of the use of such a conference was the fact that these conferences, while avoiding blocs, did tend to involve the participating countries in problems generated by anyone of them. While there is no doubt that the decision to withdraw the Aswan Dam aid which followed the Brioni Conference was appearing to this group of nations

---

[119]*Keesing's Contemporary Archives*, 1956, p. 15008.
[120]*Facts on File*, 18-24, 1956.   [121]*New York Times*, 20 July 1956.

as an attempt by the U.S. Secretary of State to deal a blow to the weakest link of the neutralist chain at this time, viz. Egypt, the violence of Egyptian reaction was unexpected and illustrated the inevitable involvement that it might imply in situations undesirable from the Indian point of view. We have quoted earlier the speech of the Indian Prime Minister that it was not India's way to deal with problems the way Nasser did; it is also the testimony of Eden that India's initial reaction to nationalization of the Suez Canal was one of uneasiness: "When Egypt first seized the Suez Canal, the Indian Government showed some embarrassment, no doubt accentuated by the fact that Mr Nehru had been the guest of Col. Nasser in Cairo only a few days before." It is also of interest to note that in the end of his political career, Eden recognized that even after all the British-Indian differences over Suez, his friendship with Nehru "was certainly unimpaired."[122]

The Belgrade Conference

Such events appear to have added to India's aversion to any attempt to create a bloc of neutral nations; the problems of their internal and external relations were viewed very differently by these countries. Some other nonaligned nations, however, particularly Indonesia, Egypt and Yugoslavia, continued to see an advantage in periodic conferences of the nonaligned countries. India virtually resisted all attempts to hold other conferences till the beginning of 1961 when she had to attend a conference at Cairo to prepare for another huge conference of the nonaligned. It is to be noted, however, that while other countries were represented at the preparatory conference by their Foreign Ministers, India sent only a civil servant to the meeting. Also, on arrival in New Delhi after the conference at Cairo, Foreign Secretary R. K. Nehru said that India was not committed to attend the Belgrade Conference and would

[122]Eden, *op. cit.*, pp. 495-650.

take a decision whether to attend it or not.[123] When the conference met at Belgrade in September 1961, India was represented by the Prime Minister.

All reports on Belgrade confirm the feeling that once again India found herself uncomfortable at the conference. The British Press was almost identical in the assessment of this aspect of the conference: the *Spectator* published a despatch from Belgrade which said *inter alia:* "Mr Nehru (was) trying to convince the other delegates that attention should be given to first things first . . . but few of the delegates were impressed. Representatives of the radical African countries even condemned Nehru as *vieuxjeu;* it is far more important, they consider, to concentrate on fighting colonialism and on stopping the loss of life in Angola and Algeria than on trying to prevent a world war."[124] The *New Statesman* wrote: "Nehru's speech was a wonderful relief after what seemed the endless succession of set documents read out by earlier speakers, mainly written for home consumption. He brushed aside the colonial issue because victory in this field was now certain. . . . Nehru was criticized for his speech."[125] The *Economist* wrote: "Although India was far from alone on most issues, there was no hiding Mr Nehru's impatience with his more parochially-minded colleagues' resentment over his demands that they should take a broader view. . . . The conference need cause the Western world no anxiety if the West . . . recognizes its own hopes for the world in Mr Nehru's remarks at Belgrade that 'we have to build in our own countries societies of free men, societies where freedom is real.' "[126] This emphasis of Nehru on the need to turn the searchlights inward was different from the one that leaders like Sukarno preferred. It is worthwhile to quote an extract from Sukarno's speech: "They cannot go on living at the expense of millions of poverty-stricken people. Their

[123]*Hindustan Times,* 16 June 1961. For a general review of India's position in regard to such conferences, *see* also *The Hindu Weekly Review,* 5 June 1961.
[124]*Spectator* (despatch by Hella Pick), 8 September 1961.
[125]*New Statesman,* 8 September 1961.
[126]*The Economist,* 9 September 1961.

affluent societies are built upon the sweat and toil and tears of millions who spend their evenings, not with their eyes glued to their television sets, but in the darkness pierced by the light of a single candle."[127]

A correspondent of the *New York Times*, A.M. Rosenthal, brought out sharply the difficulties of Nehru in a conference of this kind. Writing in the *New York Times* on 24 September 1961, he said: "Almost alone in the world, Jawaharlal Nehru has struggled against allowing the people in their ignorance and poverty to be caught in the trap of the easy way out. The others—the Nassers, the Titos, the Nkrumahs, the Toures, the Castros, the Sukarnos—have built their pedestals on their peoples' despair and strivings. At Belgrade, Nehru sat among men he must have despised ... he is no longer the automatic leader of the nonaligned nations." Again: "There are some interesting reasons why this happened (the bypassing of Nehru at Belgrade) and they bear on Mr Nehru's future influence among the uncommitted nations. He found himself among many leaders with whom he had absolutely nothing in common and small-time dictators who are contemptuous of the methods by which he lives and governs. Beyond tactics, how much influence can a man like Nehru have on a man like Sukarno? They live in different political and moral worlds."[128]

Joint Defence with Pakistan

Before concluding this discussion on the attempts at political integration, mention must be made of three other events pertaining to India's foreign affairs—the rejection of joint defence proposals from Pakistan, the initiative in rendering assistance to Burma in 1949, and the extension of military guarantees to Nepal in 1950.

The first casual mention of possible joint defence between India and Pakistan came from Prime Minister Mohammed Ali

---

[127]Quoted by Walter Laqueur and Alfred Sherman, "The Meaning of Belgrade," *New Republic*, 25 September 1961.

[128]*New York Times* (Magazine), 25 September 1961, p. 84-5.

in 1953. Nehru turned it down by asking: "Joint defence against whom?" and the Pakistan Premier complained that Nehru had "poured cold water" on his proposal.[129] The question was almost answered by China in 1959 and Pakistan President Ayub Khan promptly repeated the suggestion on 24 April: ". . . in the event of an external threat both India and Pakistan should defend the subcontinent in cooperation with each other."[130]

India turned down these suggestions. Speaking in the Rajya Sabha (the Council of States) on 4 May 1959, Prime Minister Nehru said: "It is said often in Pakistan, 'let us have a common defence policy.' Now, I am all for settling our troubles with Pakistan and living a normal friendly neighbourly life. We try for that. But I do not understand when people say that we should have a common defence policy. Against whom? Immediately, the question arises—'against whom is the common defence policy?' Are we going to become members of the Baghdad Pact or SEATO or somebody? We do not want to have a common defence policy which is almost another meaning of some kind of military alliance. The whole policy that we have pursued is opposed to this conception. . . . We are not going to tie ourselves up, our conceptions, our policies, with other countries involving military defence and attacking and all that."[131] Again: "Nonalignment . . . is a positive concept and we do not propose to have a military alliance with any country, come what may, and I want to be quite clear about it because the moment we give up that idea of nonalignment we lose every anchor that we hold on to and we drift. We may hang on to somebody or some country, but we lose our own self-respect, of the country's. . . ."[132]

In India, pro-Western newspapers and journals were anxious to explore the possibilities in this regard. Before the Prime Minister made his statement, columnist B. G. Verghese wrote in the influential daily *Times of India:* "Those who believe that

---

[129]*Dawn*, 9 June 1953.   [130]*Ibid.*, 25 April 1959.

[131]*India News*, Washington, 15 May 1959.

[132]*Ibid.* For a more recent statement by Nehru, *Asian Recorder*, 2-8 July 1961.

peace in Asia will in the future depend to a large extent on Sino-Indian friendship are perfectly right. But the formula will be incomplete unless there is a certain balance of power between them as well. The long-term interests of India therefore suggest a policy that will go towards developing and maintaining such a balance. President Ayub Khan and the Foreign Minister of Pakistan are not wrong in saying that events in Tibet underline the identity of interest between India and Pakistan. An Indo-Pakistan entente would constitute a powerful factor making for stability in Asia."[133] The Swatantra Party of India asked for serious consideration of the suggestion.[134] The former Socialist leader, Jayaprakash Narayan, also favoured the concept.[135]

After the Prime Minister's speech, the weekly *Thought* of New Delhi commented: "It may not be denied that just now, with Sino-Indian relations ruffled over the events in Tibet, talk of Indo-Pakistan joint defence arrangement could be construed as an arrangement against China. But then the better course for the Prime Minister would obviously have been not to talk about it all, rather than deliver as he did an ideological caveat against it on the grounds of non-involvement in international alliances."[136]

Others continued to advocate such a policy and even went further; the reputed author and journalist Frank Moraes wrote in March 1961: "It has been suggested that no defence arrangement is feasible with Pakistan so long as that country's foreign policy is not one of nonalignment. But ironically, Pakistan's latest moves, notably her parleys with Peking, suggest that she is moving in that direction, and with a new administration in Washington much of the sting is likely to go out of SEATO and CENTO. If Pakistan, on her part, sincerely desires to work closer with India and enter into a common defence arragement she should relinquish her membership of SEATO and CENTO which has little positive value or reality, more so against the

[133]*Times of India,* 25 April 1959.
[134]*Indian Affairs Record,* March 1960.   [135]*Ibid.,* August 1960.
[136]*Thought,* 9 May 1959.

altered background of American foreign policy.... The germ of the idea of confederation is there.... The time has come to give the idea shape and reality."[137]

Earlier the veteran Indian statesman and former Governor General, C. Rajagopalachari, had suggested a confederation between the two countries.[138] And as late as January 1961, Louis Fischer the American journalist and author, a longtime friend of India, wrote in the *New Leader:* "Nehru could if he cared confederate with Pakistan and he might find the opposition and obstacles surprisingly small."[139] Louis Fischer actually advocated such a confederation on almost the same grounds as some Indian journalists had done.

Notwithstanding these pleas, the official Indian position remained one opposed to this kind of cooperation with Pakistan.

Aid to Burma

One of the important events of India's foreign relations was her aid to Burma in her internal troubles created by Communist and Karen rebels. The Government of India convened on 28 February 1949 an informal regional conference of representatives of some Commonwealth States to find out ways and means by which they could help the Burmese Government to maintain peace and order within the country and to explore possibilities of settlement with the Karens. The question of giving aid to Burma was again discussed in April 1949 when the Commonwealth Prime Ministers met in London. They decided to give coordinated aid to Burma in the form of arms and loans and to set up a Burma Aid Committee to implement the decision. The members of the committee were the ambassadors of India, Pakistan, Ceylon and Britain in Rangoon. In their meetings, the extent and manner of financial assistance

[137]Frank Moraes, "New Look," *Seminar*, March 1961.
[138]*Hindustan Times*, 29 January 1959.
[139]Louis Fisher, "Indo-Pakistan: A Federation to Meet China," *New Leader*, 16 and 23 January 1961.

to be given to the Burmese Government were discussed. In December 1949, the Burmese Prime Minister visited New Delhi to discuss with Nehru certain matters concerning the subject. A final aid programme was drawn up in 1950 and it is known that apart from financial assistance India had also rendered military assistance to Burma. There has, however, been no public statements regarding the nature and extent of this aid.[140]

"India took a leading part in the conferences connected with the proposals for aid to Burma"; it was made clear that "India could not take an indifferent attitude to the unstable conditions within the territory of her immediate neighbour."[141] It was also well known that the aid was largely needed to tide over the Communist revolt—a situation which all the newly-freed countries were facing at this stage. As Nehru told newsmen at this time: "I feel that the fear on the part of the British and other governments was that if the present conditions continued, other elements in Burma may begin to play a more important role than either the Karens or the Burmese Government, which they did not want them to play."[142]

In a speech to the Indian Parliament, Nehru cautiously mentioned the subject on 17 March 1950: "Then there is Burma which has seen a great deal of internal trouble during the last two or three years and has faced enormous difficulties. Naturally our government and our people are interested in the present and future of Burma. It is not our purpose to interfere in any way with other countries, but wherever possible to give such help as we can to our friends. We have ventured to do so in regard to Burma...."[143] It is interesting that while aiding Burma, India refrained from taking any position regarding Indo-China, presumably because the struggle there was still largely an anti-colonial one.

While Indian opinion in general supported the Prime Minister on the issue of Burma, some criticism was heard from Communist

[140]G. N. Acharya, "India's Role in South-East Asia," *op. cit.*
[141]K. P. Karunakarn, *op. cit.*, pp. 109-11.
[142]*Ibid.*, p. 110.
[143]*Jawaharlal Nehru's Speeches, 1949-53*, p. 145.

and other elements. In an editorial, the *Republic* criticized the Indian policy toward Burma as being less than neutral and added: "Commonwealth loan to Burma is no more or less a sign of neutrality than, let us say, the United States decision to give arms aid to Bao Dai. No one can officially stop us from proclaiming neutrality. But the least we can do is to cease feeling superior to the Americans for their policy of involvement."[144]

Guarantee to Nepal

In the case of Nepal, India had made it clear shortly after the emergence of Communist China that India would consider Nepal's defence as her own and that an attack on Nepal would be considered an attack on India. After the Chinese troops had moved into Tibet, the Prime Minister of India had stated: "We cannot allow that barrier (the Himalayas) to be penetrated because it is also the principal barrier to India. Therefore, much as we appreciate the independence of Nepal, we cannot allow anything to go wrong in Nepal or permit that barrier to be crossed or weakened, because that would be a risk to our own security."[145] The statement was repeated in 1959, following Chinese invasion threats.

It should be noted that while India had not developed any positive outlook to defence arrangements with other countries, in regard to Nepal she had unilaterally extended guarantees. There is also the India-Nepal Agreement of 1951 which makes it incumbent on India to treat Nepal specially in matters of her defence needs. It may be added here that a considerable portion of India's own fighting forces are composed of Gurkhas recruited from Nepal.

Thus, when vital national security needs of India are involved, she has moved forward in identifying her interests with those of the Himalayan neighbour.

---

[144]Quoted in: Karunakaran, *op. cit.*, p. 111.
[145]*Jawaharlal Nehru's Speeches, 1949-53*, p. 177.

Economics and the Colombo Plan

The Indian difficulties in contemplating regional cooperation have been the least in the sphere of economics. The problems in this regard were obvious: the countries of the region had competitive and not complementary economies. Yet, there was a distinct Indian readiness to collaborate on the economic plane with other countries of the region. The first concrete attempt to organize some kind of regionalism in the economic sphere was the Colombo Plan. It is India which had insisted on turning the focus to the internal problems of the region at the Commonwealth conferences of the early postwar days. The Colombo Plan was born out of the attempt of the efforts of the Commonwealth to strive towards the economic better-ment of the region. It is in the Colombo meeting of the Commonwealth Foreign Ministers of January 1950 that the vital needs of the area were discussed; the meeting had set up a consultative committee for surveying the needs of the area, assessing the resources and manpower available in the region, and providing an international framework within which the cooperative effort for assisting the countries of the region could be developed. In the London meeting of the committee of September 1950 the plan was put through in the form of the adoption of the report of the committee, which incorporated reports of individual countries.[146]

The latest available figures of aid and assistance under the plan show impressive performance over the decade. According to a report submitted to the 13th meeting of the Colombo Plan Consultative Committee in November 1961 at Kuala Lumpur, the total volume of external aid that has been directed to the countries of South and South-East Asia since the inception of the Colombo Plan in 1950 to the end of June 1961 amounted to over $10,000 million. During this period, 26,373 trainees

---

[146]For an account of the development of the plan *see:* Antonin Basch, "The Colombo Plan, A Case of Regional Integration," *International Organization*, February 1955; also, N. Prasad, "The Colombo Plan," *India Quarterly*, April-June 1952.

learned new skills or attained higher standards of efficiency in skills previously learned, and over 5,755 experts visited the region to perform a wide variety of technical tasks. In the year 1960-61 alone, external assistance of the value of \$1,500 million came into the area; 4,417 men received training and 786 experts visited the region. The development expenditure incurred by the countries of the region increased from 1,187.9 million British pounds in 1957-58 to 1,724.9 million in 1959-60, and to 2,017.6 million in 1960-61. From 1954-55 the development expenditure in the region had increased by 200 per cent in a period of six years.[147]

The increase in production figures in selected commodities has been as follows: rice – increase of 40 per cent; petroleum— from 10.8 to 26.5 million tons; coal—from 35 to 54 million tons; steel—from 1.3 to over 3 million tons; cement—from 6 to 10.8 million tons.

The distinctive feature of the Colombo Plan relevant for us here is its emphasis on regional cooperation. Of the 13 countries which provided technical training to their partners in the plan, India with 266 awards comes fifth after the USA (2,356), UK (623), Australia (446), and Japan (305). In the matter of supply of experts, India comes next after the USA, with 135 as against the USA's. India has also provided both capital and technical assistance under the plan to member countries; to Nepal, India's assistance amounted to 180 million rupees during 1959-60; she has provided training to 1,694 nominees from the participating countries. Other countries in the region which have provided training are Burma (16), Ceylon (65), Indonesia (17), Malaya (30), Pakistan (116), the Philippines (14), Singapore (39), and Thailand (10).

While the plan has achieved considerable results in one sense, it is doubtful whether it can be compared with other regional plans. Frederick Benham, British economist and student of the plan, has called it "one of those voluntary and flexible arrangements based on goodwill which are not subject to any

---

[147]All facts taken from: *The Hindu Weekly Review*, 22 January 1961.

formal rules—it is not really a plan at all. It may be regarded as an envelope covering the development programs of member countries in South-East Asia."[148] The former Indian Ambassador to the United States, G. L. Mehta, said about the plan: "The most important feature of the Colombo Plan is that it is not a plan at all. It is not a blueprint of a regional development programme. While the Colombo Plan is an arrangement for international economic cooperation, it has no central organization, no irksome rules of procedure, no headquarters and no permanent secretariat."[149] A British diplomat agreed with this view in 1955: "The real strength of the Colombo Plan is the fact that it is not a rigid plan ... (the plan) has got all the amorphous characteristics of the Commonwealth ... which is its very strength."[150] The consequences, however, have appeared to an American observer as retrograde: "By leaving the so-called plan completely on bilateralism, by operating only through a consultative committee on the ministerial level, which meets annually, by making no effort to devise an integrated regional development program with a central organization, the Colombo Plan has not filled the vacuum of economic anarchy prevailing in this, as in other parts of the world."[151]

The U.S. Government had indeed attempted to help the growth of economic regionalism in the area when in 1955 it let it be known that it was prepared to set aside a sum of $200 million for projects in the region which would benefit a number of countries. The response, however, was not encouraging and it is necessary to review in this connection the Simla Conference of May 1955.

The Simla Conference, 1955

In May 1955, thirteen Asian nations of the Colombo Plan Consultative Committee—Cambodia, India, Indonesia, Japan,

[148]Quoted by Antonin Basch, *op. cit.*

[149]Quoted by Harris Wofford, "An American Interpretation of India's Asia Policy," *op. cit.*

[150]*India's Role in Asia*, p. 171.   [151]Harris Wofford, *op. cit.*, p. 140.

Laos, Nepal, Pakistan, Malaya, Singapore, Borneo, Sarawak, Thailand—met in a conference in Simla (India) to discuss a six-point agenda: (*i*) pattern of utilization of U.S. aid; (*ii*) practical problems arising in the utilization of U.S. aid; (*iii*) utilization of special allocation for development of intra-regional trade and setting up of machinery to provide credit to enable countries in Asia to tide over short-term balance of payment difficulties; (*iv*) representation of European countries which may desire to assist in the economic development of member countries; (*v*) setting up of a small permanent secretariat for the Colombo Plan Consultative Committee to provide a technical wing; and (*vi*) provision of training facilities for economic development for the people of the region.[152]

It was known that the United States was anxious to see greater regional cooperation in Asia and that much of the inspiration for the conference had come from Harold Stassen. But the United States did not attend the conference in order to allow a completely free decision by the Asians in this regard.

The decisions of the conference, as announced in a communique dated 13 May 1955,[153] were hardly encouraging from the viewpoint of regional cooperation: almost all the proposals in this regard had been rejected. The idea of a regional organization of the OEEC type was rejected; it was stated that the time had not yet come for the establishment of a permanent secretariat for the Colombo Plan; the delegates also disfavoured earmarking of funds for any project which readily lent to regional treatment. The conference also decided against any special allotment for projects designed to expand inter-Asian trade. Even European countries who desired participation in the plan were asked to do so on a bilateral basis.

In a despatch to the *New York Times*, correspondent A. M. Rosenthal said on 13 May: "The clear hope of the USA was that the experts would come up with some plans for putting the Eisenhower fund to use on a cooperative basis. But a major result of the Simla Conference has been to show that most

---

[152]*Times of India*, 9 May 1955.
[153]Text in: *ibid.*, 14 May 1955.

countries of Asia are not ready for, or are afraid of, regional planning. Instead of using the Eisenhower fund to promote the economic health of the region as a whole, most countries at Simla just want credit of the fund to be split up among the recipient countries."[154] It was Japan alone, of all the countries, which was eager for such cooperation; India was warmer than other nations but not warm enough to throw "her turban in the air with wild enthusiasm."[155] Ceylon and Burma were the most vocal in opposing all new ideas; Ceylon, "because these days she does not like anything India supports."[156] While India did not express any disappointment, the Japanese Ambassador to India, who led his country's delegation, said: "We came with advanced ideas and broader views on this regional basis but we realize that most of the member countries wanted the funds to be utilized for development of their areas through bilateral means. I think it is appropriate for the present stage to carry forward the economic development on that line."[157]

Among the reasons mentioned by the *New York Times* correspondent in his despatches for the failure of the conference were: (*i*) the fears that eventually a huge regional economic organization would grow; (*ii*) that this would lead to a side-tracking of the smaller countries' needs; (*iii*) the fear that this would lead to the emergence of a third party between the United States and the country; (*iv*) the lack of development plans of most nations of the region; (*v*) old-fashioned suspicion and fear of supra-regional organizations; (*vi*) the fear that the real interest of the USA was to develop new markets for Japan; and (*vii*) the fear, among some, that India would become too powerful.

There was an economic justification for resisting regional arrangements; with the exception of India and Japan, no other country had well-planned programmes of future development. "But," as Rosenthal said, "deeper than economic justifications and rationalizations ran the suspicions. Smaller countries

---

[154]*New York Times*, 13 May 1955.   [155]*Ibid.*, 14 May 1955.

[156]*Ibid.* (News of the Week in Review), 14 May 1955.

[157]*Times of India*, 14 May 1955.

believed that in a regional set-up they would lose the bargaining power with the U.S. and would find a third party between themselves and the source of funds. They were afraid that their own national interests might be subordinated to regional interests. They thought that sort of thing might be all right in Western Europe where most countries had foundations for developed economies, but would be disastrous for a country at the bottom of the economic ladder. . . . Regionalism was a luxury they could not afford."

The Simla Conference showed "that Asia would rather have things go on as they are than try any of those new-fangled regional ideas."[158]

The New Delhi Conference, 1961

In late September 1961, a conference of Asian Economic Planners in New Delhi again considered problems of regional cooperation. The Indian financial weekly *Eastern Economist* commented in its issue of 29 September 1961: "The Conference of Asian Economic Planners now in session in New Delhi has raised the ambitious hope that, under the sponsorship of ECAFE, there will somehow come into being in the fullness of time, an Asian economic community."[159] The direct purposes of the conference were more limited—the establishment of an Asian Institute of Economic Development and a Regional Advisory Group on Economic Development Planning. The conference succeeded in achieving the limited results envisaged; but wider cooperation, which was ably advocated by the ECAFE Secretariat in an elaborate note prepared for the occasion, was stalled by some members. "A typically cautious note was sounded by the representative of Ceylon, who while supporting the general idea of regional cooperation stated that it should not mean the colonial type of complementarity. A similar note was uttered by the representative of Pakistan. . . ."[160]

---

158 *New York Times*, 13 and 14 May 1955.
159 *Eastern Economist*, 29 September 1961.
160 *Economic Weekly*, 14 October 1961.

At the end of the conference, *Eastern Economist* wrote in agony: "Thus it would seem a great opportunity had been lost and it is necessary to explain why to those who see the obvious economic advantages of cooperation hopes of unity are still so dim and hesitant."[161] Another Indian economic journal provided the answer in advance: ". . . two pertinent questions are being currently examined in this connection. First, whether the political prerequisites exist in the region for such close cooperation, and perhaps ultimate economic integration. In Western Europe and among the Communist countries cooperation was effected primarily because of the identical political outlook of the countries concerned. Secondly, the most important argument in favour of cooperation—lack of resources and smallness of market—does not apply to India."[162]

In conclusion, the role of the ECAFE itself in regional integration in the region should be noted. Speaking in New Delhi in 1951, the Indian economist P.S. Lokanathan, the then Secretary of the ECAFE, laid considerable emphasis on this; in 1955, William Henderson wrote: ". . . (the ECAFE) has had a marked effect in developing a sense of regional unity. No doubt membership has been made attractive by the fact that the organization confers many benefits while imposing few burdens. Nevertheless, participation in its multifarious activities has strengthened the sentiment for a regional approach to the solution of common economic problems and at the same time has broadened experience in the techniques of cooperative effort."[163]

[161]*Eastern Economist*, 29 September 1961.

[162]*Economic Weekly*, 30 September 1961.

[163]William Henderson, "Regionalism in South-East Asia," *International Organization*, November 1955.

CHAPTER THREE

Problems and Prospects

TWO ALTERNATIVE models of Asian integration have been visualized by competent observers and India has been assailed, both at home and abroad, for the failure to strive more for achieving results in both the fields. The two following extracts from two American sources broadly indicate these lines of criticism.

In an editorial captioned "The Lost Leader," the *New York Times* wrote in 1951: "Instead of seizing the leadership of Asia for its good, Nehru turned aside from the responsibilities, proclaimed India's disinterestedness, and tried to set up an independent, third force India, suspended in the mid-air between the two decisive movements of our day—the communism that Russia leads and the democracy of which the United States is the chief champion. So he and India went into a limbo. It was an abnegation of greatness."[1]

Four years later an American lawyer complained in a paper on India's Asia policy: "But it is not because Nehru failed to choose our side that we feel there has been an abnegation of greatness. It is not because he tried to create a third force in Asia. The abnegation I see comes from the fact that he deliberately decided not to build such a new alternative."[2]

Most observers and students of Asian affairs have noted the tremendous complications involved in attempting regional integration in Asia. A somewhat extreme position in this matter is taken by authors like Nathaniel Peffer of the University of Columbia, who holds that there is no South-East Asia

[1]*New York Times*, 28 August 1951.
[2]Harris Wofford, *op. cit.*, p. 147.

"except for cartographic purposes. . . . In short South-East Asia is not a region that can be conceived as an effective entity in world politics. It is a place in the globe where certain groups of people, holding little in common, live contiguous to one another." Again: "A South-East Asian organization in 1954 is a rhetorical device, not a political fact."[3] As against this, scholars like William Henderson have held that "there exists among them a unity of outlook which transcends in large measure their undoubted racial, linguistic and cultural diversity." According to this view, there is considerable scope for regional cooperation, although initiative for this could hardly be expected locally. Even this view, however, takes note of the immense difficulties in the way of integration.[4] Indian authors have stressed the diversities of the Asian countries, the lack of a consensus in the region, the problems created by treaty relations of the Asian countries with outside Powers, the political fluidity of the region, the state of inter-Asian relations and economic competitiveness among them.[5]

Apart from the general difficulties, well stated by the authors quoted above, there are specific Indian problems impeding India's initiative in this regard. An attempt is made below to discuss the problems from the Indian point of view.

Keeping the political difficulties apart, for the moment, one might analyze some of the other inherent difficulties in the way of India actively striving for regional integration. In the first place, unlike Europe, Asia is not divided into countries none of which is in size, resources or population overwhelmingly greater; India, like China, represents very often the image of a giant which it may not be easy to embrace and still survive. Much of this fear of India is based on myth and legend;

[3]Nathaniel Peffer, "Regional Security in South-East Asia," *International Organization*, August 1954. This view is also stated by Guy Wint, "South Asia, Unity and Disunity," *International Conciliation*, November 1954.

[4]William Henderson, "Regionalism in South-East Asia," *International Organization*, November 1955.

[5]*See* V. P. Dutt, *India's Foreign Policy*, New Delhi, I.C.W.A., 1950, pp. 6-7; K. P. Karunakaran, *op. cit.*, pp. 85-8; H. Venkatasubbiah, "Prospects of an Asian Union," *India Quarterly*, April-June and July-September 1949.

neither is India a single nation State, united and unified to become imperialistic, nor is she as powerful as her size and population would signify. Yet, in all the neighbouring countries—Nepal, Ceylon, Burma and Pakistan—there are varying degrees of this fear; indeed, one of the writers on the subject envisaged some trend towards integration in South-East Asia because of the fear of China and India.[5a] On the other hand, India, unlike the USA in the Americas, does not have the necessary military or economic power to bring about some regional cooperation by throwing about her weight.

The Position of India: A Problem of Defining the Region

Secondly, it is difficult for India to choose the region to which she should belong. As the Prime Minister of India often declared, India was linked with both West and South-East Asia by geography, history, culture and modern political considerations; even Far Eastern problems affected India to a large extent.[6]

One of the spheres in which the uniqueness of India's position in Asia is best illustrated is that of religion. The predominant religion of India is Hinduism; only Nepal in the whole of Asia is Hindu by religion. And if one excludes the small Balinese population of Indonesia, the ten per cent Hindu minority of Pakistan and the Tamil speaking Hindus of Ceylon, there is no Asian country which has Hinduism as one of its religions. In reality, Hinduism has been coextensive with India and, unlike some other religions, has never practised conversion or attempted proselytization anywhere. Many have thus refused to call it a religion as such and regarded Hinduism as another name for the Indian way of life! Interestingly, however, this apparent uniqueness of religious thought has coexisted with another phenomenon of equal importance—the significance of India for other religious systems. Buddhism was born in India; to the

---

[5a]Milton W. Mayer, "Regional Cooperation in South-East Asia," *Journal of International Affairs*, Spring 1949.

[6]*Jawaharlal Nehru's Speeches, 1947-49*, p. 236.

devout Buddhists of East and South-East Asia, India is the Jerusalem. India itself totally moved away from Buddhism as an organized religion soon after the Buddha; but Hinduism adumbrated elements of Buddhist thought and was influenced by the great religious leader.[7] In recent years both the Indian Government and the Indian people have shown greater concern for Buddhism; it cannot be doubted that in a religious sense India is bound with some other Asian countries by ties of this religion. As for another great religion of Asia, Islam, the creation of Pakistan on the basis of a religious slogan has to an extent weakened India's position as an Islamic country. The fact, nevertheless, remains that next to Indonesia and Pakistan, India has the largest concentration of Muslims in the world (over 43 million). And as the Canadian authority on Islam, Wilfred Cantwell Smith wrote in 1959: "Today we must learn to live in collaboration. Islam like others must prove creative at this point, and perhaps it will learn this in India. For the Indo-Muslims are in India what the total Muslim group is in the world—an important minority."[8]

India's Christian population is roughly 2.3 per cent of the total; a measure of her importance in the Christian world, however, is the fact that one of the cardinals of the Catholic Church is an Indian. It is this remarkable phenomenon of a Hindu country linked both with Buddhism on the one hand and Islam and Christianity on the other, which makes India's position unique and contributes in some measure to her three-faced posture in the system of philosophical communications in Asia. One of the additional facts which complicate the situation is that the elite in Indian society has built itself up in the image of the agnostic tradition of Western Europe; unlike Burma's U Nu, India's Nehru has little or no concern for religion in his personal or political life.

[7] " . . . The essence of the Buddha's teaching . . . has been woven into the texture of Indian life and thought." (*Jawaharlal Nehru's speeches, 1949-53*, p. 430.)

[8] Wilfred Cantwell Smith, *Islam in Modern History*, New York, Mentor Book, 1959, p. 292.

The Nature of the Indian Elite

A third difficulty to be taken into account is the lack of communications between the elites in the different Asian countries and the propensity of the Indian elite to identify itself with European values and problems. Also important, in this connection, is the difficulty of India in identifying herself with a racial or revivalist cause in the name of a nebulous Asianism. It is necessary to discuss this aspect of the problem in analyzing factors in India's aversion to regional integration in Asia.

One of the major factors conditioning the Indian view of national interests is the structure and content of the opinion of the Indian elite. If foreign policy is not the function of mass opinion in any country, it is least so in the developing countries like India. For, in such countries, politics and political opinion is essentially a function of modernized elite groups—often of one man or a group of men who have come to symbolize the urges and aspirations and reflect the ideological predilections of the elite. In the case of India, for example, expert observers have agreed that the foreign policy is largely a handmaid of Jawaharlal Nehru. As Brecher observes in his definitive biography of the Indian leader: "In no other State does one man dominate the foreign policy as does Nehru in India. . . . Nehru is the philosopher, the architect, the engineer and the voice of his country's policy towards the outside world. . . . He has impressed his personality and his views with such overpowering effect that foreign policy may properly be termed a private monopoly."[9] It is not a foreign policy on which the pressures generated by democratic processes have had any discernible effect, except in a few specific instances.[10]

It is remarkable, however, that notwithstanding this somewhat limited base of foreign policy formulation, the policy itself has "called forth unstinted support from the vast majority of politically conscious Indians."[11] The explanation for this pheno-

---

[9] Michael Brecher, *op. cit.*, pp. 564-75.
[10] Examples: Hungary, Tibet and Goa.
[11] Michael Brecher, *op. cit.*, p. 569.

menon has to be sought in the undoubted capacity of Nehru to anticipate and voice the opinions of the articulate sections, viz. the opinion of the Western educated elite in Indian society. Unlike Gandhi who attempted to bridge the gap between this elite and the vast masses of the people of India by devising political slogans and techniques which would be relevant for them, Nehru has not either in the modes of his personal living or the pattern of his thinking thought it necessary or desirable to approximate to the traditional values of India, in the conservative sense of the term. Even Gandhi's political techniques were meant essentially to bring the sanction of the masses in politics without ever involving them directly; in the case of Nehru there is a distinct aversion to the short cut to mass opinion and the Indian Prime Minister is not only a relentless campaigner against the incursion of religion in politics but also a vigorous critic of such Indian practices as astrology. It is necessary to remember that as yet India's foreign policy does not give vent to the feelings of the traditionalist elements of Indian society nor does it formulate Indian interests in terms in which a revivalist right-wing element or an utterly chauvinistic militaristic left-group might elect to do. In fact, this relative purity of politics in India is based on somewhat precarious foundations; as has been pointed out, Indian democracy rests on the twin foundations of the apathy of the masses and the turbulence of the elite.[12]

What is as important as this relative isolation of foreign policy from mass urges is the nature of the elite itself. In an expert study on the subject, Edward Shils of the University of Chicago has pointed out how the Indian intellectuals are essentially "provincial" in their outlook.[13] Their provinciality is in relation to the intellectual centres of Western Europe, particularly London. Writing in the *Sewanee Review* in 1959, Shils had this to say about the Indian elite: "The truth of the matter

---

[12]Sisir Gupta, "Indian Democracy: What Gives it Stability," *Economic Weekly*, July 1960 (Special Number).

[13]Edward Shils, *The Intellectual between Tradition and Modernity: The Indian Situation*, The Hague, Mouton, 1961.

is that the British not only ruled India for a long time but also took partial possession of the Indian mind. ... It has been said that the attraction toward England will decline as the years pass. There is little sign that this is so. ... In fact, the Soviet Union, which to many Indian intellectuals vaguely figures as a leading modern country, really does not in itself attract the Indian intellectual very much. Practically no one reads books about the Soviet Union and certainly practically no one studies it in a scholarly way. ... The leftist intellectual does not care to learn about it in intimate detail. Even the leftists feel closer to England—not least when they deny what they think it stands for."[14]

This provinciality produces an intense internal conflict in the elite. In one of the oft-quoted passages of his autobiography, Nehru says about himself: "I have become a queer mixture of the East and West, out of place everywhere, at home nowhere. Perhaps, my thoughts and approach to life are more akin to what is called Western than Eastern, but India clings to me. ... I cannot get rid of either that past inheritance or my recent acquisitions. They are both part of me. ... I am a stranger and alien in the West. But in my own country also, sometime, I have an exile's feeling."[15]

It is interesting that the Indian leaders had felt a degree of emotional participation in such distant problems as the Spanish Civil War, the rise of fascism in Italy, the invasion of Abyssinia and above all the Soviet Revolution. Nehru wrote in 1940: "Munich was a shock hard to bear and the tragedy of Spain became a personal sorrow to me." Again: "There were many shocks and adjustment was difficult—the Russo-German Pact, the Soviet's invasion of Finland, the friendly approach of Russia towards Japan. Were there any principles, and standards of conduct in this world, or was it sheer opportunism?"[16]

Apart from the interest in world affairs, particularly European, one of the features of the changing structure of opinion

[14]Edward Shils, "The Culture of the Indian Intellectual," *The Sewanee Review*, April and June 1959.

[15]Jawaharlal Nehru, *Autobiography*, p. 596.   [16]*Ibid.*, pp. 599 and 609.

of the Indian elite was the appeal of the Socialist ideology. In 1936, Nehru wrote: ". . . the theory and philosophy of Marxism lightened up many a dark corner of my mind. History came to have a new meaning for me. . . . It was the essential freedom from dogma and the scientific outlook of Marxism that appeal-ed to me."[17] In subsequent years, Nehru's view changed considerably; a decade later, he wrote: "Marx's general analysis of social development seems to have been remarkably correct and yet many developments took place later which did not fit in with his outlook for the immediate future. . . . The very rapid growth of technology and the practical application of vast development in scientific knowledge are now changing the world picture with an amazing rapidity, leading to new problems."[18] In 1960, Nehru was more critical of Marxism and held it to be outdated in view of the revolutionary implications of technology and political democracy and also stressed the need for ethics and spirituality: "Yes, I have changed. The emphasis on ethical and spiritual solutions is not unconscious. It is deliberate, quite deliberate. . . . It is really the problem of creating a fully integrated human being."[19]

The gradual revision of opinion as well as the original attachment to Marxism—both indicate a distinct ideological pattern, that of the left in British politics. In fact it is the British and West European currents of thought which have for decades been determining Indian elite thinking on world affairs—resulting on the one hand in an overly enthusiastic participation in European affairs and in a broad socialistic fervour on the other. It may also be said that in the postwar years, much of left-wing opinion in Britain has found practical expression through Nehru and India.[20]

The point to be emphasized in this section is that the foreign policy of India is primarily formulated and conceived by the leaders of an elite group which is emotionally linked with Bri-

---

[17]*Ibid.*, pp. 362-3.   [18]Nehru, *Discovery of India*, pp. 30-1.
[19]R. K. Karanjia, *op. cit.*, pp. 32-3.
[20]The Socialist Party of India accuses Nehru of being the last Viceroy of Her Majesty's Government!

tain and West Europe more than with the regions to which they belong. This Anglo-Indian intellectual association coupled with the fact of India's prolonged struggle against Britain made her somewhat of a "meeting ground between the East and the West." The point was stressed by Nehru himself in one of his early speeches in the Indian Parliament: "India becomes a kind of meeting ground for various trends and forces and meeting ground between what might roughly be called the East and the West."[21]

It has been stressed by other observers of Indian foreign policy also that in this sense India occupies a unique position in the world. At a seminar on India's role in Asia held at Chicago in 1955,[22] several speakers laid emphasis on this aspect. Horace Poleman of the Library of the Congress said: "I feel that India is the focal point as far as the West is concerned in Asia from an intellectual point of view, as the crossroads through which we have to work with the rest of the Orient. . . . India is more of a Western nation in many respects than she is an Asiatic nation." D.J.C. Crawley of the British Embassy in America said: "I think we would all agree with Mr Poleman when he says that as Occidentals we do feel more at home intellectually, socially, culturally and so on, with Indians than with most other Asians."

This factor in Indian thinking on world affairs is of particular importance in Indian attitudes to regional integration in Asia. It should be added, however, that this phenomenon has no inevitable permanence about it. As one of the participants in the Chicago seminar pointed out: ". . . there might be an 'utter Indianness' in the future, as that part of the Indian population which bears upon policy formation comes to include greater number of Indians without strong commitments to the West."[23] India's aversion to a super-nationalism in Asia might in such an eventuality vanish but the cost of it would apparently be tre-

---

[21]*Jawaharlal Nehru's Speeches, 1947-49*, p. 236.
[22]Robert I. Crane (Ed.), *India's Role in Asia*, Chicago, 1955, pp. 88-105.
[23]*Ibid.*, p. 100.

mendous and its consequences unhealthy for international cooperation.

The Economic Scene

A fourth difficulty inherent in the structural system of Asia is that, economically, the countries of the region are not complementary but competitive. As P.S. Lokanathan said: "In the field of trade the scope for regional development is limited by a variety of factors, not the least of which is the non-complementary character of the region's economy. With the exception of Japan and to a lesser extent India and China, all the countries of Asia and the Far East are still largely in the stage of primary mineral and agricultural production, with similar commodities to export and having to import the greater proportion of their requirements in terms of manufactured articles. ... This state of affairs is in contrast with that in Europe where there is a complementary relationship." Another difficulty mentioned by the ECAFE dignitary was that the area could not provide her own resources for development even if integrated and "this indeed is a basic limitation on regional economic cooperation in Asia."[24]

A look at India's trade pattern would be interesting in this connection. Economically, India is an inward oriented economy; the proportion of imports to national income is only eight per cent in India, as against 35 per cent in Ceylon, 31 per cent in Burma, 27 per cent in Malaya and 21 per cent in Thailand. What is more, India's foreign trade is really declining; according to the Indian Planning Commission, while the world's total export trade doubled in the last decade, India's share in it declined from 2.1 per cent in 1950 to 1.1 per cent in 1960. India's imports expanded rapidly, but were financed mainly by foreign aid.

The pattern of trade with the ECAFE countries has been dismal; "the dispatches to ECAFE countries as a proportion of total

[24]P.S. Lokanathan, "Regional Cooperation in Asia," *India Quarterly,* January-March 1951.

exports were 25.7 per cent in 1952, 16.3 per cent in 1956 and 17 per cent in 1960. The imports from ECAFE countries were 13.6 per cent in 1952, 12.4 per cent in 1956, 13.1 per cent in 1960."[25] Only with Japan there has been a perceptible improvement in trade, owing largely to the export of iron ore to that country. Both official and non-official accounts of India's trade prospects and needs have emphasized the potentiality of the South-East Asian market; specially with the emergence of an efficient light and heavy industry structure, it is this region which will be the major goal of India's export drives. But apart from the increasing competition with Japan, a new and formidable competitor in the field is Communist China; "China is in the South Asian market with several products similar in range to those which India could hope to supply, and her sales are supported by extensive aid and loan agreements against which India has found no answer yet."[26]

It is inevitable that much of India's trade policy in the future will be determined by this competition. It is not inevitable but likely that this economic background of the political rivalries would also influence the Asian policies of both the governments. The table on page 96 would illustrate Indian trade directions and their relative rigidity over the years.

The Problem of Domestic Politics

A fifth difficulty which is not easy to substantiate from documents and speeches is the fact that the major problem of India internally is the integration of her various linguistic, cultural groups into a unified nation State; many of the South Asian countries contain portions of the same linguistic groups as are existing in the outlying regions of India. The Bengalis, totalling about 75 million are divided between India and Pakistan; there are Hindi speaking people in Nepal; the Tamils are a powerful minority in the south of India and north of Ceylon; the Punjabis again are divided between India and Pakistan.

[25]K. Krishna Moorty, "The Dismally Stagnant Trade Picture," *Far Eastern Economic Review*, 21 September 1960.   [26]*Ibid*.

INDIA'S TRADE WITH SOUTH AND EAST ASIA
(value in million rupees)

		1960	1957	1954	1952
JAPAN	Imports	542.0	544.2	166.9	199.9
	Exports	342.8	273.4	162.7	254.7
	Balance	−199.2	−270.8	−6.2	+54.8
PAKISTAN	Imports	151.8	134.0	178.2	291.4
	Exports	101.2	67.7	100.9	463.4
	Balance	−50.6	−66.3	−77.3	+172.0
BURMA	Imports	195.1	131.9	433.6	311.4
	Exports	69.4	133.0	165.9	236.8
	Balance	−125.7	+1.1	−267.7	−74.6
SINGAPORE	Imports	115.9	126.7	167.8	138.2
	Exports	69.2	90.8	72.3	154.0
	Balance	−46.7	−35.9	−95.5	+15.8
CEYLON	Imports	39.2	57.6	73.1	48.2
	Exports	184.8	170.4	184.1	202.3
	Balance	+145.6	+112.8	+111.0	+154.1
CHINA	Imports	32.6	48.6	15.3	154.5
	Exports	56.0	37.0	18.0	31.0
	Balance	+23.4	−11.6	+2.7	−123.5
MALAYA	Imports	136.6	141.9	62.5	26.6
	Exports	46.8	41.2	35.3	34.9
	Balance	−99.8	−100.7	−27.2	+8.3
INDONESIA	Imports	39.9	38.1	14.5	15.6
	Exports	43.2	57.1	53.7	54.4
	Balance	+3.5	+19.0	+39.2	+38.8
THAILAND	Imports	5.9	5.6	5.2	91.5
	Exports	23.8	36.2	25.0	46.8
	Balance	+17.9	+30.6	+19.8	−44.7
TOTAL	Imports	1258.8	1228.6	1119.1	1277.3
	Exports	937.2	906.8	817.9	1418.3
	Balance	−321.6	−321.8	−301.2	+201.0

SOURCE: *Far Eastern Economic Review*, 2 September 1961.

Any attempt at regional integration in the South Asian region may well lend new meaning to sub-national loyalties and open the floodgates of irresistible demands for recasting national boundaries cutting across existing political boundaries.

A problem of the same kind is posed by the fact that most of India's neighbouring countries—Nepal and Pakistan in particular—have a still less developed political infra-structure and integration might tend to overwhelm existing Indian political values and the democratic system. The most important aspect of India's Asian role is what she does with herself; if for the sake of a larger grouping India were to lose her distinctive political system and impair the integrity of existing political units, the purpose would be defeated. Internally, India is still largely in search of a stable level of politics and economics; being engaged in a deep ideological and political conflict with China, India has got to constantly improvise her system, recast her internal emphases, and discover new sources of social vitality which can cope with the Chinese challenge. In designing a new pattern of social, political and economic values, India is constantly in need of at once underlining her differences with the Communist system and approximating her own system to the apparent advantages of the Communist. The supreme need from this point of view is of maintaining a large measure of flexibility in foreign and domestic policies. A study of the political techniques and programmes adopted by the ruling party of India would point to a conscious attempt on its part to avoid commitments of any kind, while attempting an approximation to a vague ideological pattern. To the extent that any attempt to coordinate regional policies would be a limiting factor for this crucial flexibility in all spheres of policy, regionalism has a distinctly difficult implication for India.

A paper by Morris E. Opler in the Chicago Seminar of 1955, referred to earlier, entitled "Non-Political Factors Conditioning India's Asia Policy" noted this in the following words: "The point to be made here is that the recency of independence, this fluidity, this consciousness that the formative process is still going on has become involved with the relations with the outside world and perceptions of the outside world." It is interesting to note in this connection that as early as 1948, Nehru had said: "If today by any chance I were offered the reunion of India and Pakistan, I would decline it for obvious reasons. I do not want to carry the burden of Pakistan's great problems."[27]

Political Difficulties of Integration

The major political difficulties for India adopting a more positive attitude to regional integration would be evident from the brief history of attempts toward this goal and the understanding of the assumptions, motivations and style of India's foreign policy. It would be a negation of India's foreign policy objectives if attempts at regional integration would be tantamount to incurring the antagonism or hostility of either of the great Powers; the attempts made to form regional military alliances fall under this category. It was impossible for any Asian country to join any Western-sponsored defence pacts and still call itself nonaligned and friendly to the USSR. It would involve a thorough change in national politics, in the style of foreign policy and in the internal emphases in India. An emergence of a right-wing dictatorship in India, an alignment with the Western bloc and an additional stress on the security problems of the region vis-a-vis communism would convert India into a clear-cut model in Asia, the other exponents of which have had lesser success either in accomplishing a minimum level of social change or reducing communism's attraction for the people.

Has not Chinese action against India in 1959 changed the context? The answer has to be complex; the Chinese invasion of India and the persistent attempt from Peking to brand India as pro-imperialist, capitalist and anti-Communist are but tributes to the modest gains made by India as an alternative model for Asia and Africa. It may be deduced from the nature of the sudden Chinese outbursts against India that the real purpose of her aggression was precisely to disturb the foundations on which the alternative model rested. If under the impact of the Chinese invasion of her northern borders, India would overly stress the military threat and divert resources from her vital economic plans to her defence, if she would abandon her nonalignment

[27]*Jawaharlal Nehru's Speeches, 1947-49*, pp. 338-9.

and openly state her decision to join the Western bloc, if she would suddenly move away from her accepted policies, the purposes of Peking would be served. In this sense, in the first round of India-China conflict, it is China, not India, which has lost notwithstanding her advances on the northern frontier.

It is also relevant to note that the China-India problem is not a problem between the Communist world and India. Soviet neutrality on this issue, coupled with the growing difficulties of inner bloc unity in the Communist world, makes it abundantly clear that any presumption of a monolithic Communist bloc attempting to take over India would be utterly wrong. In fact, one might even interpret this as but one of the signs of an inevitable Soviet stake in the containment of China in the region. There is no easy answer to the innumerable posers one might raise about the Sino-Soviet rivalries and their relevance for the non-Communist world. There is no denying, however, that the Indian experience of recent years suggests a potentiality for the nonaligned nations bordering China, specially India, to use, at least for a time, the USSR as their first line of defence against China. It is interesting to note that the period of India-China rivalry has been the period of growing protestations of Indo-Soviet friendship from both sides.

During these years (1959-62), the Indian and Russian Presidents and Prime Ministers exchanged visits, India secured Soviet assistance for use in her northern borders,[28] increased Soviet technical and economic assistance was announced, declarations made not only of Soviet neutrality in the India-China conflict but also of the inviolability of Indo-Russian friendship and open issue made of India-China relations in the Communist Party meetings. In short, India has been able to play an important role and make herself a key issue in the politics of the Communist world;[29] a sudden Indian decision to join the West or to reverse her foreign policy might greatly limit the potentialities of the anti-Chinese argument within the Communist bloc.

[28]*See* statement by Krishna Menon, *Asian Recorder*, 1961, p. 3865.
[29]*See* despatch by Tilman Durdin in *New York Times*, 29 October 1961.

Difficulties in the way of any attempt to provide machineries of cooperation among the nonaligned would be two-fold: in the first place such cooperation would presume a large measure of positive commonness of outlook and objectives in internal and external policies; secondly, a third force or bloc in the world will either have to be strong enough to act as a balancing power or reconcile itself with the status of a mere nuisance in politics. On both counts the problems are apparently stupendous. Nonalignment is primarily a negative approach and indeed a very broad statement of policy. Within the limits set by nonalignment, nations could still have a widely divergent set of policies in various spheres. The Suez conflict brought out one such divergence into the open; to Egypt, Britain now was the major enemy—precisely the country with which India maintained the closest relations. Again, to many African countries, colonialism is still the major problem; to India it is receding and does not present the picture of an inveterate foe, except for such countries as Portugal. Any attempt to integrate such outlooks would considerably affect their flexibility of approach. It would almost ruin India's foreign policy style.

What is more important than foreign policy, however, is that India is not a powerful enough country to underwrite weak political infra-structures. And many of the nonaligned countries do not have any greater elements of stability than the allies who have been embarrassing even such powerful countries as the United States. It is not without reason that, at Belgrade, Nehru pointedly advised his neutralist colleagues to turn the searchlight inward and stressed the need for greater internal efforts for these countries. Indeed, some of the nonaligned countries had almost made nonalignment an aggressive foreign policy attitude and bypassed vital internal issues by raising this policy to the status of the greatest single symbol of national greatness. It is also not impossible that an integrated third bloc of nations would, in attempting to voice the extreme nationalistic feelings of Asia and Africa, convert itself into an even greater threat to world peace and stability than the Communist bloc led by the developed Soviet Union. For, while they would in case of any conflict have no prospect of a victory, they would have little prospect of defeat. An integrated Afro-Asia might become a magnified China in world politics.[30]

Why, it might be asked, does India fear exacerbation of conflicts and underlining of the various lines dividing the developed and the underdeveloped world? Is not India as much a part of the Afro-Asian world as China? The answer is partly to be found in the twin factors of India's relatively contented status as a nation and the structure of elite opinion discussed earlier. China's enthusiasm for Afro-Asianism, likewise, arises out of the conviction of the Chinese rulers that it is the surest way to advance their national interests and extend China's influence over the smaller countries of the region.

The problems of regional cooperation and integration in Asia may be summarized as follows:

(*a*) One of the most important problems inherent in Asia is that the geo-political realities of the region, unlike those of Africa or Latin America, are bound to create a difficult problem of defining the region. Where does the region for possible integration begin?

(*b*) There is no apparent cultural, religious or racial commonness of the peoples of the region.

(*c*) If traditional values and other loyalties do not bring the countries closer together, nor do the present intellectual loyalties of the elites in these countries.

(*d*) In Asia, unlike in Europe, the States are not roughly equal in size or status. India and China are two giants in Asia and it may be a hard decision for the smaller countries to come closer to either of them.

(*e*) On the other hand, unlike the Americas, Asia does not yet have a country big and powerful enough to wield its military and economic strength to bring about a regional association.

---

[30]For a discussion of the arguments for and against "third force" *see:* "Our Foreign Policy" number of *Seminar,* March 1961; also the Chicago seminar discussions, *India's Role in Asia.*

India is only potentially a Power of this kind; China is advancing faster to this position.

(*f*) The countries of the region are incapable as yet of defending themselves even with their combined might against any onslaught from a great Power.

(*g*) Communications between the various Asian countries are little. Particularly among the political parties and functional groups, which are said to play a vital role in the integration of regions, there is meagre contact. Even exchange of ideas and dialogues between elites of the various countries is for all practical purposes non-existent.

(*h*) In the matter of political systems, values and ideas, the countries of the region vary widely; the four predominant patterns being the dictatorship of the Communists, the dictatorship of the left-of-centre nationalists, the dictatorship of the right wing, and the democratic States. To these may be added the paternalistic monarchy of Nepal or Cambodia as a special category. In economic and social ideals there is an equal degree of divergence—from Communist to feudal, all social patterns exist in Asia.

(*i*) The foreign policies of these countries vary as much as their political systems. Not only are there the three main divisions—the aligned, the nonaligned, and Communists—but among the nonaligned there is no community of outlook.

(*j*) The foreign policy problems are further aggravated by the existence of traditional rivalries and serious political disputes among the countries of the region. Afghanistan and Pakistan, Pakistan and India, the Philippines and Malaya, Thailand and Cambodia, Malaya and Indonesia, are all involved in serious quarrels.

(*k*) A very serious hindrance is caused by the fact that most of these countries are yet to emerge as strong unified nation States. The problem of sub-nationalism is rampant in most of these countries and often the groups clamouring for autonomy are cut across by national boundaries; the cultivation of regional loyalties may make these demands more difficult to solve.

(*I*) In the economic sphere, the realization of the values of regional cooperation has been slow among the smaller States. Fear of economic domination by India, China and Japan is pronounced; also obvious are the advantanges of continuing to deal bilaterally with the aiding countries and the agencies of the United Nations. Finally, the economies of these countries are still largely not complementary but competitive.

It is apparent from the above that there are serious impediments in the way of India playing a major role in Asian integration. Yet it would be wrong to end this discussion on a pessimistic note. For one thing, if the Indian assumption of Soviet intentions in the region has any validity, and hopes of a common U.S.-USSR approach to the problems of the region eventually materialize, many of the political difficulties might be easily resolved. It is not inconsistent with India's needs that the southern neighbours of China are brought together in a common effort to resist the intrusion of the dangerous doctrines being propagated from Peking. In the conflict between China and her adversaries, India can no longer hope to remain nonaligned. For, nonalignment is essentially based on an agreement among competing Powers not to push the other side to alignment. Thus it may not be impossible to expect Soviet readiness to tolerate, if not endorse, reasonably well thought out schemes of integration. Should China, on the other hand, become normalized and tamed she herself might become the corner-stone, along with India, for an integrated development effort in Asia. This far-fetched calculation is nonetheless important to bear in mind in considering future possibilities in the Asian region, just as it is important to be aware of the fact that if Sino-Soviet relations are restored to the level of Stalinist internationalism, now on China's terms, there will be the need for integration with overt and covert Western support.

Prospects of Integration: Economics

The realm of speculations apart, there are specific areas in ·

which integration attempts are conceivable even on the basis of the existing evidences of great Power interest in the region.

At least in two spheres—economics and Indo-Pakistan relations—the prospects of integration are not entirely dim. There is a growing volume of opinion in India, specially among organized interest groups, which has shown an increasing awareness of the need for such integration and the government have never shown aversion to it. It is not India which marred the Simla Conference of 1955; and a year later, the Indian second Plan stated: "It is evident that as developmental planning proceeds in this region, the problems of mutual adjustments in the matter of specialization in certain lines of production and mutually advantageous trade and exchange of know-how and experience will assume increasing importance. Planning in the different countries in the region is at different stages and it is only to be expected that the prime consideration for each country will be the fullest development of its own resources in the light of its needs and along lines it finds economically and socially most promising. Nevertheless, it is essential that the programmes of development are so framed as to give the scope for mutually advantageous exchange of products and technical know-how. Even countries which are, on the whole, short of technical know-how and personnel can still render assistance to others in a limited way. This is the basis on which co-operation within the Colombo Plan has been organized. It would be desirable to think along similar lines in respect of problems confronting this region and to arrange for interchange of ideas and of technical personnel. Planning in India has thus to be viewed in its wider regional perspective and it has to be borne in mind that poverty, low standards of living and economic backwardness are problems of common interest, and the efforts and experiences in each country are bound to be of value to the others in the area faced with similar problems."[31]

The *Eastern Economist*, organ of the House of Birlas, wrote after the 1961 conference of the ECAFE countries: "The truth is that the element of trust between the nations of South-East

[31]*India—The Second Five-Year Plan*, New Delhi, 1956, pp. 19-20.

Asia is not large enough for an edifice yet to be built. . . . Unless South-East Asia feels the crisis of its own survival much more keenly, it is extremely unlikely to take the plunge in anything like the direction which the ECAFE working paper has coherently suggested. The conference has thus still a purely academic ring. Nevertheless the contribution has been significant. Some imperfect seed has been sown. One must rest with that unless the political imagination runs to the dimensions required by our responsibilities to our peoples. This week the trumpets have given forth only a very uncertain sound."[32]

It was the view expressed by a correspondent in an independent and somewhat left-inclined journal at this time that "a growing and influential lobby is at work in Delhi to convince the Government of India that if a South Asian market is insulated against the economic penetration of China and the leakage of goods through the free port of Hong Kong is plugged, Japan and India can divide the market without undue friction."[33]

There would still be many questions left unanswered. Would Japan, for example, be ready to share a market for which she has aspired for long and with great tenacity? Would the other countries be prepared for a reasonable tariff system in the interest of the region as a whole?

Notwithstanding these difficulties, it is of tremendous consequence, from the viewpoint of Indian attitude to regional integration, that such "lobbies" are at work now. With a free market economy—not more than 12 per cent of the Indian economy is State-owned—business interests such as those represented by the *Eastern Economist*[34] would be or should be expected to be in a position to partially mould governmental attitudes in such matters. In any event, India's aversion to

[32]*Eastern Economist*, 29 September 1961.
[33]*Economic Weekly*, 30 September 1961.
[34]The House of Birlas own considerable segments of India's jute, tea, paper, automobile, machine tools and newspaper industry; it was also one of the major supports behind the Indian national movement and is known to have retained its good relations with the ruling party after freedom.

regional cooperation or integration in Asia is likely to be the least in the economic sphere.

India and Pakistan: Units of Possible Integration

As has been stated earlier, one of the factors impeding regional integration in the area is the state of India's relations with her neighbours. With Pakistan, in particular, relations have been strained and by far less than friendly; the unnatural division of the Indian subcontinent has left a legacy of conflict and rivalry and led to the continuation of a minor cold war in the subcontinent. The very absurdity of the division has exacerbated tensions and lent new meaning to archaic political slogans. Paradoxically, therefore, the process of integration must start precisely in the region where disintegration was at work in 1947—the Indo-Pakistan subcontinent.

Difficulties in its way cannot be exaggerated but certainly the advantages and potentialities of such an effort may be understated. There are no other two countries of the region with as much in common as India and Pakistan; viewed from the angles of race, culture, language, historical memories, the extent of communications and the interdependence of the two States in economic and military terms, India and Pakistan have between them the most fertile ground for attempted integration in Asia.

What are today two countries developed for ages as integral parts of a single economic and political entity; Mohenjodaro in Pakistan is as much a chapter of India's history as Delhi, Agra, Lucknow and Aligarh are of Pakistan's. Even their more recent aspirations grew under the common impact of the West. The political leaders who conceived Pakistan and the leaders of India's struggle for freedom were close associates and colleagues believing in a common set of values. Economically the two countries have been traditionally interdependent. The two main languages of Pakistan are also languages of India, the same literary figures are held in esteem by Indians and Pakistanis. The two main religious groups of India are also the two main religious groups of Pakistan; members of the same family often reside in both countries.[35] It is interesting but not well known that the brother of the Vice-President of India was the Vice-Chancellor of the University of Dacca in East Pakistan; two brothers are among the highest officials in the two foreign offices; the brother of the former Secretary of Pakistan's Communist Party is a Minister in a provincial government in India.

It is, perhaps, these commonnesses that make the partition of India tragic and the mutual relations of the succeeding States bitter. What is also possible and an advantage is that it is the country which fought for secession that has failed to reconcile with the consequences. The Pakistan that came into being in 1947 is far less in size and weaker in resources than the one its leaders had contemplated. Also there is the growing evidence that the demand for separation was advanced as a bargaining counter for achieving a higher status in an Indian confederation rather than to have a separate State as such. In any case neither the Indian communal problem nor the problem of the stability of the region has been solved by the partition of India and the very emergence of a geographically absurd, economically unviable, politically unstable State in the subcontinent has tended to affect the stability of the region as a whole. A state of abnormality has been perpetuated in the vital South Asian region.

It is not necessary to deny the existence of disputes and problems between the countries to see their natural interdependence and the need for greater Indo-Pakistan cooperation, leading toward some kind of integration in the South Asian region. The leaders of both the countries have been aware of this and often talked of the logical path they must tread. Talking to C. L. Sulzberger of the *New York Times* in March 1957, Nehru said: "Twenty years ago I would have said that certainly we should have some kind of confederation—not federation—of independent States with common defence and economic possibility. ... The difficulty is now if we talk about it. This upsets our neighbours, because we are so much bigger. Nevertheless,

---

[35]*See* Sisir Gupta, *India's Relations with Pakistan, 1954-57*, New Delhi, 1958, p. 1.

of course, this remains the logical future path—confederation with each member maintaining its independence intact!"[36] Writing in the *Foreign Affairs* in July 1960, President Ayub Khan repeated what he had said earlier: "As a student of war and strategy, I can see quite clearly the inexorable push of the north in the direction of the warm waters of the Indian Ocean. This push is bound to increase if India and Pakistan go on squabbling with each other. If, on the other hand, we resolve our problems and disengage our armed forces from facing inwards as they do today, and face them outwards, I feel we shall have a good chance of preventing a recurrence of the history of the past, which was that whenever this subcontinent was divided—and it was often divided—someone or other invited an outsider to step in."[37]

Behind this apparent identity of views, however, was a wide gap in the conceptions of timing and the motivations for such integration. To India, no such integration was possible or desirable so long as Pakistan's foreign and domestic policies remain so glaringly at variance with India's. To Pakistan military cooperation was an immediate necessity and foreign policy differences were immaterial in so far as the security of the subcontinent was concerned. India would wait till Pakistan throws up a leadership identical in outlook and orientation: Pakistan would desire an urgent get-together to face an imminent danger.

This statement oversimplifies the problems involved. In the first place, Pakistan's offer of joint defence was not unconditional; progress depended on the solution of the Kashmir question to her satisfaction.[38] This made many in India wonder whether Pakistan wanted joint defence or Kashmir! Secondly, there is a distinct aversion in India to any association of this kind with an army group or a feudal-theocratic elite; India, as Nehru, said, would not also add to her own problems by

[36]*New York Times*, 2 March 1957.

[37]Mohammed Ayub Khan, "Pakistan Perspective," *Foreign Affairs*, July 1960.

[38]*Indian Affairs Record*, January 1960.

associating with Pakistan on underwriting her politics. Thirdly, some of Pakistan's activities and the expression of opinions in prominent organs of opinion indicated a continuation of the old jealousies and rivalries and no lessening of the pre-Partition zeal for religion. A superstructure of unity or cooperation built on such insecure foundations might easily give way to the forces of disruption thus leading the two countries once again into the quagmire of conflict and tension.

These factors need to be repeated with annotations. It so happens that the political infra-structure of Pakistan is among the weakest in Asia; much of India's stability and capacity to deal with vital internal problems has been due to the Partition and the removal it implied of the dangerous cankers from the body politic. Any attempt to reintegrate India and Pakistan might regenerate the kind of politics in the subcontinent which had led to mass violence and a collapse of sophisticated politics (in 1947 communal killings on a massive scale took place in the subcontinent). It should also be noted that in Pakistan there has been a continued deterioration in the quality of politics, necessitating army rule, and the gaps between India and Pakistan in several vital spheres of policy have widened. It should be remembered that in the years after freedom the gulf between India and Pakistan has been yawning and involving the entire range of State policies.

The differences in foreign policy have been the most oft-cited symbol of these differences. In reality, however, their significance would appear lesser than of the differences on other counts. In recent years, Pakistan has attempted to develop closer relations with such neutralists as Nasser, Tito and Sukarno; it has signed an oil exploration agreement with the USSR and declared its friendly feelings for China. On the other hand, notwithstanding her nonalignment, India's proximity to the West has been in a way underlined by the Chinese decision to invade her borders. India's continued membership of the Commonwealth, the identity in recent months of Indian and American views on problems of South-East Asia and the increasing sign of the Western involvement in India's developmental planning are also indications of the continued relationship between India and the West.

As against these factors, it should be noted that in the spheres of domestic politics and economic policies, India and Pakistan are treading different grounds. Combined with the foreign policy differences, these structural differences have almost made India and Pakistan representative of two of the three competing models in Asia, viz. communism, democratic socialism, and anti-Communist dictatorship. It should also be noted that on all the three counts of foreign policy, domestic politics and economic policies, India and Pakistan had started with an identical approach; their differences in policy matters at that time were confined to the one important sphere of the role of religion in politics. The differences in two of the three fields—politics and foreign policy—arose out of Pakistan's gradual transformation; in the sphere of economic policy, it is India which accepted socialism as its official goal in 1955 marking a vital shift in ideological orientation. Even here Pakistan has moved somewhat in the opposite direction—from mixed economy to free enterprise.[39]

More than these policy differences has been the apparent incapacity of Pakistan to settle down to the status of the smaller State in South Asia. So intense is the resulting frustration that Pakistan has applied only one criterion in determining her foreign policy—India. Fearing an impending U.S. foreign policy change, the *Dawn* wrote on 24 February 1961: "India is to be built as a counterpoise to China and, therefore, upon India's head must be set the crown of the economic and political leadership of the East ... because the USA has decided she should become the leader. ... It is not necessary to create such a leadership at all. ... Speaking again in the name of the people of Pakistan we can say without the slightest hesitation that if other people were forced to a position where they must make a choice between the leadership of India and the leadership of China, they would most certainly decide against the former

[39]Preface, *Pakistan: Second Five-Year Plan*, Karachi, 1960.

kind of leadership."[40] Some of the hysterical outbursts of this newspaper after Vice-President Johnson had asked for an Asian conference and hinted at the possibility of Indian leadership of the area are also instructive. The *Dawn* asked: "Is it going to be an attempt to create another bloc in opposition to China on the one hand and Nasser-led nations on the other?"[41] Again: "First, it may be the first act of the Nehru worshippers to set up that most unscrupulous of Asian heads of nations in the role of Asian leadership which some people have been talking about in Johnson's country. Secondly, will such a conference be allowed to discuss Kashmir?"[42] In repeated editorials (21, 23 and 29 May and 3 June 1961) the daily gave vent to its anger at this suggestion, finally saying: "The present U.S. leadership is looking in our peoples' eyes like sinking men who are clutching at every straw.... Whatever befalls Mr Kennedy in Vienna he needs above all the mercy of God so that his eyes, his mind and his ears may be awakened to truth."[43]

The persistent and violent criticism from an "ally" had its impact; on 9 June 1961, Ambassador Rowntree made it clear in a statement to the Press that Johnson did not mean to suggest that the leadership of any country would be imposed and what he really meant was the possibility of the emergence of a collective leadership in the region.[44] It was not until the Pakistan President was accorded a great reception in the United States in July 1961, and the Asian military leader compared to George Washington, that Pakistan's anger was to be removed.[45]

A special mention also needs to be made here of Pakistan's increasing friendliness towards China in an attempt to harm the common enemy—India. In a dispatch from Karachi, the *Christian Science Monitor* said in March 1962 what has often been feared in India: "If by opening up a bridge to Peking, Pakistan could obtain equipment and financing for a guerilla conflict in Kashmir there plainly would be great temptation to

[40]*Dawn*, 24 February 1961.   [41]*Ibid.*, 23 May 1961.   [42]*Ibid.*
[43]*Ibid.*, 3 June 1961.   [44]*Ibid.*, 10 June 1961.
[45]*See* "George Washington Ayub," *New Republic*, 30 October 1961.

do so. Matters have not gone that far as yet by any means but few here doubt that Peking would regard such conflict as a desirable war of liberation. President Ayub's soft words in describing Peking's foreign policy are consistent with an effort to entice such help. They also are consistent with a bluff in Peking's direction for frightening the West."[46] It is a tragic but fascinating drama of international politics being enacted in the South Asian region—the military ally of the United States and the military ally of the USSR combining to undo what has become an area of agreement between the USA and the USSR. The greatest problem, in this sense, in the great Powers' Asian policies is their Asian allies!

Another difficulty in Indo-Pakistan integration is the continued religious sense of belonging in some circles of Pakistan; transcending considerations of race, language, culture, history, traditions, geography and politics is this one single sense of belonging to Islam. The conception of future integration possibilities of this section is essentially oriented towards the Islamic countries of West Asia. In 1949, Pakistan sounded other Muslim countries about an Islamic conference without much success; an international Islamic economic conference was, however, held in November 1949, where the Finance Minister of Pakistan in his presidential address outlined the philosophy of an Islamic "third force." The intensely secular nationalism of the Arabs, and others prevented any further moves in this direction; "... the political upsurge elsewhere was based largely on territorial or racial nationalism, anti-Western, anti-White."[47] The disappointment with the Arabs, however, did not entirely convince the Pakistanis of the impossibility of such moves. The Baghdad Pact was interpreted in Pakistan as a pact among Muslim countries; and the major scheme of integration mentioned in public discussions so far in Pakistan is of a federation between Iran, Afghanistan and

[46]*Christian Science Monitor*, 21 March 1962.
[47]Keith Callard, *Pakistan, A Political Study*, London, Allen and Unwin, 1957, p. 314.

Pakistan.[48] In 1960, a Pakistani author wrote: "In this struggle for survival (of Islam) these three nations must come closer together and resist attempts by the Soviet Union or the West to impose allegiance on them. The danger is very real.... Pakistanis believe that Islam itself is a nationality.... Such a development is possible in this region only on the basis of Islam and not on racialism or geographical nationalism."[49]

We have discussed above the importance of Indo-Pakistan integration and also noted the difficulties involved. Many sympathetic observers of the South Asian developments like Louis Fischer have favoured such a step and even predicted that "Nehru could, if he cared, confederate with Pakistan and he might find the opposition and obstacles surprisingly small." There is no doubt that much of the vehemence in Pakistani views against India is a result and not the cause of disintegration or lack of integration; there can be no doubt, however, that much of this antipathy is built in the political infrastructure of Pakistan, the nature of its elite and the abnormality of their past when an apparently modernized elite was to struggle in the name of religion to protect their vital interests as they conceived them. In India also it would be necessary to curb the apparent vested interests that have grown against such integration; a section of the extreme right and of the extreme left in Indian politics flourish on a certain degree of antipathy to Pakistan. The advantage lies in the fact that in India none can easily discard such ideas as antagonistic to India's interests; the national leadership was on record against Partition and Gandhi once said that Partition would come over his dead body. Apparently, it is not the annulment of Partition which is the immediate prospect but closer and cooperative relations of the two States. It is impossible for anyone in India to reject reasonable schemes for such cooperation without disowning the traditions of our national struggle.

[48]Cited by Aslam Siddiqui, *Pakistan Seeks Security*, Karachi, 1960, p. 158.
[49]*Ibid.*, pp. 158-62.

Postscript

MOMENTOUS EVENTS have taken place in Asia in 1962-63, at once underlining the complex problems of regional cooperation in Asia and the importance of it. Serious conflicts have broken out in two parts of Asia. An open military confrontation between India and China following China's unprovoked aggression against India and the Indonesian opposition to the formation of Malaysia have brought out into the open the fact that inter-Asian disputes can become intensely acute and that nationalism still remains the predominant factor in the making of the policies of Asian countries. There are indeed other problem spots in Asia: India's relations with Pakistan are at an all-time low in October 1963; the situation in Laos is a matter of concern for almost all the countries involved in it; the persecution of the Buddhists in South Viet Nam has angered many Asian nations and the Philippines are reluctant to accept Malaysia.

As against these factors, there are of course some signs of a trend towards cooperation. The formation of Malaysia is itself a significant pointer that larger federations may come into being in some parts of Asia; the leaders of Malaya, the Philippines and Indonesia have at least once talked of a confederation or Maphilindo. Another favourable indicator is that Japan which had withdrawn from the Asian scene ever since the end of the World War is showing signs of playing an active role again in the affairs of South-East Asia.

. What is most relevant for this book, however, is that for the first time the possibility has opened up of a different kind of integration, at least in some parts of Asia. It has been stated earlier that one natural form of integration is. when a great Power by exercising the sheer weight of its military and economic strength organizes a neighbouring region into some kind of an integrated unit. This type of integration is hardly an immaculate federation and it often becomes difficult to differentiate between this form of integration and the traditional concept of empire-building. However, in the world of today, there are other regional associations which resemble this pattern. The Organization of the American States or the Comecon are basically associations dominated by one great Power. It is of course still a long way for China to tread to become as great and powerful as the Soviet Union or the United States, but there is no doubt that it aspires today to extend its power penumbra over the neighbouring regions and make out of parts of Asia and, if possible, Africa an integrated block under the leadership of China.

China has various advantages in these matters. An overseas Chinese population in South-East Asia would be intensely interested in this form of Asian integration; there are elements in the Communist parties of almost all the Asian countries, who are pro-Chinese; the simple racialistic slogans raised by China may have an appeal to some non-Communist Asian minds; and finally there is the previous history of many parts of Asia owing allegiance to China. A determined bid has been made by China in recent months to increase its communications with South-East Asia and to replace the former front organizations of the international Communist movement by purely "Asian" or "Afro-Asian" bodies. Institutions like the Ganefo and the proposed Asian News Service are as much straws in the wind as the Journalists Conference in Jakarta or the air agreement between China and Pakistan. The most important single element behind this kind of Chinese moves, of course, is China's expanding power and the ever-increasing desire of China to emerge as a great Power with its own sphere of influence.

There are many factors impeding the success of China's efforts. The existence of India as another potential Asian power, the possible entry of Japan as a contender, the intense urgency of the Soviet Union to prevent such a development, the continued capacity of the Western Powers to play a role in Asia, and above all the vigilant nationalism of the countries of South-East Asia, are all factors with which China would have to reckon.

Inevitably, in a situation of this kind, India's role in Asia has to be one of preventing integration on the lines set forth by China. If India can accumulate the minimum power that is necessary to prevent the extension of China's power influence to its smaller neighbours, it will help the prevention of such a development.

Looked at from the viewpoint of regional cooperation and integration, however, the India-China situation has also some other hopeful possibilities. It is unlikely that many countries of Asia would voluntarily elect to integrate with such an overwhelming power in China and risk the loss of their identity. In fact, there is a possibility that some of them would cooperate among themselves to withstand the Chinese power thrust. It is also unlikely that Asian countries will for long ignore the patent reality that compared to China, India is a smaller Power, that it is not probable that she would emerge in a similar role in Asia, or that in preventing the extension of Chinese sphere of influence they would walk into India's.

The most hopeful element in the situation, however, is different. India in a way is a symbol of Soviet-American cooperation and notwithstanding the verbal outbursts in some of the Asian countries, basically the policies of their governments remain similar to India's. China's capacity to do harm is unlimited but its capacity to do good is little. India in this basic sense is an entirely different factor in Asian politics than China. The essence of the difference between India and China is that India is attempting to demonstrate an alternative road for the salvation of the coloured, underdeveloped and overpopulated nations—the road of international cooperation. Whether it is Ceylon or Indonesia, Nepal or Pakistan, Afghanistan or Cambodia, it has been the objective of all the Asian governments to secure such cooperation and sympathy of the great Powers of the world for their development. In this basic sense, the Indian path has proved attractive to most Asian countries and it is not impossible that with the support and sympathy of the great Powers of the world vitally interested in the triumph of the Indian path, it will be possible to think of cooperation in Asia.

There are apparently a large number of irritants in the matter of India's relations with many of the neighbouring countries. Personal vanities some time play an important role; Indian advocacy of a democratic form of government is not liked by many rulers who believe in different forms of "democracy"; and the Indians abroad are not always the best ambassadors that a country can send to another. There may also be the supreme factor of the suspicion that there will be little eventually to choose between a powerful India and a powerful China.

It will be wrong for India to start working towards regional integration or cooperation in Asia on the basis of its own experiences with China. So long as other countries do not share similar experiences, they will be reluctant to accept totally the Indian view of China. Secondly, all our policies must be guided by the recognition of the fact that while we know that we are not as powerful and strong as would make us expansionists and while we have no desire to be so, there is a subdued element of apprehension about India also in many countries. It will be particularly wrong for us to overstep our natural region of cooperation and begin to confront China in its present posture in distant Africa or even South-East Asia. We should, on the other hand, recognize that regional cooperation among Arabs or Africans or in South-East Asia and the emergence of larger political units in some of these areas are the best guarantees against China's predominance. Instead of ourselves trying to get involved in such agencies of regional cooperation as these countries envisage, we might quietly help them to have their own larger political units and then try to deal with them on a basis of equality and mutual advantage.

The case of Pakistan is different. It is not conceivable that Pakistan can solve either its problem of identity or its problem of status by joining any other regional association. Pakistan essentially belongs to South Asia and shares its problems and aspirations. It also cannot escape any large scale instability or disaster that will overtake India. Paradoxically, no country seems to be more interested at the moment to bring about that disaster than Pakistan. Caught in a peculiar psychological mould in which Pakistan considers herself a logical projection of anybody who is anti-Indian in any part of the world, it has completely gone over to the side of China and is selling the Chinese line to other Asian countries.

It is not necessary for India to overlook these factors in order to keep the long-term goal in view of Indo-Pakistan friendship, cooperation and, if possible, integration. The very absurdity of Pakistan's obsession with India and its present posture is a matter of hope in the long run.

In the short term, however, the reality may be that the Pakistan-China alliance, almost like the Hitler-Stalin pact, is a prelude to renewed military pressure on India from two sides in order to crumble her spirit of resistance. But there are other realities about Pakistan, apart from its present alliance with China. For one thing, the dependence on the Western nations for Pakistan's subsistence remains. For another, the growing signs of Pakistan-Soviet cooperation are a hopeful indicator.

Many in Pakistan may soon discover that in real material terms, China has little to offer to Pakistan. On the other hand, the advantages of Indo-Pakistan cooperation in the context of the hopeful trends in the larger international background are too obvious to be ignored. Furthermore, there are so many things in common between India and Pakistan that they are bound to assert in the course of time. As the bigger country of the South Asian region, it is India's privilege and obligation to pave the way for the growth of a new South Asian loyalty, without, of course, minimizing the threat from the monstrous alliance between China and Pakistan.

APPENDIX

*A Note on Pakistan's Attitude to Regional Integration and the Emotional Involvement with Islam**

PAKISTAN ACQUIRED her international personality in August 1947 with relatively few emotional or intellectual international commitments. Unlike the Indian National Congress, the Muslim League had remained largely silent and never committed itself on such issues as Spain and China, Abyssinia and Czechoslovakia, fascism and communism.[1] Several reasons can be adduced for this relative absence of an international orientation of the Muslim League. In the first place, the period between the League's demand for a sovereign State and its coming into being was extremely brief and was a period of rather simplified world politics, viz. war. Secondly, even during these years there was little certainty about the nature and form in which the Muslim demand would be fulfilled in the future constitutional set-up in India. Thirdly, the Muslim League's internal task was in a sense more difficult and absorbing than that of the Congress. In a period of growing cynicism about religion in the world as a whole, the chances of the League's success depended precisely on keeping up such loyalties. Fourthly, there was no internationally-oriented personality in the higher echelons of the Muslim League. Fifthly, articulate left-wing opinion which might have related internal and

*Based on my article originally published in *India Quarterly*, July-September 1962.

[1]Jawaharlal Nehru, *Discovery Of India*, Calcutta, Signet Press, 1946, p. 447.

international developments was either non-existent or silent in the League. Lastly, the League had a somewhat unique role within the general pattern of developments in Asia—to emphasize the internal problems of the region rather than the external problems that the Asian countries faced in common. It is interesting to note that when the Indian Council of World Affairs organized the first Asian Relations Conference in New Delhi in 1947, the League declined to attend it on the ground that it was "a thinly disguised attempt on the part of the Hindu Congress to boost itself politically as the prospective leader of Asian peoples."[2]

Against this general lack of a foreign affairs orientation, however, must be noted the fact of the historical sympathy and interest of the Muslims of India for other Muslim countries of West Asia and North Africa. In the decades following the Indian Mutiny which ended in the smashing of the archaic symbols of India's freedom and of the prospects of a return to the *ancien regime*, there was a search among the Indian *elites* for past glory and greatness. In this, the immediate past was overlooked; the Hindus looked back for psychological sustenance to Sanskrit and ancient Indian culture and the Muslims to the early Islamic period of West Asian history.[3] It is interesting to note the comment of a Muslim historian: "While we have historical literature by Bengali Muslims on Islam, Arabia, Egypt, Turkey, Afghanistan, etc. we have very few works from Muslims on Bengal or India."[4]

Like many other aspects of the Muslim movement and thought this reflected the unique social structure that the Indian Muslims had evolved at this time: the old aristocratic and conservative attitudes persisted in isolation from the new attitudes and trends which the Western impact on India had created.[5]

[2]Quoted in: Werner Levi, *Free India in Asia*, Minneapolis, University of Minnesota, 1952, p. 38.

[3]Jawaharlal Nehru, *op. cit.*, p. 364.

[4]A.R. Mallick, "Modern Historical Writing in Bengali," *Historians of India, Pakistan and Ceylon*, Ed. C. H. Philips, London, Oxford University Press, 1961, pp. 446-60.

[5]Jawaharlal Nehru, *op. cit.*, pp. 363-7.

Sir Syed Ahmed Khan attempted to correct this outward orientation of the Muslims; he was openly opposed to any allegiance to the Turkish Khilafat,[6] and stated that Indian Muslims had little reason to get excited if the British Government attacked Afghanistan.[7] However, once the grip of this Aligarh outlook loosened and the Indian Muslims discovered the need and possibility of participating in Indian politics, the pan-Islamic attitude re-asserted itself. Muslim leaders within the Indian National Congress often expressed their emotional attachment to other Muslim peoples of West Asia. In 1923, Azad in his presidential address to the Congress said that "India must make common cause with the universal struggles of Eastern nations to shake off the fetters of slavery and should assure Egypt, Syria, and Palestine and Morocco of her sympathy with their struggle."[8] Mohammed Ali, presiding over the Congress in 1926, commended the idea of an Eastern Federation.[9] The Khilafat Movement was the organized expression of such sentiments.

Interestingly, there was a difference between these typical, Muslim sentiments and the overall Congress outlook; this was dramatically illustrated by the Congress decision to alter the terms of its support to West Asian countries between 1922 and 1923. In 1922 the Congress had asked not only for the restoration of Turkey's sovereign rights but also for her guardianship of the world of Islam; in 1923, it dropped all reference to Islam and congratulated the Turkish people on their success which was "a presage of the freedom of all nations of the East." Again in 1922, the Congress had wanted all mandated territories to be freed from non-Muslim control; in 1923, it asked for removal of all alien control from them.[10] While the Muslim leaders in the Congress stressed the need for an Eastern Federation, with India as its eastern-most unit, the non-Muslim

[6]*Ibid.,* p. 367.

[7]Nehru, *Autobiography*, London, Bodley Head, 1936 p. 462.

[8]Quoted in Levi, *op. cit.*, p. 22.

[9]Bimla Prasad, *The Origins of Indian Foreign Policy*, Calcutta, Bookland, 1960, p. 72.   [10]*Ibid.*, p. 69.

Congressmen pleaded for a large Asian Federation. It was only Dr Ansari, among the Congress Muslim leaders, who envisaged an Asian Federation, adding that India was fortunately placed in that a part of its population had affinities with the West Asian countries and another with the East Asian ones.[11]

The Muslim League itself had little to do with such ideas at this stage and, with the exception of Iqbal, none of its leaders expressed an open preference for any pan-Islamic grouping. The League, however, did develop a broad sense of sympathy for the "Muslim" causes in the world. In December 1924, the League condemned British actions in Egypt; in January 1926, it protested against the mandate system; in 1929, sympathy was expressed for King Amanullah of Afghanistan; in 1931, Italy was condemned for her atrocities in Tripoli; in 1933, it urged the scrapping of the Balfour Declaration and protested against the British policy in Palestine. In 1937, Jinnah said: "May I point out to the British Government that this question of Palestine, if not fairly and squarely met, boldly and courageously decided, is going to be the turning point in the history of the British Empire."[12] In 1938, the League expressed its confidence in the Grand Mufti; in 1939, the League was represented in the Palestine Conference at Cairo by Chaudhuri Khaliquzzaman. In 1941, the League adopted the following resolution after the Allied troops had moved into Iran and Iraq to depose pro-Nazi governments: "The Mussalmans of India are greatly perturbed at and view with alarm the military occupation of certain Muslim States in the Near East by Great Britain and her allies. The Working Committee, therefore, urge upon the British Government and her allies to declare unequivocally that the sovereignty and independence of those Muslim States will be immediately restored as soon as circumstances permit and that the pernicious system of mandates and the creation of zones of influence for European Powers will not be resorted to."

---

[11]*Ibid.*, p. 76.

[12]M. Ahmad, *Pakistan and the Middle East*, Karachi, Kitabi Markaz, 1948, p. 162.

A later resolution on Iran was more strongly worded: "The Working Committee learnt with dismay the news of the unprovoked aggression against Iran by Great Britain and Russia and warn the Allies that this action will still more complicate the Near Eastern situation and alienate the sympathies of Muslim India and create bitterness in their hearts, which will result in the withdrawal of every help by them to the Allied cause."[13] In 1943, the League adopted three other resolutions: one urging the freedom of Muslim colonies of Italy; another, asking for the abolition of mandates; and the third, condemning the French action in Lebanon.[14]

More than these resolutions, an event in the Muslim League Session of 1941 illustrated the intensity of Indian Muslims' feeling for the peoples of West Asia. The loyalist Premier of the Punjab, Sir Sikander Hayat Khan, attempted to stop the League from adopting a resolution on Iran stating that Reza Shah was pro-Nazi and the people of Iran might have disliked him. He was hooted in the meeting and prolonged shouts greeted the cause of Reza Shah.[15]

In the Muslim League's emphasis on Muslim causes in the world, two elements may be noted: one, the broad anti-imperialist urge of all the colonial peoples at this stage; and two, the need and urgency of cultivating a "Muslim" sense of belonging among the adherents of the organization. There was a degree of contradiction in this dual posture: and the attitude of other Muslim countries toward the Muslim League was not one of great enthusiasm. In the 1941 session of the League, the Raja of Mahmudabad complained that no Muslim outside India had expressed any sympathy with Indian Muslims and yet they were pouring money and blood in support of the non-Indian Muslims.[16] A Pakistani author, complained in 1948: "When Indian Muslims under severe handicaps were striving to establish Pakistan, they received no encouragement from the Middle Eastern Powers. Some of the Arab dignitaries, led away by the false mischievous propaganda of the enemies of Islam, even

---

[13]*Ibid.*, p. 165-6.　　[14]*Ibid.*, p. 167.
[15]*Indian Annual Register*, 1941, II.　　[16]*Ibid.*

condemned the creation of Pakistan. The isolationist stand taken by the Kemalist Turkey, to which Indian Muslims had pinned great hopes, made their disappointment all the more acute."[17] Keith Callard has referred to the same phenomenon in different terms: "For many Muslims outside it has been more important to align Asians and Africans against the colonial Powers than to defend Muslim causes against non-Muslims. The Congress argument that specifically Muslim demands hampered national independence found wide acceptance in other Asian and Middle Eastern countries."[18]

Another observation that might be made in this introductory section is the unique nature of the provinciality of the Muslims in India, inasmuch as it reflected no existing inferiority of theirs but a situation of the distant past. In the Muslim world the Indian Muslim was among the most advanced; but his provinciality in relation to archaic societies like Saudi Arabia impeded, on the one hand, the much-needed exposure to the impact of the West and, on the other, a realization of modern realities of world politics.

Nature of Pakistani Foreign Policy

It was with this commitment of support to the Muslim causes that Pakistan was born. In conducting her foreign policy, however, the one single factor of overriding consequence was her relation with India. Most observers of Pakistan's foreign policy have been struck by this; "relations with India have been the main preoccupation of the foreign policy of Pakistan," said Callard.[19] Recent Pakistani publications on foreign policy have frankly accepted this. In *Pakistan and the United Nations*, written on behalf of a high-level study group, Sarwar Hasan says: "Robert Schuman, former Prime Minister of France, once observed that since 1871 the foreign policy of his country had been continuously dominated by one main

[17]Ahmad, *op. cit.*, p. 207.
[18]Keith Callard, *Pakistan: A Political Study*, London, Allen and Unwin, 1957, p. 314.   [19]*Ibid.*, p. 313.

preoccupation, that of ensuring her security and independence from her neighbour, Germany. Unfortunately, the foreign policy of Pakistan has in a similar manner been dominated by considerations of security and independence from its neighbour, India."[20] It is of some significance that since 1956, the military alignments of Pakistan have been officially explained in terms of threats from India, not from any other source. Suhrawardy, when Prime Minister, defended Pakistan's alliances in these terms: "Now if there are some amongst you who hold that it is better for us to remain friendless and alone, or who think that there is no danger, or if the danger comes it will be a good thing to be absorbed by India, then they should not accept the policy which I am now laying down."[21] Explaining his policy of alignment to an Indonesian audience at Bandung in December 1960, President Ayub said: "Please remember that it is an Asian country which has been oppressing us and continues to oppress us."[22] Russia and China .were not the possible enemies that Pakistan feared; Suhrawardy said in 1957: "I seek the friendship of China. I am not isolated. I feel perfectly certain that when the crucial time comes, China will come to our assistance. It has already done so.... When I have nothing against Russia and against China, and have no desire to be against them, why should they be against us."[23] Recently, there have been cordial exchanges of notes regarding the border between China and Pakistan.*

What has made India the major factor in Pakistan's foreign policy are not merely the disputes which bedevil their mutual relations, but also the more basic factors involved in the making of attitudes. Keith Callard has summed up some

---

[20]K. Sarwar Hasan, *Pakistan and the United Nations*, New York, Manhattan, 1960, p. 50.

[21]*Prime Minister's Statement on Foreign Policy*, 9 December 1956, Karachi, Government of Pakistan, 1957.

[22]*Asian Recorder*, 1960, p. 3748.

[23]*Winding up of Foreign Policy Debates*, Karachi, Government of Pakistan, 1957.

*Agreements have now been signed regarding the border and other matters between China and Pakistan.

of these in his political study of Pakistan. Maintaining that problems of relations with India have "dominated foreign affairs, defence and economic policy and have lain behind many of the moves of internal politics," Callard continues: "In large measure Pakistani feeling toward India has been a continuation of the political struggle before Partition. . . . The idea that a country has a foreign enemy is easy for the mass of the people to understand, and it also provides a powerful stimulus to unity. For Pakistan, India has filled this role."[24]

This internal aspect apart, issues of prestige have also played an important part. "Mr Jinnah had never agreed to any constitutional formula which would have denoted a lesser status for the Muslim League. India contained two nations: one sovereign nation is the equal of any other sovereign nation. . . . Many political leaders and most of the articulate section of the population have reacted with emotional intensity to any suggestion of Indian superiority in any field. . . . The degree of passion has been heightened by the feeling, largely justified, that on every matter on which the real interests of the two nations have come into conflict, India has contrived to emerge victorious."[25]

It is against this background of Pakistan's foreign policy and attitudes that developments in relation to the Muslim world have to be viewed. On the morrow of its freedom, Pakistan felt the pressing need of attracting sympathy and attention from other peoples of the world. It was symbolic of Pakistan's difficulties that the UN Legal Department decided that while independent India continued as a Member-State, Pakistan had to apply for membership of the United Nations. What heightened this sense of helplessness was the fact that the Commonweath failed to give any help to Pakistan in the Kashmir dispute. In 1949, Liaquat Ali said in London: "Pakistan must not be taken for granted; Pakistan is not a camp-follower of the Commonwealth."[26] The *Dawn* demanded in an editorial at this time: "British elements should be eliminated from civilian

---

[24]Callard, *op. cit.*, p. 17.   [25]*Ibid.*, p. 304.   [26]*Dawn*, 14 May 1949.

positions and from those positions in the armed forces for which Pakistani substitutes can be found. Even for those positions in which foreigners must be appointed, because suitable Pakistani personnel are lacking, search should first be made outside the British Isles."[27] As for others, "Russia was an enemy of the empires of Western Europe, but had shown no enthusiasm for Pakistan as a separate unit";[28] "China was still under Chiang Kai-shek—a personal friend of Nehru and an admirer of the Congress"; the United States "knew and sympathized much more with the land of Gandhi and Nehru than with that of Jinnah."[29]

Suggestive of Pakistan's plight was the incident of the Moscow invitation. When the Truman administration invited Nehru to visit the United States in 1949, the Pakistan Prime Minister secured an invitation from Moscow soon afterwards. However, the visit never came off, because, it is said, the Soviet Government did not reply to the Pakistani Prime Minister's communication asking for a date. The *Newsweek* reported on 21 December 1949: "After several weeks of unsuccessful attempts, Liaquat Ali Khan gave up in disgust and announced that it would not be possible for him to make a trip. No one in Karachi has any idea why Moscow failed to carry through its invitation."

As Callard noted: "In the first appraisal of her position among the community of self-governing nations, Pakistan could find no single country which could be counted as an unfailing friend and ally willing to lend aid and comfort in time of need."[30] In this bleak situation, Islam appeared to Pakistan to offer the only bond of belonging, in whose name she could appeal for other nations' support.

Apart from this inevitable search for friends was the continued need to cultivate a distinctive sense of belonging in a country which was cut out of a natural historical, geographical and cultural unit. Also important was the urgency of stressing the continued difference with India. Maintaining that Pakistan

---

[27]*Ibid.*, 8 May 1949.   [28]Callard, *op. cit.*, p. 303.   [29]*Ibid.*
[30]*Ibid.*

had no other security against the natural tendency of one government absorbing another in a topographical basin, Aslam Siddiqui says: "To escape the consequences of this axiomatic development Pakistan has to put up some shield. That shield obviously is religion, on the basis of which partition of the Indo-Pakistani subcontinent took place."[31]

Search for Muslim Unity

There was a large measure of confidence in Pakistan, immediately after Partition, that the Muslim countries of the world will draw closer to Pakistan and, indeed, might move toward a pan-Islamic grouping of nations. Muslim unity, according to this view, was the natural corollary of a renewed Islamic sense of belonging; the creation of Pakistan itself was a symbol of this postwar phenomenon. A. B. Rajput wrote in his book on the Muslim League: "Thus with the birth of Pakistan the hope of pan-Islamic unity and brotherhood brightened afresh amongst the Islamic States of Asia."[32] Another author, M. Ahmad, wrote in the same year: "The younger generation of the Arab leaders consider the Arab League as the authentic answer to their longheld and mounting desire for the unification of Muslim States which possess the common bond of the Muslim religion and the urge for complete freedom. The fact is that even without the Caliphate, a more powerful idea of Islamic solidarity has originated."[33] It is interesting to note the terms in which this solidarity was sought by Pakistani intellectuals. To quote Ahmad: "A real agreement among these potential allies can alone ward off the menace of Hindu, Russian, American and British imperialisms. The Muslim State or States, which may be inhibited from making a common cause in the fatuous hope that these menacing imperialisms will attack others and leave them in peace, will be left in isolation and condemned to annihilation."[34]

[31]Aslam Siddiqui, *Pakistan Seeks Security*, Lahore, Longmans, 1960, p. 17.
[32]A. B. Rajput, *The Muslim League*, Lahore, 1948, p. 204.
[33]Ahmad, *op. cit.*, pp. 205-6.   [34]*Ibid.*, p. 213.

While such ideas were germinating in some minds even in 1948, concerted attempts for Muslim unity were made only during 1949 after the Prime Minister had made a statement in London that Muslim nations between Cairo and Karachi could play an important role between the two Power blocs. On his way home from London in May 1949, he stopped in Cairo, Baghdad and Teheran and in his speeches stressed the Islamic ideals of Pakistan: "In the laboratory of Pakistan we are experimenting with the principles and ideals of Islam and hope to put before the world a progressive code of life."[35] In Teheran he said: "My hope for the future is that Iran and Pakistan will be like one soul in two bodies."[36] Earlier, an organization called the "Motamar-e-Alam-e-Islam" (Muslim World Conference) had started functioning in Karachi; in February 1949 its first session was attended by delegates from 19 Muslim countries. On his return from London, Liaquat Ali made moves for a conference at the governmental level. However, the Arab and non-Arab countries did not show much interest.[37]

Their lack of interest became more evident when an exploring mission by Chaudhary Khaliquzzaman, the then President of the Muslim League, ended in a fiasco. The Pakistan leader had earlier propagated his ideas of an "Islamistan" in a pamphlet on the subject[38] and had in 1949 visited the West Asian countries and London in order to promote the idea. Although ostensibly concerned only with a people-to-people campaign for an Islamic bloc, the League leader exceeded his brief and canvassed a security pact with British support. The reactions in Arab countries to his mission were unfavourable, if not hostile. The *Dawn*, in an editorial, "Caution Islamistan," wrote: "His approach was to have been on a people-to-people basis, but within a few days of his tour he seems to have directed attention to the governments of the countries that he visited rather than to their peoples.... He set out to sell the idea to Muslims alone, but if we are not mistaken he went to London to discuss the issue with the Commonwealth Relations Office and the Foreign Office

---

[35]Siddiqui, *op. cit.*, p. 88.　　　[36]*Ibid.*　　　[37]*Ibid.*
[38]W. C. Smith, *Islam in Modern History*, New York, Mentor, 1959, p. 88 n.

of the British Government. . . . Furthermore, the idea of getting together of the peoples of the various countries, it appears, has developed into the suggestion of a security pact on the enlarged pattern of the pact agreed upon by the Arab League countries . . . even if such a security pact were practicable, apart from the question of being desirable in the present world context, it will have to be underwritten militarily as well as politically by certain non-Muslim foreign Powers. . . . In fact . . . he has been attempting . . . to enlist the active support of those foreign Powers . . . (this) naturally prompts some quarters to ask: Security against whom?"[39]

While the overtly political attempts at pan-Islamic integration failed, an International Islamic Economic Conference was held in Karachi in November 1949 under non-official auspices. At the conference, the Prime Minister of Pakistan said in his inaugural address: "Pakistan has one and only one ambition—to serve Islam and humanity. . . . We all belong to the great brotherhood of Islam. Islam alone can solve some of the problems facing the world today."[40] Finance Minister, Ghulam Mohammad, envisaged Islamic unity and cooperation leading to the creation of a third bloc of nations. He held: "Besides being united in a common faith, a common outlook and a common way of life, we form also a geographic unity." More interesting than this stereotyped appeal for unity was the ideological basis on which coming together was sought at this time: "We are now under pressure from two different ideologies, both striving to gain our allegiance. We are told that there are only two ideologies; you must accept one and repudiate the other. . . . One purpose of convening this conference is to grapple with this dilemma and determine objectively and frankly whether we are constrained to subscribe to the one or the other." Ghulam Mohammad continued and gave his answer: "We cannot put implicit faith in the Western democratic system nor can we subscribe to communism, although there are some aspects of this vast and comprehensive experi-

[39]*Dawn,* 15 November 1949.
[40]*Ibid.,* 26 November 1949.

ment which we must appreciate.... Islamic society has never been subjected to the stress and strains of class war and morbid hatred of the rich has never been one of its characteristics.... Islam is the golden mean between these two extremes; it is a non-violent method of rectifying unsocial and detrimental inequalities."[41] The conference ended on notes of high hopes of regional economic cooperation among Muslim nations as a prelude to political integration.

The second "Motamar" Conference in Karachi held in February 1951 also raised high hopes of Muslim unity. Delegates came from all countries containing Muslims, including the People's Republic of China but excluding the USSR and India; the Grand Mufti of Jerusalem presided over the conference. In the Muslim Women's Session, Begum Liaquat Ali stressed the need for bringing up children on Islamic principles; in the general conference the Prime Minister of Pakistan set the political tone: "The underlying idea of the movement for the achievement of Pakistan was... to secure a territory, however limited, where the Islamic ideology and way of life could be practised and demonstrated to the world. A cardinal feature of this ideology is to make Muslim brotherhood a living reality. It is therefore part of the mission which Pakistan has set before itself to do everything in its power to promote closer fellowship and cooperation between Muslim countries.... The world is in sore need of light. I have no doubt that light can be provided by Islam."[42] The Grand Mufti endorsed this call for unity and asked for the creation of a Muslim bloc, cooperating in matters of culture, economics, politics and defence.

Another organization, the Muslim Peoples' Organization, held a conference in early 1952, again attended by delegates from several Muslim countries.

All the three organizations—the International Islamic Economic Conference, the Motamar-e-Alam-e-Islam and the Muslim Peoples' Organization—had their headquarters in Karachi and maintained permanent secretariats there. These pan-Islamic organizations reflected the internal political groupings within

41*Ibid.*   42*Ibid.*, 10 February 1951.

Pakistan: "One member of the Pakistan Cabinet is the founder-President of the International Islamic Economic Conference; another member of the same cabinet is, we believe less officially, closely associated with the Motamar, and the former head of Pakistan's national political organization is bestowing his foster care on the embryonic Muslim Peoples' Organization."[43] The references are to Ghulam Mohammed, Fazlur Rahman and Khaliquzzaman—a Punjabi, a Bengali and a Hindustani—and the involvement of internal politics with this aspect of foreign policy becomes obvious. A certain degree of pan-Islamism had become thus at this stage in Pakistan the *sine qua non* for furthering political ambitions.

It should be noted that none of the conferences that Pakistan could arrange was official or inter-governmental. The attempt in 1949 to hold an official conference had failed; another attempt made in 1952 to hold an official Islamic Conference also failed. In a Press conference, on 2 May 1952, Foreign Minister Zafarullah tried to remove some of the fears and apprehensions in the minds of other governments. The points he made, noted below, illustrate the nature of the criticism made elsewhere of Pakistan's attempts for Islamic solidarity. Zafarullah said: "In some quarters it has been said that this is an attempt by Pakistan to destroy their League. This is an attempt by Pakistan to lead the Muslim world. This is to restrict cooperation among the Asian and African States. Every one of these and similar other assertions, if they are not due to misunderstanding and misconception, are deliberate falsehoods by mischievous people. . . . It is also said that there is some game Pakistan wants to play: that it desires the States whom it wants to invite to participate in this system, so that they should pull Pakistani chestnuts out of the fire. If such an idea exists I wish to completely refute it." A third plank of the criticism was not refuted by the Foreign Minister but only referred to: "It has become a fashion to charge Pakistan of being a theocratic State. But why is it that at least the Muslims, a greater part of them, claim that the world

---

[43]*Ibid.*, 9 February 1951.

can be led back to human happiness and prosperity through Islam? Why do we make that claim? Why is it that the claim is not made by other communities on behalf of their faiths? ... There must be something in that." Finally, the Foreign Minister made one more appeal to the Islamic antipathy to the West: "Our emotions are today held in greater bondage to the West than before Independence.... We are sinking deeper and deeper into intellectual slavery."[44]

Despite the Foreign Minister's earnest explanation that Pakistan had no other motives in calling the conference except to serve humanity and Islam, the other Muslim countries still held back and the government conference failed to materialize.

Subsequently Islamic conferences did take place in Pakistan, but they evoked less and less enthusiasm. In April 1954, Karachi was the venue for a third session of the International Islamic Economic Conference (the second was held in Teheran); it confined itself to purely economic affairs;[45] "after this it became dormant and its activities have remained confined to Pakistan."[46] In 1957, Lahore was the venue for an Islamic Colloquium; there was little political significance attached to it and many of the participants were Western scholars on Islam. An International Assembly of Muslim Youth was started in Karachi in 1955; the chief organizer of the association was the secretary of the Motamar. But the high pitch of Islamic enthusiasm of the 1949-52 period was not reached again. It was during the period of Muslim League rule that this enthusiasm reached its highest point. This period began after the death of Jinnah in September 1948—Jinnah had little enthusiasm for pan-Islam—and ended in 1953, with the dismissal of Nazimuddin when the civil servants virtually took over the government.

Disillusionment with the Arabs

It became clear at this time that the realities of the Muslim world were different from those expected by Pakistan and the

[44]*Ibid.*, 3 May 1952.   [45]*Ibid.*, 26 April 1954.
[46]Siddiqui, *op. cit.* p. 90.

enthusiasm for pan-Islamism began to decline. Two days after the Foreign Minister's Press conference, referred to above, the *Dawn* wrote: "The time has come for Pakistan's intelligentsia to realize that Pakistan is not adding to its prestige in the international field by running after certain other countries which are economically and otherwise in a far less stable position than Pakistan itself and which can really be of little help to us. If we concentrate on building up our resources and our strength . . . the day will come when many will be candidates for our friendship without our chasing them. Let us not forget that we in Pakistan constitute a Muslim world in ourselves. We say to our nation: give up sloganism and be realists."[47]

More important in this connection was the political transformation that was now under way in Western Asia. The Egyptian Revolution of 1952 opened up entirely new dimensions of Arab aspirations and paved the way for further secularization of Arab politics. It brought to the fore the dormant contradictions between the interests of West Asian and Western European countries, of which Mossadeq's nationalization of the Anglo-Iranian Oil Company in 1951 was a forerunner.

What prevented Pakistan's fuller participation in this new milieu was Pakistan's alliance with the Western Powers, which began to take shape about this time. There are two views of the development of this alignment. The one held by most Pakistanis is that after trying to maintain a neutralist position for five years, they discovered that Pakistan needed strong allies against India and it joined the United States in defence pacts. The other view is the one held by some U.S. observers (e.g. Selig Harrison) and some Indians that Pakistan was always anxious to do so and it is the United States which now had an administration which welcomed Pakistan. In fact, Harrison traces the story further back.[48] In any event, 1952-53 marked the turning point in Pakistan's foreign policy: "In 1953 two changes took place. In the United States, Eisenhower was installed as Presi-

[47]*Dawn*, 4 May 1952.

[48]Selig S. Harrison, "Case History of a Mistake," *New Republic*, 10 August 1959.

dent with John Foster Dulles as Secretary of State; in Pakistan, Ghulam Mohammed dismissed Nazimuddin and replaced him by Prime Minister Mohammed Ali, formerly Ambassador to Washington. Mr Dulles wanted pacts; Mohammed Ali liked the Americans. Pakistan wanted money and arms."[49]

Developments followed in quick succession. In February 1954, Pakistan accepted military aid from the United States, in September 1954 she joined the SEATO and in September 1955 the Baghdad Pact.

The latter pact projected Pakistan in West Asia in an entirely different role than the one envisaged earlier by the various Islamic conferences, namely as a third force, a golden mean between "capitalism" and "communism." Apart from India, Egypt, Syria, Jordan and Saudi Arabia vigorously criticized the pact. It was interpreted in these countries as an anti-Arab move, an extension of Western domination and one designed to divide the Arabs. Typical of the criticism in these countries is the following broadcast from Radio Mecca: "Is it, therefore, possible for any person to believe that an Islamic State, such as that of Pakistan, should accede to those who have joined hands with Zionist Jews. ... Whatever may be the case, Pakistan, a country so dear to us and to other Arab countries, cannot be expected to put her hand in the hands of those who have bad intention towards the Arabs."[50] Official apologists of Pakistan, on the other hand, have maintained that it was to help the Muslim countries and to unite them that the Baghdad Pact was created. In 1956 the *Dawn* had advised other Muslim countries: "Let them shake off their illusions, their vanities, and jealousies—*and join the Baghdad Pact*. If they do so that body can immediately be transformed as to become a Muslim NATO with plenty of teeth in it. Nehru does not want it because he wants a Hindu hegemony; Moscow does not want it because it wants a Red hegemony. And the Arabs foolishly rise to the bait. Our suggestion may sound fantastic in Cairo and Riyadh in their present moods, but if

---

[49]Callard, *op. cit.*, p. 321.

[50]Quoted by: Sarwar Hasan, *op. cit.*, p. 76.

their hearts and minds could be freed from the mesmeric influence of Islam's enemies masquerading as friends they might wake up with a shudder of guilt to discover that theirs today is the fantastic and suicidal policy."[51] Suhrawardy claimed in 1957 that Pakistan belonged to the pact which had $12\frac{1}{2}$ crores of Muslims in it and that those who kept out had only $2\frac{1}{2}$ crores.[52] Ayub Khan said in April 1961, that it was Pakistan's desire to forge a united front with the Muslim countries, to strengthen them and ensure their progress and prosperity which led her to join the Baghdad Pact.[53]

There may be considerable merit in this claim that Pakistan joined the Baghdad Pact to promote Muslim interests. It is, however, to be noted that the Baghdad Pact was not the only pact to which she has elected to belong nor was it the first of which she agreed to become a member.

In any event, some students of foreign affairs in Pakistan have not failed to note that the Baghdad Pact has tarnished the image of Pakistan in the Muslim world. Sarwar Hasan noted the following disadvantages of the pact: (*i*) It led to a setback for Pakistan among the African and Asian nations; (*ii*) instead of hleping, the pact worsened the position of Pakistan in her disputes with India; and (*iii*) "Pakistan has fallen in the estimation of the Arabs." Elaborating the third point, Hasan says: "The Baghdad Pact undoubtedly divided the Arab world. Pakistan by its membership of the pact was held responsible for contributing to that division. By destroying Arab unity and by making the Arabs more suspicious of Western intentions, the Baghdad Pact increased instability in the region."[54]

Pakistan's relations with the Arab world in general entered their most critical phase a year after the signing of the Baghdad Pact. Following the U.S. decision to withdraw the aid for Aswan Dam, Nasser nationalized the Suez Canal in July 1956. Pakistan upheld Egypt's sovereign rights over the Suez Canal and her right to nationalize it. But at the London conferences on Suez shortly after this, Pakistan's role was different from

---

[51]*Dawn*, 6 October 1956.   [52]*Winding up of Foreign Policy Debates.*
[53]*Pakistan Times*, 5 April 1961.   [54]Sarwar Hasan, *op. cit.*, p. 76.

that of Ceylon, Indonesia, India and the USSR; and, Pakistan was publicly criticized in Egypt for her failure to disassociate herself from the Dulles Plan which was totally unacceptable to Egypt.[55] In the first London Conference on Suez, the countries which supported the Dulles Plan included the Baghdad Pact countries of Turkey, Iran and Pakistan; those who opposed it included India and Indonesia.

Eight days before the invasion of Suez, the Foreign Minister of Pakistan deprecated unthinking enthusiasm for pan-Islamism. The days of pan-Islamism, he said, were over and Pakistanis should first guard the interests of their own Muslims and then of other Muslims of the world. He said: "Pak-Islamism and not pan-Islamism should now be the new slogan. You have no future if you indiscriminately fight or die for Muslims outside Pakistan even though they be the dearest friends of your enemy."[56]

Yet when Suez was invaded, protests came not only from the left-oriented groups in East Pakistan—the British Consulate in Dacca was burnt down[57]—but also from the Islam-oriented groups in West Pakistan. An editorial comment in the *Dawn* said: "They (the people of Pakistan) are asking and we are giving voice to their questions: Is this not the rise once again of bigoted and perverted Christendom against the world of Islam in alliance with the Jews! Is this not a threat poised against the Muslims from the Atlantic to the Pacific?"[58] The government's role was, however, less spectacular. Along with the other Baghdad Pact members, Pakistan did protest against the invasion, but her protest was not among the strongest. When at this time the Colombo Powers met in New Delhi to discuss the Suez issue, the Pakistan Prime Minister excused himself from this meeting.[59] Although Prime Minister Suhrawardy later maintained that it was "partly as a result of our efforts that the Anglo-French forces were withdrawn from

[55] *Ibid.*, p. 183.
[56] *Asian Recorder*, 1956, p. 1116.
[57] *Ibid.*, p. 1153.   [58] *Dawn*, 1 November 1956.
[59] *Indian Affairs Record*, December 1956.

the Egyptian territory,"[60] Pakistan lost many friends among the Arab peoples.

The Egyptians, particularly, were unimpressed and showed their distaste of Pakistan when they refused to accept a Pakistani contingent in the UN troops in the Gaza strip. When Prime Minister Suhrawardy proposed a visit to President Nasser in November, the Egyptian Government regretted its inability to receive the Pakistani leader.[61]

Smarting under this rebuff, Suhrawardy said at Lahore that the Anglo-French action in Suez was merely "an attempt on the part of these Powers to see that the Suez Canal remained free for international navigation. The invasion aimed at restricting the sovereignty of one country for the benefit of the world."[62] He also derided the concept of a Muslim bloc as against the Baghdad Pact: "The question is asked, why don't we get together rather than be tied to a big Power like the UK or America? My answer to that is that zero plus zero plus zero is after all equal to zero."[63] He also said: "The fact is that the Muslim countries today are so divided amongst themselves that it is difficult for them to sit together." Again: "We find that whereas we go out in sympathy for them, there is hardly any reciprocity on the other side for us. We find that Egypt, for instance, has declared that it is on the side of India on the Kashmir issue."[64]

The intense conflict between Pakistani and Arab opinion was reflected in newspaper comments even before the Suez invasion. King Saud, on an earlier visit to India, had expressed satisfaction that in India Muslims were well treated. Again, when Nehru paid a return visit to Riyadh, in September 1956, he was greeted there as "Rasul-ul-Salam" (messenger of peace). In Pakistan the word "Rasul" is used only for the Prophet and Pakistani papers launched a severe attack on the Saudi Arabian

---

[60]Suhrawardy, *Statement on Foreign Relations and Defence*, Karachi, Government of Pakistan, 1957.

[61]*Asian Recorder*, 1956, p. 1174.   [62]*Ibid.*, p. 1179.

[63]*Prime Minister's Statement on Foreign Policy*, 9 December 1956.

[64]*Ibid.*

Government. The *Dawn* ended an editorial thus: "However disappointing may be the policies of the governments in most of the Muslim countries, the Muslim people are sound at heart and share the broader Islamic outlook. Some day they will assert themselves and the Muslim world will re-discover its soul which selfish rulers and juntas are now foolishly mortgaging to the enemies of Islam."[65] In another article in early October, the *Dawn* complained: "When it is the cause of some other Muslim country, the Egyptians and most other Arabs pooh-pooh the Islamic appeal. Our own Kashmir issue is the most striking example. They do not realize how thin is such hypocrisy."[66] In an editorial "So this is Nasser" the *Dawn* wrote on 1 December 1956: "Nasser's hatred of Pakistan, and love of Bharat and its Nehru, is an attitude of mind not warranted by facts but conditioned by insensate bias and blind prejudice the source of which may well be examined by psychiatrists. It is nevertheless a matter of deep regret that in the veins of this turbulent egotist not the blood of Islam should seem to flow but the turbid waters of the Nile. Nasser will never be our friend; he will never think in terms of Islam. . . ."[67]

Relations with Afghanistan

Pakistan's appeal as an upholder of the idea of Islamic integration was greatly curtailed by the state of her relations with Afghanistan. These relations were often strained to the breaking point. The Afghan Government had not accepted the boundaries between the two countries and had challenged the Durand Line on the ground that it was signed under duress. Even in 1942, the Afghans had attempted to raise the question when Sir Stafford Cripps was discussing his plan for India's freedom. When Pakistan became independent, Afghanistan was the only country to voice its protest and its inability to vote for her admission to the United Nations. Shortly afterwards, Jinnah entered into negotiations with Afghanistan but the

[65]*Dawn*, 27 September 1956.
[66]*Ibid.*, 6 October 1956. [67]*Ibid.*, 1 December 1956.

negotiations broke down and the status of the tribes along the Pak-Afghan border remained unsettled. By 1949, relations between Pakistan and Afghanistan had become strained over this issue: while Pakistan claimed that the "Pakhtoonistan" movement was an Afghan "stunt," Afghanistan charged Pakistan of having violently suppressed their people's urge for the freedom in the tribal areas. On 12 June 1949, Pakistan planes bombed a village within the Afghan territory; although Pakistan apologized soon afterwards, relations from this time onwards have remained intensely strained. In the following years clashes were often reported. The integration of West Pakistan into one federal unit, which forced the Pushto-speaking areas into an unwilling marriage with West Pakistan, predominated by the Punjabis, led to a fresh outburst of propaganda war in 1955; on 30 March, the Pakistan Embassy building in Kabul was attacked by rioters; on 1 April, mobs in Peshawar attacked the Afghan Consulate and tore down the Afghan flag.[68] On 6 May 1955, the *Dawn* demanded: "Our embassy in Afghanistan is, according to international law, a part of Pakistani territory, and the sanctity and security of that territory has been violated. After having given the Kabuli junta, in vain, sufficient time to make honourable amends for the aggression, it should now be perfectly legitimate for us to resort to police action to chastize the aggressor."[69]

This friction with Afghanistan has continued. In March 1961, Afghanistan complained of a major offensive by Pakistani troops in the tribal areas. Pakistan admitted bombing the Pathan areas but said that it was done to blow up the ammunition dumps of Afghan agents.[70] Relations deteriorated in the following months: on 22 August, Pakistan closed down its consulates in Afghanistan and demanded the closing down of Afghan Consulates in Pakistan. On 30 August, Afghanistan said that diplomatic relations with Pakistan would be severed if they did not withdraw their demand for closing down the

[68]For a further discussion of the issues involved, *see:* Sisir Gupta, "Pakistan's Relations With Afghanistan," *Foreign Affairs Reports,* July 1955.

[69]*Dawn,* 6 May 1955.   [70]*Asian Recorder,* 1961, p. 3935.

consulates. On 3 September, the border between Pakistan and Afghanistan was closed and on 6 September diplomatic relations between the two countries were severed. The United States and Iran have offered mediation but so far failed to bring about any improvement in Pak-Afghan relations; most of Afghanistan's trade is now conducted through Soviet ports.[71]

Problems and Prospects

Notwithstanding these grave problems and the occasional statements deriding Muslim unity, the urge for Muslim solidarity has characterized the policies of the Pakistani Governments. Even when the Pak-Egyptian relations were at their nadir, the Muslim League—the major opposition party—revived the demand for a united Muslim world bloc for their "security and survival."[72] Feroz Khan Noon, the then Prime Minister, talked in 1958 of a Pakistan-Iran-Afghanistan federation—a slogan earlier given by League leader Qayum Khan. In 1960 a Pakistani author made this the main theme of his book on Pakistan's security: "In this struggle for survival, these three nations must come close together and resist attempts by the Soviet Union or the West to impose allegiance on them. The danger is very real. Already Central Asia is lost; Bokhara and Merv are no longer Muslim; part of the Islamic homeland is lost to the Jews."[73] The Arabs were regarded as lost and the lament continued: "At present nationalism is strongest in the Arab world, which is unfortunate in two respects. Modernism has been introduced with little regard for Islam and its intellectual revival is considerably indebted to Christian writers. The recent cordiality with communism may prove a third complicating factor. All this might lead to an unbridgeable gulf between the Arabs and the non-Arabs in the Islamic civilization and finally to its disintegration. Pakistanis believe that Islam itself is a nationality."[74] It may be noted here that in Pakistan

[71]*Ibid.*, p. 4211. Pak-Afghan relations have now been re-established, but the dispute over Pakhtunistan continues.   [72]Callard, *op. cit.*, p. 315.
[73]Siddiqui, *op. cit.*, p. 159; *cf.* also pp. 33, 132 and 162.   [74]*Ibid.*, p. 160.

many regarded the Arab League as a retrograde development.[75]

Even Ayub Khan, who functioned in a relative political vacuum, found it necessary to strive for Muslim solidarity or at least to pay lip service to it. We have quoted already his view on the Baghdad Pact. Speaking at Layalpur on 4 April 1961, the President said that he favoured the idea of a Muslim Commonwealth, to which the Malayan Prime Minister had made a reference earlier in London.[76] In June 1961, the Prime Minister of Northern Nigeria, Sir Ahmadu Bello, discussed this idea with Ayub Khan.[77] However, Pakistan has not made any progress in this direction. On the other hand, it has drifted farther apart from most other Muslim countries. The Belgrade Conference of September 1961, attended by most of the Muslim countries, illustrated the increasing isolation of Pakistan from other Muslim peoples. By and large her foreign policy still remains different from that of the large majority of Muslim States.

In fact, one obstacle standing in the way of Pakistan's ties with other Muslim countries is the striking similarity between the outlook of most Muslim States and India in regard to many international issues. There is also a deliberate attempt on the part of India to cultivate cultural and political ties with Muslim countries. And so long as it is an "either India or Pakistan" proposition, it is unlikely that Pakistan will be able to claim the larger share of the Muslim world's sympathy, just as even her allies are finding it increasingly difficult to choose Pakistan and ignore India. It is important to point out that India has as many treaties of friendship with the Muslim countries as Pakistan has, excluding the military pacts with the CENTO countries. Callard has noted: "Once Partition was accomplished, many of the other Muslim States were reluctant to make a choice between friendship for India or Pakistan. If a choice had to be made, India, as more powerful, more stable, and more influential, was likely to have the advantage."[78] The problem for Pakistan is precisely this: it is only in terms of her difficulties with India that she has invoked the cause of Muslim unity.

Another impediment for Pakistan has been that while she is engaged in building up an Islamic State, in many Muslim countries, leaders like Sukarno and Nasser are engaged in internal struggles against minority groups which share the Pakistani view of Islam's potentialities in the modern world. The Masjumi in Indonesia and the Muslim Brotherhood in the UAR are banned and their activities regarded as anti-State.[79]

There are other difficulties in the way of Pakistan in moving towards closer cooperation with other Muslim countries on the basis of a common faith. In the first place, any attempt at a West Asian regional integration into a Muslim bloc pre-supposes a similar urge for Islamic belonging in other Muslim peoples. In other words, it projects into the Muslim world an assumed Muslimness which is unique in the case of Pakistan, reflecting its continued problems in the South Asian context; secondly, it assumes that there are non-religious factors in their commonness; thirdly, that other Muslim countries will see the threat of "Hindu" imperialism which Pakistan allegedly faces; fourthly, it involves problems of defining the region of Muslim cooperation. The Muslim world extends from Indonesia to Nigeria and its politics differs from one country to another. Even in Pakistan itself, on the major political problems, viz. national integration and the role of religion in politics, there is no unanimity or even a consensus. Lastly, in the politics of the Muslim world, Pakistan is somewhat on the periphery. To say the least, it is very doubtful whether a peripherial State can become the cornerstone of Islamic unity.

As Callard says: "The political upsurge elsewhere was based largely on territorial and racial nationalism, anti-Western, anti-White. Religion played a part in this, but it was a lesser part

---

[79]In 1958 a Pakistani writer, after a visit to Indonesia, reported that while some political parties there admired Pakistan, the ruling circles were enamoured of India and were reluctant to take any stand on Kashmir. Rais Ahmad Khan, "Pakistan in South-East Asia," *Pakistan Horizon*, December 1958.

than colour, language and political theory of violent opposition to colonialism and exploitation. For many Muslims, elsewhere, it has been more important to align Asians and Africans against the colonial Powers than to defend Muslim causes against non-Muslims."[80] John S. Badeau describes the same obstacle to Muslim unity in more abstract terms: "Pan-Islam is difficult to conceive as the basis for a modern empire, because it is almost impossible for any group of States to become integrated into the international structure when they are based upon a political and ideological pattern at variance with the rest of the world. So long as Islamdom contained the centre of its gravity and was self-sustaining politically and economically, it could afford to maintain its distinctive political organization. But, today, it is difficult to perpetuate such isolated political monads and to assume that they will move together with the rest of the world in a pre-established harmony. . . . No group of States can set up a bloc built upon radically different political concepts without being in continuous tension with the rest of the world. Islamdom cannot insulate itself against the seepage of the most universally accepted political concept of our times—nationalism."[81]

Some Pakistani intellectuals, however, regard this as a temporary phenomenon and feel convinced of the inevitability of the ultimate assertion of Islam. Samin Khan blames the Christian Arabs for deliberately infusing secularism in the Arab world and for reviving the pre-Islamic past of the Arabs; but regarding the future he has no doubt: "Arab nationalism does not rest either on ethnographic or territorial chauvinism. It is based first on the Arabic language and, secondly, though indirectly, on Islam. . . . The history of the Arabs is the history of Islam. . . . Once nationalism has taken its normal course and achieved its objectives . . . it then looks for an ideal—permanent and sublime ideal. Since Arab nationalism will not serve the purpose, the forces of history which are much stronger than

[80]Callard, *op. cit.*, p. 314.

[81]John S. Badeau, "Islam in the Modern Middle East," *Foreign Affairs*, October 1959.

the temporary transient factors of nationalism shall assert themselves."[82] In another article the same author has pointed out how the Kemalist "reaction" in Turkey was defeated: "After the Second World War the country emancipated itself from the split personality which it had to endure for a quarter of a century. In this conflict between religion and nationalism, nationalism suffered its first important defeat in the Muslim world. . . . The defeat of nationalism was possible, for its espousal by the leaders of Turkey was the great betrayal of the aspirations and ideals of the Turks."[83] While only the future can reveal the validity of these two views, there is no doubt that Pakistan is often poised not only as a detractor of Afro-Asian solidarity but, what is more, as one of the parties in the most serious dispute in the Muslim world—the dispute over Pakhtoonistan.

It is possible that behind Pakistan's policy to seek Muslim solidarity lie more basic factors of history. Says Dr Brown: "Pakistan as a Muslim nation looks westward to the lands where Islam was born and became great. Western Pakistan, especially, illustrates the same phenomenon of association with western regions, which it has exhibited in the past. It feels itself culturally akin to those areas ouside the subcontinent, rather than to the areas east of it, though they are geographically close to it and economically its natural partners."[84]

A significant aspect of this observation is the difference implied in it between East and West Pakistan. Indeed, this difference cannot be exaggerated. Cultural difference apart, the East Pakistanis may well prefer closer relations with Malaya and Indonesia, to those with Afghanistan and Iran. An Iran-Pakistan federation, for example, would completely alter the political power structure in Pakistan and reduce the advantage of the larger population, that East Pakistan enjoys, to nothing.

[82]Samin Khan, "Arab Nationalism," *Pakistan Horizon,* December 1958.

[83]Samin Khan, "Religion and State in Turkey," *Pakistan Horizon,* December 1958.

[84]W. N. Brown, "Pakistan and West Asia," *Pakistan Miscellany,* Karachi, Pakistan Publications, Vol. 22, 1958, p. 30.

Moreover, East Pakistani politics centres round many secular issues which were thrown up in 1954.[85] It is unlikely that any sudden Islamic resurgence can push them into the background.

Yet, in this age of super Powers, Pakistan must belong to a larger group. In a sense, it is correct that the age of nationalism is becoming outdated. The trend is everywhere towards the evolution of higher loyalties—Arab unity, West European Community, the Free and the Communist Worlds, the Alliance for Progress in the Western Hemisphere, the African personality and Malaysia in South-East Asia, are all indications of the growing tempo of regionalism. Muslims of the world too, like other peoples, have fallen in step and are getting integrated regionally. Nigeria is seeking the cooperation of her African neighbours; the Arab States are searching for bases of their own unity; Turkey is primarily a NATO country; Malaya has already achieved a Malaysian Union; Indonesia might become the keystone of another South-East Asian regional group. Where then does Pakistan stand in this emerging pattern? It is here that inevitably South Asia becomes more than a mere cartographic expression.

Even keeping apart other considerations, it may be said that there is an element called the unity of Indian Islam in the thought-pattern of the Muslims of the subcontinent. It is not easy for the Muslims of Pakistan, in promoting their Islamic sense of belonging, to ignore this obvious unity, and any scheme which bypasses the Indian Muslims could only have half-hearted support in Pakistan. One thing, therefore, is certain: whatever be the approach that Pakistan brings to bear on the question of her future association with other nations or her future partnership in a regional organization, the rest of South Asia will remain a strong contender for her supra-national loyalty. In fact, the continued emphasis on Islam in Pakistan, even after being constituted as a Muslim majority State, may well be regarded as a measure of her inability to run away from her minority status in the complex of South Asian realities.

[85]This election resulted in the most spectacular upset in Pakistan's political life.

Select Bibliography

BOOKS AND PAMPHLETS

ARORA, S.K., *American Foreign Policy Towards India*, New Delhi, Suneja, 1954.

BABU, V. VITHAL, *The Colombo Plan and India*, New Delhi, Atma Ram, 1951.

BOWLES, CHESTER, *Ambassador's Report*, London, Gollancz, 1954.

BRECHER, MICHAEL, *Nehru: A Political Biography*, London, Oxford, 1959.

BRIGHT, J.S. (Ed.), *Before and After Independence* (collection of Nehru's speeches, 1922-50), New Delhi, 1950.

BROWN, W.N., *The United States and India and Pakistan*, Cambridge, Harvard, 1953.

CALLARD, KEITH C., *Pakistan, A Political Study*, London, Allen and Unwin, 1957.

COUSINS, NORMAN, *Talks With Nehru*, New York, John Day, 1951.

CRANE, ROBERT I. (Ed.), *India's Role in Asia*, Chicago University, 1955 (mimeo.).

DAS GUPTA, J.B., *Indo-Pakistan Relations*, Amsterdam, Djambatan, 1958.

DEAN, VERA MICHAELS, *India: New Patterns of Democracy*, Cambridge, Harvard, 1959.

DUTT, V. P., *India's Foreign Policy*, New Delhi, Indian Council of World Affairs, 1950 (mimeo.).

DUTT, V. P., and SINGH, VISHAL, *Indian Policy and Attitude towards Indo-China and SEATO*, New York, IPR, 1954 (mimeo.).

EDEN, ANTHONY, *Full Circle*, Boston, Houghton Miffin, 1960.

GUPTA, K., *Indian Foreign Policy, In Defence of National Interests*, Calcutta, World Press, 1956.

GUPTA, SISIR, *India's Relations With Pakistan, 1954-57*, New Delhi, I.C.W.A., 1958.

HASAN, K. SARWAR, *Pakistan and the United Nations*, New York, Manhattan, 1960.

INDIA, *Jawaharlal Nehru's Speeches, 1946-49*, New Delhi, 1949.

——, *Jawaharlal Nehru's Speeches, 1949-53*, New Delhi, 1953.

——, *Jawaharlal Nehru's Speeches, 1953-57*, New Delhi, 1957.

INDIA (LOK SABHA), *Foreign Policy of India: Texts of Documents*, New Delhi, 1959.

——, *Indian-American Relations*, New Delhi, I.C.W.A., 1951.

KARANJIA, R. K., *The Mind of Mr Nehru*, London, Allen and Unwin, 1960.

KARUNAKARAN, K. P., *India in World Affairs, 1947-50*, Bombay, Oxford (prepared under the auspices of the Indian Council of World Affairs), 1952.

——, *India in World Affairs, 1950-53*, Bombay, Oxford, 1957.

KOTHARI, S., *India's Emerging Foreign Policies*, Bombay, Vora, 1951.

KUNDRA, J. C., *Indian Foreign Policy, 1947-54*, Groningen, Wotlers, 1955.

LEVI, WERNER, *Free India in Asia*, Minneapolis, University of Minnesota, 1953.

MALENBAUM, WILFRED, *East and West in India's Economic Development*, Washington, National Planning Association, 1959.

MENDE, TIBOR, *Nehru: Conversations on Indian and World Affairs*, New York, Braziller, 1956.

MURTI, B. S. N., *Nehru's Foreign Policy*, New Delhi, 1954.

NEHRU, JAWAHARLAL, *An Autobiography*, London, Bodley Head, 1958 (22nd Edition).

——, *The Discovery of India*, Calcutta, Signet Press, 1946.

POPLAI, S. L. AND TALBOT, PHILIPS, *India and America*, New Delhi, I.C.W.A., 1958.

PRASAD, BIMLA, *The Origins of Indian Foreign Policy*, Calcutta, Bookland, 1960.

RAJKUMAR, N. V., *The Background of India's Foreign Policy*, New Delhi, A.I.C.C., 1953.

ROSINGER, L. K., *India and the United States*, New York, Macmillan, 1950.

SHEAN, VINCENT, *Nehru: The Years of Power*, New York, Random House, 1960.

SHILS, EDWARD, *The Intellectual Between Tradition and Modernity: The Indian Situation*, The Hague, Mouton, 1961.

SIDDIQUI, ASLAM, *Pakistan Seeks Security*, Karachi, Longmans, 1961.

WARD, BARBARA, *India and the West*, New York, Norton, 1961.

ARTICLES

ACHARYA, G. N., "India's Role in Asia," *Far Eastern Economic Review*, 21 September 1961.
(The whole of the above issue of the *Review* contains useful articles on India's role in Asia.)

BASCH, ANTONIN, "The Colombo Plan, A Case of Regional Integration," *International Organization*, February 1955.

BIRDWOOD, LORD, "The Defense of South-East Asia," *International Affairs*, January 1953.

DEUTSCHER, ISAAC, "Khruschov Plays the Waiting Game," *Reporter*, 21 January 1960.

FISCHER, LOUIS, "Indo-Pakistan: A Federation to Meet China," *New Leader*, 16 and 23 January 1961.

GUPTA, SISIR, "The Problem," *Seminar*, March 1961.

HARRISON, SELIG S., "The Case History of a Mistake," *New Republic*, 10 August 1959.

———, "The Cost of a Mistake," *New Republic*, 24 August 1959.

———, "The United States, India and Pakistan," *New Republic*, 2 September 1959.

HENDERSON, WILLIAM, "Regionalism in South-East Asia," *International Organization*, November 1955.

KHAN, MOHAMMED AYUB, "Pakistan Perspective," *Foreign Affairs*, July 1960.

LEVI, WERNER, "Union in Asia," *Far Eastern Survey*, 16 August 1950.

LOKANATHAN, P.S., "Regional Economic Cooperation in Asia," *India Quarterly*, January-March 1951.

MENON, LAKSHMI N., "Our Policy," *Seminar*, March 1961.

MICHIE, ALLAN J., "The Growth of an African Power Bloc," *Reporter*, 17 March 1960.

MILTON, W. M., "Regionalism in South-East Asia," *Journal of International Affairs*, No. 3, 1949.

MOORTHY, K. KRISHNA, "The Dismally Stagnant Trade Picture," *Far Eastern Economic Review*, 21 September 1960.

MORAES, FRANK, "New Look," *Seminar*, March 1961.

MORGENTHAEU, HANS J., "Military Illusions," *New Republic*, 19 March 1961.

NEHRU, JAWAHARLAL, "The Basic Approach," *AICC Economic Review*, 15 August 1958.

NIKHAMIN, V., "New International Role of Eastern Countries," *International Affairs* (Moscow), May 1960.

——, "India's Role in World Affairs," *International Affairs* (Moscow), January 1958.

PADELFORD, NORMAN J., "Regional Organization and the United Nations," *International Organization*, May 1954.

PANIKKAR, K.M., "Regional Organization of the Indian Ocean Area," *Pacific Affairs*, September 1945.

PEFFER, NATHANIEL, "Regional Security in South-East Asia," *International Organization*, August 1954.

PRASAD, N., "The Colombo Plan," *India Quarterly*, April-June 1952.

RAJAN, M.S., "India's Foreign Policy in Action," *India Quarterly*, July-September 1960.

SHEAN, VINCENT, "The Case for India," *Foreign Affairs*, October 1961.

SPAIN, JAMES W., "Military Assistance for Pakistan," *American Political Science Review*, September 1954.

SURI, SURINDAR, "Economics," *Seminar*, March 1961.

THAPAR, ROMESH, "Realities," *Seminar*, March 1961.

VENKATASUBBIAH, H., "Prospects of an Asian Union," *India Quarterly*, April-June and July-September 1949.

——, "Political Alignments of Asian Countries," *India Quarterly*, July-September 1951.

WILBUR, C. MARTIN, "South-East Asia Between India and China," *Journal of International Affairs*, 1956.

YUDIN, P., "A Reply to the Basic Approach by Shri Jawaharlal Nehru," *World Marxist Review*, December 1958.

Index

BAREFOOT IN THE CHURCH

BAREFOOT IN THE CHURCH

DONALD R. ALLEN

JOHN KNOX PRESS
Richmond, Virginia

Scripture quotations are taken from *The Jerusalem Bible,* copyright © 1966 by Darton, Longman & Todd, Ltd. and Doubleday & Company, Inc.

Second Printing 1973

Library of Congress Cataloging in Publication Data

Allen, Donald R   1930–
    Barefoot in the church.

    Bibliography: p.
    1.   Church renewal—Case studies. 2.   Harrisonburg, Va. Trinity Presbyterian Church. I. Title.
BV600.2.A4   262'.001   72-1759
ISBN 0–8042–1540–5
© John Knox Press 1972
Printed in the United States of America

To
my wife
and extended family

ACKNOWLEDGMENTS

I wish to express my sincere thanks to the many friends and acquaintances across this country and in Europe who assisted in the progress of this work by providing encouragement, accommodations, and research assistance.

Through the interest of the Board of National Ministries of the Presbyterian Church, U.S., the effort to write was intensified. The faculty and student body of Union Theological Seminary, Richmond, Virginia assisted greatly by providing a variety of facilities, not the least of which was understanding companionship.

To my wife and four daughters who willingly accepted additional burdens during my sabbatical I owe the inner peace and freedom to have continued self-assured.

There are two without whose assistance, patience, and support this work could not have been completed. My eternal gratitude is acknowledged to Mrs. Virginia Aliotti who bore the weight of the grammatical revisions and granted perspective by discussing theme developments over many years, and to Mrs. G. Don Whitmore whose labors and patient encouragement from the typewriter far exceeded that due any "boss" by his esteemed secretary.

Finally, I am aware that this writing would be without interest or purpose were it not for those whose radiant and open lives called forth this story. To those in the emerging Christian communities called house churches and especially to the congregation called Trinity, I am forever indebted.

CONTENTS

There the angel of Yahweh appeared
to him in the shape of a flame of fire,
coming from the middle of a bush. . . .

"Moses, Moses!" he said.

"Here I am" he answered.

"Come no nearer" he said.
"Take off your shoes, for the place
on which you stand is holy ground."

—EXODUS 3:2,4–5

PROLOGUE

The dignified chalice had been joined by an odd assortment of crude handcrafts—a pinwheel, decorated paper plates, a paper cup "bug," pipe cleaner figures, a tambourine, and an irregular wooden box. This unlikely arrangement graced the communion table to remind the dozen workers of their imminent service of worship. The room which they were now cleaning—removing traces of paste, stardust, and colored construction paper—measures fifteen feet wide by sixty feet long. A low ceiling emphasizes the shoe-box atmosphere. Known as the sanctuary, this room for the past month had been the place where children were doing the hokey-pokey, an engaging group dance that fused teacher and student into a unit of joyous sharing. Since it was their last day, Tess, the volunteer director, had asked that the staff follow the closing summer day camp for the retarded with a service of worship suitable for the occasion.

In the center of the room, folding chairs encircled the communion table which had been moved out from its hiding place behind a curtain. It had been banished along with the pulpit and baptismal font to that undignified spot when the room was converted to its temporary use as an arts and crafts center.

To lend some degree of awesomeness and praise to the last hour of a taxing yet exhilarating month, the children's handcrafts, unusual aids to worship, were placed on the table beside the chalice. What was not planned in the sharing of this holy spotlight was a day camp participant resting his head in the middle of these offerings. Yet, with that addition, we found ourselves experiencing again the oft-learned truth that love is a happening.

Brenton, eighteen years old, was one of the two dozen beloved participants in the day camp. His ride had not yet come. When we gathered around the table his normal friendly curiosity brought him to the door where he peered in bashfully. Worship progressed. Matthew 9:35–38 was read and the participants began to respond to its meaning in light of their experiences throughout the past month. The open discussion gave Brenton the courage he needed to enter. Everyone had been trying to put into words what the work in the day camp had meant. Hearing expressions of gratitude, Brenton circled the communion table shaking hands with everyone he could reach saying, "Thankful. We're friends. Thankful. We're friends." Then, satisfied, feeling totally at home, he took the chair beside Sherry, the teen-ager who had been his "buddy" helper, reached for her hand, placed his head down on the communion table amid the other offerings, and smiling, closed his eyes. We realized that nothing more was needed to clasp the feelings all were sharing. The climax of the worship service as well as the day camp had come as an unexpected gift which brought us to that moment of highest communication when no words are adequate, when communion is a sudden unveiling of God's holy presence. In this familiar setting we were a small community overwhelmed by our experience of joy in worship. It was a celebration born out of efforts to release joy in others.

This occurred in the summer of 1968 as a result of five years of searching by a group of people known as a house church. This particular house church, responsible for a ministry to the retarded, is only one of a handful of house churches within a small congregation struggling for its unique existence in the settled Shenandoah Valley of Virginia. This cluster of house churches, known together as Trinity Presbyterian Church, is in turn only one of a growing number of similar congregations which are developing their own creative thrusts within and outside the settled institutions of denominationalism. To widen the perspective further, this disconnected unfolding of house churches in their many varieties of forms is only one type of expression that is calling the church to new life.

What is a house church? A small change in our vastly changing culture, it has the potential of a mustard seed. Not an organized movement, the house church belongs to all who would claim it, from the highest courts of the denominations to the most casual fellowship living in some drug-therapy center or halfway house. House church groups are cropping up more and more—sometimes as a part of a congregation, sometimes as an entirely new expression of the church. The house church has no single definition and does no set predictable thing. Still there are common characteristics underlying all house churches. The Most Reverend E. W. Southcott, Provost of Southwark Cathedral in London, spoke in 1969 to a group of twenty American clergymen interested in the concept of a house church. As one who has written of the house church and worked with its many nuances, Provost Southcott has witnessed its successes and failures, its rise and fall. He spoke of elusive identity: ". . . I don't know what the house church is except that I see Jesus' body exposed in a way that often it isn't exposed in the church building. Often the church building hides Christ from people."[1]

To envisage our sanctuaries as hiding God is to recognize a similarity to those circumstances recorded in Mark 15:38 which brought about the act of God's unveiling. At the point of Jesus' crucifixion, when he had "breathed his last" (Mark 15:37), it is said: "And the veil of the Temple was torn in two from top to bottom." Jesus' death brought about the full revelation of God's purposes and his dwelling place. God was no more to be hidden behind the holy of holies within the sanctuary.

In a day when, for many persons, the body of Christ seems veiled within the church on the corner, when people are uncertain about what they mean to one another, and when the worlds of work and leisure appear more demonic than liberating, the desire for meaning presses for something to rip open, revealing purpose. The rise of the church in the house is one promising way to move toward meaning, making known God's gift of life which is at hand.

To understand this development of the house church we shall look in some detail at the experiences of one congregation, while examining broad concepts of the house church as seen historically and theologically. In addition, a number of other house church communities will be reviewed as examples of the diversity and current development of this particular style of Christian life. No attempt has been made to list all house churches presently in existence. Instead, the effort has been to suggest the varieties of styles, emphases, and purposes from random samples of house churches across the nation.

This book is written to tell of the unfolding of such house churches and particularly of Trinity's cluster. The story focuses upon the Trinity congregation—its growing pains and its moments of celebration—but as only one of the exciting developments related to the house church. This exploration does not hold up one particular congregation for emulation by those disenchanted with their present life. It would not suffice. Neither does it present a form to be duplicated, but rather the evidence of a truth not to be forgotten: the body of Christ is not an organization to be developed but a living organism constantly to be rediscovered. Out of this style of church life may spring hope for meaningful existence.

Is it possible to experience a new awareness of the body of Christ more real than has been known for centuries? Are we able to meet in expectation of receiving gifts of life from one another? Do we dare allow ourselves to be exposed to the challenge of maturing in Christ? Or must the church forever mean a program to be attended or a slot to be filled in the organizational makeup? In our day, after a plethora of pronouncements, bundles of books, and endless experiments pointing to new signs of life for the church, there are still few actual avenues open to people to act on their concerns inside the institutional church. The most vital signs of new life seem to have left the church or are only allowed to probe around its fringe observed by a cautious and wide-eyed church officialdom. A person can become more than a little uneasy when, in addition to the resistance to renewal, he sees those supposedly renewed meeting one another running in opposite ways. It is disturbing that much of the institutional church's efforts to renew herself continue to reflect limited denominational points of view.

Many denominations seem to understand church renewal as the act of reversing their former positions rather than as a search for the basic purpose of the church's existence. Thus, those who have moved to the other side of the altar, a radical adjustment after centuries of tradition, are perhaps surprised to see their brothers passing them by as they exchange sides. Whereas new life to some means speaking in the vernacular, others are interpreting new life as a discovery of unknown tongues. Those denominations with a history of aristocratic formality are leading the way in "shoes-off" human interaction, while those low churches who have had their shoes off for decades are wondering where the renewal is in all of this. Renewal to those raised with simple methods seems to be a new discovery in theology, while those branches of the church that have always lived on heavy doctrine are turning away to find new birth in the plainness of their feelings. Certainly such exchanges of experiences can benefit us all, but they still fall short of answering the cries for a true breakthrough in what it means to be Christ's man in today's world.

What is needed is a renewal of life that rediscovers the locale of God. Christians need to know that here is the church when there is no building. We need to see the holy when there is nothing religious around, to be moved toward need when there is no program calling, and to experience the dance when there is no music. We need an awareness of the grace that surrounds us.

Those who love the church and pray for its renewal are learning that it will require more than words to enable the church to meet such a demand for true effectiveness. We are learning that the system itself is a powerful influence over our lives. In other words, we are realizing how the form of the church speaks to us and shapes us, equally as much as the concerns spoken of within the form. What is being considered is the possibility that the house church, in its truest radical departure from all present expressions of church life, can place us where the form is more consistent with the essence of the body of Christ. Is it possible to discern the hand of God in the midst of life?

Elizabeth Barrett Browning expressed this possibility of finding the holy in the commonplace when she wrote in "Aurora Leigh":

> Earth's crammed with heaven,
> And every common bush afire with God;
> But only he who sees, takes off his shoes,
> The rest sit round it and pluck blackberries. . . .

BECOMING

† The small group that was to become Trinity Presbyterian Church began to move toward their unique growth with traditional birth pangs. For most of us, it began in the fall of 1962. The First Presbyterian Church in the valley town of Harrisonburg, Virginia had voted not to move out to their new property. In an attempt to make the best use of the beautiful four and one-half acres of land, complete with a majestic antebellum home built in 1825, First Church had offered it to the presbytery. The presbytery, accepting graciously, determined the presence of "new church potential." I was called by the presbytery as the organizing minister. The moves happened quickly and followed the usual steps of any typical new church development. Predictions of rapid growth and a beautiful edifice were proudly voiced by the church authorities. But as one visitor to the area has written, "A funny thing happened on the way to that

showpiece. The church a-borning got to thinking: What kind of building does a church need? What is a church, anyhow?"[1]

An important initial decision helped in great measure to determine the alternate path of the new congregation. Instead of razing the large old home on the site to make way for "building a church," a committee of the presbytery had suggested remodeling the house. It was to be temporary, of course; only a few thousand dollars were used to renew wiring and plumbing and to knock out a couple of walls for sufficient room in which to worship. Nonetheless, this decision provided two ingredients that, in retrospect, seem vital. It released the new group from any pressure to build, thus altering their priorities. It also gave them a local immediate challenge in working together to "fix up" the place so that it would serve their purposes, thereby accelerating their growth as a close community.

It was late in September when about twenty white, middle-class, "older" young adults responded to the challenge of seeing what it might be like to begin a church from the ground up. Most of them had come from the parent body with the encouragement of their minister and the official board, the session. We met that first night in a large room in the antebellum house which had been deserted for three years. The twenty by twenty foot room was filled with broken glass from the tall sedate windows that overlooked what was once a most majestic lawn of plantation bearing and proportions. The lawn had since grown knee high with weeds. Someone had filled the room we were in with stacks of abandoned straight-backed wooden chairs and an old piano.

Now, with twenty interested people, a roof over our heads, and chairs plus a piano provided, one might expect that the rest of the traditional accouterments fell providentially into place. One might well imagine a knock on the door, with well-wishers from nearby congregations handing us boxes of hymnbooks. Miraculously the roof might open up to permit a dossal cloth and cross to be reverently lowered into place. Everyone would feel proud that in so short a time another standard model of the church had come off the ecclesiastical assembly line.

Certainly there were enough subtle pressures brought upon us in those early months to convince us that, if we allowed it, the beckoning stream of tradition would carry us along. With little effort we could follow the current. Indeed, it now seems possible to find a new course to steer in the church only if the seeker can discover a quiet cove that enables him to get out of the organizational rapids —a place where he can stop the headlong torrential rush of forces that now move on their own momentum. There is also a fearful overeagerness by those already caught up in the system to catch others up in its engulfing plunge. We have seen how one needs to pause awhile in calmer waters, near the banks away from the central stream . . . and ponder.

The little group continuing to meet each Wednesday evening experienced the pressures of organizational momentum. We took time, however, to stop the expected trends long enough to ask: Why? We began asking the quiet questions on that first Wednesday. The nucleus which continued searching week by week slowly grew. We grew in our excitement as we realized the potential for creativity. We grew in joy as we found fast friends through the sharing of paint buckets and through the laughter over how hideous the others looked with polka-dot rags bound over their hair to ward off at least some of the spattered paint. Never has a house been painted by such disorganized, carefree novices. At first our weekly gatherings included time to scrub, paint, and repair, as well as time to discuss, sing, and share. I suppose it was then through prayer with hammer in hand that we first glimpsed the possibilities of finding a new dimension of community. As we moved toward the self-appointed time of beginning Sunday services, our mid-week task intensified our closeness to one another. Soon unspoken questions could be aired. Doubts and desires could be shared. It was in this early period that the seeds were planted which grew into later efforts to do a new thing in responding to the challenge to be a church.

Meanwhile, mistakes were made that tended to counteract the newly planted seeds of renewal. My own zeal for beginning the Sunday morning routines of church school and worship was that kind of error. This immediately limited the creative processes by leading others to repeat the well-known instead of probing the unknown. In this way we set limits on what we presumed might fall within God's call to do a new thing. This step also brought about an increase in the traditional interest in Sunday attendance as the primary appeal to potential new members. Another equally innocent move that thwarted the creative processes came from the presbytery's committee on new church development when they urged us to organize by winter (an inadequate period of less than six months for preparation). A less effective but interestingly subtle pressure came from women's organizations in our area. They made continued efforts to bring our own ladies into their pre-cut mold with bold assumptions that there could be no other legitimate way to develop the church.

As we completed our official organizational tasks, a new wave of searching by the now-official session again opened the way for exploring. Visits were made to the Church of the Saviour in Washington, D.C. Books were studied on the nature and mission of the church. The few pamphlets published at that time concerning new directions for the church were eagerly dissected at weekly session meetings. During our first four months as an "official" church, the session refused all other tasks to give themselves totally to the search for a proper response to God's calling for our own day. A required training class was begun for all members. With every new piece of material uncovered that spoke to the challenge of the Christian community in the twentieth century, this class increased in depth and in length. Soon it was to reach its level, offering approximately two months or twenty hours of class time in preparation for membership. (Even so small a training requirement has made its impact through the years—in action born within and reaction against it from without.) A continuing mid-week gathering of those people who were searching for newness, a concentrated response to that searching by elected leaders, and the decision to require training for membership all helped stem the inevitable pressure of traditional patterns throughout that first year.

By that first spring, the session had seen the need for a mission-oriented congregation as well as for one which made "belonging" worthwhile through small-group life. The result was that on May 5, 1963 at a worship service under the trees at Massanetta Springs, a retreat site three miles from town, the congregation began their response to the challenge of the session: to say "no" to all traditional committees and functions of the church and "yes" to seeking through house churches their reason for being. The initial groups were created by arbitrary assignment so that our approximately eighty-five members comprised four house churches. We knew we wouldn't have true house churches with such arbitrary assignments, but there were expectations that out of this structural pilgrimage would come a new dimension of the body of Christ.

The response was enthusiastic and for a number of months each meeting promised more of the joy that comes in a first blush of new discoveries. I, for my part, surely played the role of a foolish kid as I darted across town on the given meeting night visiting first one house church, then another and, during the drives in between, delightedly sensing the moving of the Creating Spirit in each group's growing individuality. My other drives where their agony and despair preoccupied me were to come farther down the road.

After the May launching of the house church as the primary structure of the congregation, the session sought to clarify its growing concerns for the challenge of developing a new church. To give some tangible form to the many convictions expressed, they printed a brochure. While not yet canonized, this explicit statement of purpose has served well as a reminder of the vision of those earlier and simpler days in our development. Through the years there have been those who have felt the many pressures created by the statement of purpose and consequently would rather forget that it was ever expressed; on the other hand, there are many who see this youthful vision as a proper, shall we say, bench mark for continual use. The final draft appears as follows:

WHAT IS GOD SAYING TO HIS CHURCH?
WE BELIEVE . . .

that God is alive and at work in the world today
therefore we seek to listen to His voice that can lead us in new pathways through the eternal newness that is in the living Christ

that we are not called to "business as usual"
the church is never static or matter of fact—but expectant and exciting in its awareness that our Lord can remold it according to the circumstances and needs of His world

that a voice speaks out of the disenchanted and disinterested world

therefore new structures must be found to make known God's redemptive activity in the world

that total commitment is the realistic command of Christ Jesus for discipleship

therefore a training class is required for membership and small-group studies are offered for members to find disciplined renewal in the life of the church

that the church exists for the world and not for itself

therefore its own buildings and programs are secondary to the actual life, service, and witness to the world of a redemptive society

that where Christ is known human barriers are broken down

therefore we seek to become a Christian group truly open to every person regardless of race, nationality, or economic status who would respond to our Lord's call to commitment

that laymen and laywomen are called and equipped for a particular ministry

therefore we seek to become a company of ministers enabled by the Holy Spirit to minister to and penetrate society where we live

that the church is more than an institution; it is the household of God

therefore we strive in house churches to become a community of awareness, a fellowship of the forgiven, a company of the committed

that "success" for God's church is not measured by statistics and budgets, but by losing itself in its concern for God's world

therefore we seek to reverse the world's view of the church as an institution pulling in, to that of an organism reaching out

that the Holy Spirit offers us freedom even from new molds of our own making

therefore we rejoice in the "worldy insecurity" that will enable us to continue in an open-ended search for the will of God, wondering and eagerly listening for what He will say to His church tomorrow

You are invited to share with us in this fellowship to become a part of our common search to know and to respond to—WHAT GOD *IS* SAYING TO HIS CHURCH!
> The Session, August 1963
> Trinity Presbyterian Church
> South High and Maryland Ave.
> Harrisonburg, Virginia

With that statement, more bold a decade ago than now, the course was set. Temptation to disclaim and challenges to apply these beliefs were yet to come.

This review of our first year together illuminates a common plight in new church development. Our fellowship began even in that early state to experience the tensions between the expected procedures and the only hoped for returns; the pressure of tradition and the call of new life; the inclination toward security and the desire for obedient action.[2] These tensions have remained with us in varying degrees to this day. The birth of house churches after those first nine months has known no small measure of growing pains. Nonetheless, it is within such tensions that the search for renewal is taking place. Our struggles are painfully real but out of them we discover what is genuine. It is this experience which makes Trinity's life worth sharing.

DISCOVERING

† It was after this first year as a congregation that some of us in Trinity discovered, to our surprise, that groups elsewhere called themselves house churches. Through our reading we were discovering, too, that the house church had appeared in the early life of the church. The importance of its historical roots and its contemporary emergence slowly dawned upon us.

Because house churches have hitherto risen to any noticeable degree of prominence only in times of great stress and insecurity in the church, it seems especially fitting to consider the forces that are giving rise to the house church in our day. A comparison of past and present influences upon the Christian community may suggest what role the house church will play in our century. Can we understand the rise of house church groupings as well as their full potential by viewing their ancient past?

So many centuries have passed with the church maintaining the same basic relationship to its cultural surroundings that it is very difficult for most of us really to imagine the church in any other stance. The fact that the Christian community, for a number of centuries, had few public buildings but met primarily in the homes of its members is known by some but comprehended by few. That it survived these centuries with vigor while having no legitimate place or status in its own cities or villages—indeed that to "join" such a community and attend such a house meeting put one in physical danger—is understood by even fewer.

From the New Testament we read of Christians greeting one another in letters which were sent to the homes where they gathered to worship through breaking bread and participating in study and prayer. The words of greeting were directed to the *oikon ekklesia* or the *house church.* (Examples can be found in Romans 16:5, 1 Corinthians 16:19, Colossians 4:15, and Philemon 2, where in translation *oikon ekklesia* reads as *the church in your house.*) In a book by J. G. Davies, entitled *Daily Life in the Early Church*, there is a clear picture of the primary use of homes for training members and for the worship of those early communities. Clement of Alexandria carried out his daily teaching tasks in a house. Clement's own home was the focal point for his students' training in discipleship. Referring to a new class of members who had just finished their probation period to join the church and who had just had their ceremonial, Clement of Alexandria wrote: "The memory of the simple but impressive ceremonial is still fresh in their minds. As night was falling on Easter Eve they had gone to the house, which through the generosity of a wealthy member of the congregation had been placed at the disposal of the Church as a place of worship."[1] Literature of the early Christian period implies that in some areas separate buildings may have been set aside as churches, but private dwellings served congregations as meeting places for worship. "It is impossible to say what was the situation in Alexandria in Clement's day as his references are ambiguous . . . but it is assumed that a house-church was in existence. The description in the text is based upon that of the Christian house-church *c.* A.D. 232, discovered at Dura-Europos on the Euphrates *vide* M. Rostovtzeff. . . ."[2] The reference made is to one of the oldest actual locations of a Christian meeting place yet discovered. In the Syrian desert, midway between Baghdad and Aleppo, stand the ruins of Dura-Europos. The ancient city rests on the road that, for time immemorial, had followed the Euphrates. It would not be surprising to find evidence there of a Christian group for, according to M. Rostovtzeff, their small communities had ceased to be a novelty in the life of the cities of Mesopotamia in the late Roman times.

"In 1931–32 we found under the sloping embankment of the desert wall to the south of the main gate a private house, part of it in excellent preservation, which had been built in the early third century and was transformed very soon, probably about A.D. 232 into a Christian meeting place and place of worship. One little room was used as a baptistery."[3]

The relationship of the small Christian cult to the life of the city as a whole was at best a tenuous one. The church existed in a climate where the obvious religious landmarks that were known to the citizens were the many temples dedicated to their numerous gods. In going to the market one would take the usual route past the temple of Zeus on one corner and thence to the center of the city's marketplace where in Dura was to be found the great temple of Artemis. In such a society Christians could not expect popular acceptance, nor could they expect the tolerance that might permit them to erect a public building for worship. The alternative was a house church.

"As was done for the Synagogue, a private house of medium size was reconstructed for the use of the Christian community. The house was adapted to the requirements of the Christian cult soon after A.D. 232. . . . The house was well hidden in a cluster of other similar houses, and its appearance remained exactly that of a private house even after its transformation into a Christian church. The Christians in the third century A.D. had every reason not to make their house of prayer conspicuous."[4] Artwork on the walls revealed some early Christian themes put there to impress the catechumens at their baptism. Drawings depicting the miracles of Jesus, the figure of the good shepherd, Adam and Eve, David and Goliath, Christ reaching to Peter in the miracle of the lake, and the Resurrection were uncovered on the baptistery walls. The drawings were those commonly used to represent central themes which bound the members of the Dura house church to other similar Christian communities already well scattered in this period, little more than a hundred years after the writings of our New Testament.

This is not to romanticize the house church because of its antiquity. Rather, the house church in Dura was in another time when the Christian community existed as a minority, in a day of transition, in an alien environment. Then the people of God found the church in the house suitable to their needs. This example of early house churches should emphasize to the present-day Christian that the church has survived, and indeed thrived, in such circumstances. The church is quite capable of moving in similar ways today. The prime difference would be that, whereas the ancient house churches sought to grow in virgin soil, the house church of today must rediscover its roots in an overworked ground.

The early house church was not determined merely by conditions of numbers and income as though it depended upon time and growth to "arrive" in the community by building the church on the corner. On the contrary, the early Christians who lived under persecutions that began with Emperor Nero in A.D. 64 and continued in localized areas until the reign of Diocletian in the fourth century, could not have purchased public property to raise their steeples if they had so desired. As long as they took a public stand, regarding the Empire as an evil institution—godless, corrupt, and contrary to the will of God—they had little chance of having public property. Whenever they were a revolutionary force disrupting popular attitudes, they were bound to gather in hidden sanctuaries where, through instruction, they reinforced their way of life in opposition to the surrounding culture. The house church, then, has represented not only a necessary place for the church but an attitude as well—a stance in relation to one's society. In addition, the house church during this time came to symbolize the transitory state which the members of the body of Christ were experiencing. These earliest Christian communities, composed of Jews and Gentiles, were in a state of fluidity. They operated with a little of the old while moving toward the new. They were leaving their temples and synagogues.

This they knew, but what they were moving toward they did not know. House churches, although not considered temporary, served them well in the transitional times in which they lived.

An additional perspective which enables us to understand the house church as signaling a life-style more than a specific location comes from the broad interpretations given to the terms *house* and *church* as they were used in the New Testament.

"It is significant to note that in the New Testament the same term, *ekklesia*, is used to designate (i) the universal church, (ii) the church of God in a certain province or region, (iii) a particular local church, and (iv) the actual assembly of believers in any place, for instance in the upper room of a home."[5] To the writers of our New Testament, then, the church as the people of God could appear as a reality in any setting with any number of persons. Obviously, the church was never seen as a building, be it house or temple; it was and is wherever people gather and live out their life in God's name.

As the New Testament writers used the term church broadly, so too did they define *house* more broadly than we generally perceive.

"The New Testament term for 'house' *(oikos)* designates first of all a place, the place where people live and work. . . .

"It is important to note that already in the New Testament the meaning of the term *oikos* is not restricted to the house as a building. Very often it rather means house in a social context. *Oikos* then becomes almost synonymous with 'family,' 'tribe,' or the concrete social environment of a person."[6] Applying this understanding to our day, the house church becomes the church in the world when the activity of any gathering of God's people takes place in the concreteness of man's secular and social context in life. House church occurs wherever men are acting out of their basic "frame" of reference and there unveil the presence of God.

The impact of the house church of the first and second centuries upon the church of this century demonstrates that the Christian community cannot only survive, it can exercise powerful influence in the midst of an alien and totally secularized society. It would be tempting to call for a return to the ancient form of the church for nostalgic motives alone, but that would miss the vital truth that the call is not to duplicate ancient form but to duplicate the capacity to re-form. Early Christians were able to adjust from their temples and synagogues to the underground style called for by their situation.

It would be tempting also to suggest a return to their stance wherein the house church existed in opposition to the dominant cultural beliefs of the day. But this too would overlook the far more basic contribution, which is an awareness that, by means of their flexible adjustments in the house church, the Christians were themselves able to determine what their stance might be, whether in sympathy to the society of the day or in opposition. They were able to exist in the stance they chose out of obedience to God; they were not molded by the principalities and powers, i.e. the political and economic influences, but by the calling of the Holy Spirit. For centuries since, beginning with the acceptance of the Christian church by the Emperor Constantine, the church has modeled much of its life, from shapes of buildings to ethical teachings, according to what was acceptable by the dominant culture in which it has become popular. Today we may use the early house church *form* and *stance* if it fits our situation, but we must take seriously the *concept* and the *style* of the house church if we are again to locate the holy in the midst of life.

† The twentieth century has seen a small reemergence of the house church. It had its sudden rise in Europe, mostly in England and Scotland, during the closing years of World War II. Examples of house churches could be found in America approximately a decade later. Mr. Edwin H. Robertson, Associate Director to the World Association for Christian Communication, has written about the European rise in house churches. His observations, recorded in the book *Basileia* in 1959, indicate that several distinct pressures caused this rise. Contemporary pressures were the real reason for the return of the house church, according to Dr. Robertson, and their appearing on the modern scene was "only afterwards interpreted as a movement back to the primitive Church."[7]

In England saturation bombing was a continuous element in life. Even though their churches had never been closed, the British were now forced to consider alternatives. It was impossible for members to come together in the customary large groups so far from their homes. Small groups within their homes were, of course, possible. One evening a week the church kept in touch with itself and its Lord through these house meetings. They soon discovered advantages in this arrangement so that the practice was continued in many areas long after the initial cause—the war—had ended.

Of all subsequent house church developments in England the most notable has been the oft-cited work of E. W. Southcott as vicar of Halton Parish in Leeds, London.[8] It was through his spirited leadership in the beginning of the fifties that the congregation at Halton began to experience the moving of worship services, including the Eucharist, out into the streets and into their homes. Provost Southcott's book depicting those experiences displays clearly the new grappling with life made possible by the discovery of the church in the houses of the parishioners. Throughout *The Parish Comes Alive,* Southcott emphasizes that besides establishing a new location, the house church challenges the body of Christ to face the commission placed upon it to be the church. The vicar brought contemporary relevance to the house church when he wrote: "It is much more out on the frontier that one experiences the weakness and the strength of the Church as the Body of Christ."[9]

"The house-Church represents, so to speak, the tap-roots of the vine, the Church underground, that of the life of the tree most closely in contact with the clinging soil of everyday existence: it is the tree as it is embedded in the deepest crevices and seams of the secular world."[10]

The leading pressure at Halton was the appalling failure of the majority of the baptized within the parish ever to return to church again. As Southcott put it, they came to be hatched, matched, or dispatched.

Another kind of pressure during this same post World War II period was at work in the Church of Scotland. This pressure appears to have been the absence of the kind of fellowship within a congregation which could support a true ministry of the laity, one to another.

Naturally, the Church of Scotland with its presbyterian form of government sought to revitalize its lay ministry through the office of the elder. Neighborhoods were divided into sectors with an elder of the congregation responsible for holding occasional home meetings for those families within his sector. This example was followed extensively in the congregation in Greenock as they gave the name house church to these monthly home meetings.

Another strong influence toward the development of house churches came from the Iona Community. Their concern was to bring the church into a new relationship with the industrial community. To this end, specific guidelines were offered to those congregations interested through a pamphlet published by the Iona Community, written by the Reverend David Orr, entitled simply *The House Church.* It is a practical "how to" manual written chiefly within the perspective of the Church of Scotland offering concise guidelines for those who wish to develop house churches through the eldership.

In Norway, the home group meeting sprang up as a result of the influence of the Moral Re-Armament movement. The Moral Re-Armament movement left in its wake a continuing interest in the possibilities derived from the small group. Intimate conversations, relevant study, and in time, a concern for the neighborhood beyond the group all became a part of the spontaneous beginnings of house churches in Norway. Although leaderless in the beginning, these small groups eventually organized for an improved area distribution within their neighborhoods. Study helps in the form of outlines were provided by the church. Ten years ago Mr. Robertson reported more than 1,000 such groups in Norway.

† The sporadic development of house churches in Europe found its American counterpart in the next decade. If the 1950's marked the major effort in England, Scotland, Norway, and Holland, the 1960's brought the first brief acquaintance of the house church to the States. The one outstanding exception to this timetable would be the Church of the Saviour in Washington, D.C. This ecumenical

church pioneered the renewal trend, of which the house church is a part, and has been well documented.[11]

The present rise of the house church in the States continues the variety of patterns found in Europe but, as could be expected, includes additional types. In the United States, those house churches within the institution seem to be finding themselves involved in the many interacting influences controlling denominational thrusts today. Thus the house church reflects the many nuances of church development found in United States history with its hundreds of denominational and sectarian emphases.

Recently I sent a questionnaire to churches in several sections of the country where the house church is a part of their experience. The following response to just two of the questions—those concerning the purpose and the marks of the house church as they see them —reveals the great diversity with which this movement is being viewed.

From the Valley United Church of Christ, Concord, California:

PURPOSE: "We strive to affirm our humanity in a de-personalizing period. We look for purpose and value in ways that are meaningful to the mid-twentieth century. We experience what it means to belong to each other."

MARKS: "Our group is distinguished in that it does not feel insecure without the institutional markings and program of the church."

From the Diocese of Lansing, Michigan:

PURPOSE: "To bring people in a neighborhood to become aware of current needs and to become better acquainted."

MARKS: "The place where meetings occur."

From The Church Without Walls, Kansas City, Missouri:

PURPOSE: "Mission—mutual support and some study."

MARKS: "A small group of persons who are the church to each other who function together for the purpose of mission, fellowship, education and worship in meetings at least once every two weeks."

From the Oreland Presbyterian Church, Oreland, Pennsylvania:

PURPOSE: Their purpose, printed in a submitted constitution, reads: "The purpose of these groups shall be to follow Jesus Christ by enacting certain agreed disciplines as defined in Article IX of the By-Laws."

MARKS: "Equal division of time allotted in meeting for prayer and Bible study. Complete reforming of groups every four to six months. Ingathering—meeting of all groups together for inspiration and public witness every four months."

From Christ Church, Presbyterian, Burlington, Vermont:

PURPOSE: "Common reflection and celebration of the faith."

MARKS: "Self-conscious and overt celebration and reflection of the faith."

These churches are finding through a variety of approaches some expression of the church-in-the-house helpful for their development.

Despite diversity in house church styles, there is a willingness among many house church representatives to confer in an effort to realize what is common between them. To this end several house church consultations have been held in the past few years. One such consultation was held in Louisville, Kentucky in November 1971 at the Presbyterian Theological Seminary. Approximately twenty-five participants in house churches attended with others who were interested in exploring the movement. This particular group was called together by leaders in the United Church of Christ and the Presbyterian Church, U.S. Their purpose was to look at the various models of the house church, its theological and institutional implications. They also anticipated a positive experience in simply sharing together.

Representatives of house churches came from such diverse places as the Sycamore Community, State College, Pennsylvania; Genesis II, in Rochester, New York; Church of the Foothills, Ventura, California; The Experimental Church, Winston-Salem, North Carolina; a house church of the Colorado Conference, U.C.C., Denver, Colorado; The Grand Valley Ministry, Allendale, Michigan; the

Three Chopt Presbyterian Church, Richmond, Virginia; and about a dozen others. During those three days it was almost impossible to ascertain any unifying factor within the group. No theological basis unified them, nor were there similar goals. There was no single model design for house church nor common life-style within house churches. What did appear to be their common ground was a disenchantment with the institutional church. Their sentiments ranged all the way from mild disappointment to abhorrent rejection. Most agreed that whatever its varied expressions, the house church was an attempt to find a better way to respond to the Christian challenge than that allowed by present institutional forms. These twentieth-century house churches represent, as did those of the third century, a particular stance in relationship to society even more than they represent a new place for the church to meet.

While most of those attending were attempting to exist within the institutional framework, all felt some estrangement due to their unconventional stance. This alone accounted for a great deal of the support felt through this opportunity to share. Although this particular gathering remained loose knit and adjourned with no expressed interest in a planned continuity, there was an obvious increase in understanding within the house church movement. Most left strengthened and reassured that their particular efforts toward church renewal were not carried on in vain or in isolation.

† **O**ne current expression of the house church is located in a pleasant residential district of Claremont, California. The night I attended one of their home meetings, I was told by Father Dan Brown that this was the first gathering of most of those present. The sixteen men, women, and children were personally known to the host and his invitation alone established the reason for their presence. They were not likely to meet in that exact context again.

The guests gradually shifted from their informal conversation to hear Father Brown. Standing behind a card table adorned with candles and flowers, he was explaining to those closest to him the reason for the liturgical vestments he was donning. Worship began quietly but with careful attention to the revised liturgical forms of the Roman Catholic Church. Scripture was read by a layman. The Priest expounded upon the meaning of the Word and invited discussion by those seated around the room. The theme was Acts 2:42 on the meaning of the church as the gathered people of God. "The church is what's there when the walls fall down,"[12] Father Brown explained. Discussion followed, beginning slowly at first with only the most proper kinds of questions. Soon, however, the group relaxed into lively exchanges on the pros and cons of new forms of worship.

"Do you think there will be the time when we will play down a little bit all this jazz in our church?" asked one woman.

"I like the new worship. I can follow it word for word. The Latin I could follow, but I didn't know what I was saying," offered another. The group closed the discussion with prayers—prayers for their experience of community, for a couple about to get married, for a teen-ager who had lost her father.

The home mass followed with a young boy assisting in bringing the elements to the card table in the center of the room. After a number of liturgical responses, Father Brown moved to each person in turn, asking as he passed the bread, "The body of Christ?" Each member responded in turn, "Amen!" It was just a beginning in this group's experience of the church through the ages coming to them in a new way. The event was warmly received and brought new interest to many of the participants.

During the refreshment period that followed, Father Brown explained that home mass was currently being celebrated in his congregation through three approaches. There were those personally invited by the host, as we were experiencing. There were other groups called together by their proximity to one another in some neighborhood. And there were still other groups which met frequently for home study who celebrated mass together on occasion. This latter grouping would, of course, lend itself to less formality and easier dialogue because they would have established a fellowship by the time the mass was brought into one of their homes. Through this procedure one could see the church gradually making new inroads into the awareness of its members in first one neighborhood and then the next. Slowly a movement was beginning for them wherein time-honored concepts were perceived in a new light, offering new challenges in being the people of God.

I have discovered that most house church groups do not know of one another. They have not derived from any common source, and what's more, are not particularly anxious to organize or even to start a chain news letter. Any preoccupation with their unique ties to the church, historical or ecumenical, through the house church specifically, would seem to be equally trivial in their minds, I suspect. The person who dares to be involved and become exposed in some such group, the person who is anxious to get on with the job of being the church, is the person who can neither wait for any mass ecumenical formula nor desire any preoccupation with further crossties, either organizational or historical.

† "Look at it this way. This is a very hang-loose group and we adore it that way." So spoke one male member of a house church in Concord, California. His description came in the middle of an evening's gathering where ten young adults were responding to questions about their style of house church living. The terms he used accurately described their life together. As a hang-loose fellowship they meet approximately once a month for worship and educational work with the children and gather on other weekends at times and places that fit their need for the moment. They do not go to meetings together so much as they get involved together for a day or a weekend on a concern of mutual interest. His term "adore" also suits them well, as together they manifest an adoration of life itself. They have determined to be responsible for influencing the forces which affect their life in modern society rather than remaining passive victims of life's forces. A politically active group, the members are often found in the forefront of community improvement meetings and projects, from low-cost housing to new models of education. Their minister, Bill Smith, whose salary is supplemented by secular work, functions as a helper and a catalyst for their group, leaving a great amount of the leadership to the laity.

The twenty-five family units have been meeting in homes for a little over three years now. They have no church building and plan to have none. A bona fide congregation in the eyes of the United Church of Christ, the group is anti-institutional enough to refuse to submit a list of members to the authorities. They feel that membership is of the heart and that an emphasis on numbers detracts from their meaning together. This group did not choose the identity of house church; it was put upon them by others in the area for lack of a more fitting description. They could as well be known as a mini-church, as delineated by Dr. Dietrich Ritschl.[13]

The Valley Church actually had its beginnings in a traditional fashion in 1963. They had a plot of land and plans to build. The minister wore a robe, and white tablecloths were used on the communion table. The institutional signs were obviously present. A growing concern over the Vietnam War and a desire not to build were the issues which in time turned the group to new directions.

They are still evolving. Their latest area of interest is in exploring the advantages of a communal or collective style for their Christian community. They are looking closely at the needless duplication of homes and property, from twenty cars for every dozen families to row upon row of duplicate power mowers and swing sets. Twelve households, in an established partnership, have purchased twelve acres of land in their area. Twelve homes, clustered for extended family sharing, are planned. The families involved are committed to work and live together to find deeper community and personal fulfillment.

The Valley United Church of Christ does not expect to become a large church, mainly because their own style of life and interest is not that popular. Remaining small, however, does not worry them. As one young mother put it, "There are a lot of things you can't be as a church when you are big. In our church we see the value of the community that means something special to one another—kind of an extended family. When we go camping together and my kids need a grown-up, my friend Barbara is often that adult, not me. We try to see what we have that we can give to each other."

They might hang loose in organization and doctrinal emphasis, but this group of young adults believes that they can be a church based upon zest for life and concern for others. Some observers might be disturbed by their total abandon to a spontaneous community, but it is obvious that the members of the Valley United Church of Christ "adore it that way."

When the church can blossom spontaneously, free to respond to so many diverse callings, we realize that the church belongs not to man but to God. This realization can thrust us back into our own small group with an invigorating sense of the broader community of Christ's body.

This strength stemming from a sense of community—of the constant awareness of others who share our concerns, fears, and hopes—has been one of the obvious needs calling for the rise of house churches across our land. Indeed, this concern for community was one of the earliest pressure points at work in the development of the congregation of Trinity. We had to discover that such a desired community could not simply be decreed. It, too, was a happening.

BELONGING

† **O**ne of our first observable growth areas in the house churches within Trinity was in understanding what it really meant to be "in community." One could observe it at our first major spring retreat in May 1964. The entire congregation was again gathered at Massanetta Springs. We had come to the closing hours of our retreat when a member came up to me and said, "I'm looking forward to being with this new group. . . . We've had an exciting experience here this weekend, and have grown together, but . . . I don't want to leave the house church I've been with for a year." This concern, expressed in passing, evidences an important development in our first year's experiences with house church living. They had, of course, had many difficult hours together. Now that the effort was being made to have all new assignments for the next year, as an outgrowth of the retreat, they became aware of a growing relation-

ship. The comment was typical of the expressions that revealed how house churches were slowly becoming more than an organization of the church; they were becoming a family, a community, a brotherhood. Many other members, excited over their past twelve hours of cumulative growth through a communications workshop, were expressing anxiety as well as anticipation as they packed up the nursery toys and collected mimeographed materials. Typical thoughts were: "Why can't we stay with the house church we have had for a year, where despite our dislikes, we are at least known now and still accepted?" "What if I am not able to be *me* in the new group?" "But what if I'm now able to be more *me* than before?"

A short year had passed since at the same retreat site through a service of worship, sitting in casual clothing under the trees, we had begun our house churches. None of us had known what we were getting into then, and I had secretly wondered how long the innovation would continue. To call people to weekly home meetings with poorly prepared leaders and a still uncertain purpose seemed foolhardy, to say the least. I had forgotten how our lives thrive on the uncertainties of an open road with its hope and promise in the unknown. At least with us, the fresh, the new, and the possible were sufficient incentives to ride out the difficult times and overcome in some measure our lack of training.

It is impossible to measure our growth in that first year in house churches. For some members very little had taken place: a study book or two, a lot of talk, perhaps a slow relaxing. But even for those who saw little as well as for those who were aware of more, there was a common transition from thinking of house church as "that meeting I have to attend," to "that's my group getting together tonight, and I'm a part of it."

Thus, belonging crept up on us. It was desired more than actually expected. For many, that call to change house churches after one year was the first awareness of something happening to us —despite ourselves.

Through the years we were reminded in much the same unexpected way that our growth in Christian community "happened" more than it was discussed or programmed. There was the night, years later, when the Community Service House Church said good-bye to the Davidson family. They met that week in the apartment of Mrs. Funkhouser, a grandmother whose spirit had kept this group struggling for their purpose and identity when all signs pointed to its demise. On this particular January evening most members of the house church family had turned out. The atmosphere appeared a bit more jovial than usual—almost a party. Then it began to happen. Someone expressed, on this occasion for farewells, what the group had meant to him; the spark immediately began its chain igniting. Spontaneously and quickly, person after person made known his present desire to affirm the love, support, and challenge the house church experience had brought. This was not done piously, as if it were testimony time and one needed to get his credentials of acceptability out on the table, but simply and naturally, as a confirmation of what we knew must be there all along—the presence of a bond between people which simply had to be expressed at such a time as this. Occurrences such as these keep us aware of the possibility of community, even when the group seems more fractured than whole. For true community is realistic. It lives with the awareness that closeness brings disappointment and opposition as often as it provides support and fulfillment. The significant value of the house church rests in its ability to provide growth in acceptance through the difficult times as well as the joyful ones.

The cause or causes of developing community are difficult to perceive. No set of exercises or rules will guarantee its happening. Frankly, the more I am witness to it, the more I must confess that I do not know how it comes about except that it is a gift of God. Often when we worked for it, the sense of a real community would disappear. On the other hand, when we least expected it to be strong, there it would appear in obvious signs of concern, acts of forgiveness, and determination to see the group through the rough spots. If asked what contributed to our sense of community, I could only point to the constant confrontation through weekly, open-ended sharing in our living rooms. Without the props of administration or religious symbolism we have been able to see more clearly the gifts of belonging which otherwise may have passed unnoticed, obscured by religious exercises that continue to veil us from one another. A house church does not create Christian community, but it does provide a setting where the participants have to look hard the other way not to see it happening.

Running *from* a growth in fellowship is as inevitable as running *toward* it. We discovered that there is a natural resistance to belonging just as there is a natural desire for it. To observe an individual running from the involvement inherent in a house church even while regularly participating in its mission is not uncommon. Dr. J. C. Hoekendijk correctly reminds us that "there is no universal longing for inspired relationships and it is not true that everyone wants to overcome his skeptic reservations in animated thought, if he only knew how. We have become contact-poor and contact-shy."[1] His statement has accurately described the experience and struggle of a number of our house churches. This is due to the fact that our desire to relate on a deeper level to others outside our own home is matched by our years of experience wherein we have learned to distrust or even fear the possibility of honest, authentic sharing. We must expect an ebb and flow of the trust level in a house church. This fluidity can be endured if, as we have usually found, there are enough determined, fearless participants to challenge the entire group to face their tendency to become formal, simply sweet to one another, very bookish, or too busy at the project to observe how the "guards" have come up.

Another reason for retreating from the group encounter, beyond our fear of relationships, stems from our refusal to face the possibility of not belonging at all anywhere. Much of the time, we are playing with such topics as discipline and hope, for we do not see them as seriously related to the base issue of life and death. Small group community remains something organizational and "nice" so long as we deny our yearning to know we belong before we die. We enter into a community search hoping to discover our own identities only to find ourselves promoting "busy work" so that no one will know the depth of our need. We must confess our fear of finiteness before we are able to look realistically at what promises our infinite worth. Yet, too often the church has allowed us to "belong" on the same good citizen level to which we might "belong" through a number of civic service organizations. In this way, the church protects us in our maneuvering to escape searching in depth at the level required to bring the hope desired.

Because real community becomes difficult to achieve even when desired, at Trinity we have developed certain measures to aid the process. The leadership positions which have evolved in Trinity's house churches are, when properly functioning, representations of the balance sought in the life of the community itself. There is a trilogy of offices with a congregationally elected elder at the top of the triangle while a nurture leader and a mission leader maintain the balance in direction of the group as they grow together and move outward to others. The elder, known locally as the pastoral leader, serves as the main line of communication to the core of the church's governing body and thus to the core of the resources that might be requested by a house church to aid its health as a group. As the other two leaders concentrate on developing their respective areas of growth, the elder is freed to be a process observer, overseer, and general coordinator of the group's desires. This diffusion of leadership alleviates the weight of total responsibility from one person and also increases the opportunity for a variety of leadership skills which may come to the total group.

† In those first few years of growing together, we exerted little effort to make overt use of the techniques and knowledge found within the behavioral sciences. Science has developed approaches to group behavior known variously as group dynamics, T groups, encounter groups, and therapy groups. Obviously such dynamics were taking place but there was only an occasional look at the process. The spring retreats, membership classes, and special training sessions for all the nurture leaders or elders attempted to keep members and leaders alike sensitive to the groups' interaction. Our aim was to make clear its importance without elevating the group process to the level of a central purpose or goal.

With only spotty lay training offered at Trinity, I marveled at the new growth periods following each slump. Commitment to intended purposes and impatience with present apathy have often led house church members to call for renewed evaluation of the group, an evaluation which included their own interaction.

I have felt guilty that more group awareness has not been developed within the leadership. Its absence has frequently hindered internal ministry as well as the mission of the house church. Because of this situation, I was pleasantly surprised when, on a weekend retreat for the entire congregation, increased awareness of the group process became obvious. We had planned this retreat after letting too many years pass without one. Its announced purpose was to discover anew an experience in community. The weekend was designed to bring in leaders and other resources to confront the congregation with the need for corporate life as well as to introduce those features of group interaction which would enable the experience to become a reality, not just a discussion. Out of the hope-filled weekend was heard a large negative cry. The general complaint was that the new groupings, formed just for the weekend to include visitors, were not groups at all. Members complained loudly that they were not hearing one another at any meaningful level, that they each came with a built-in agenda, and that the vying for leadership was atrocious. You can imagine our disappointment when so much positive confrontation had been anticipated. Then it came to me—the actual list of negative incidents within the retreat was no more significant than those recorded at former retreats. If our members now knew so quickly what a bad community experience was, it must be because in the interim they had actually experienced real community where these negative aspects were less apparent. A few years before, they would have thought this a fine retreat, but growth had again outstripped expectations and the process of community was becoming more and more refined. It took a negative experience to point to positive growth, but few things could have spoken more clearly to the determination of the participants not to settle for any pretended community interaction.

The preceding example of group growth was selected to make clear two important truths concerning group dynamics in the house church. The first is that such awareness training is very important for the most effective growth of the house church. Had we developed more leadership in group relations, many of Trinity's problems could have been overcome. The second is that we do not need to wait for specialists in the field before daring to meet together to be exposed to the process of a group experience. The Trinity members have grown in group awareness despite a lack in formal training.

One form of community building stemming from the behavioral sciences is known as the human potential movement. In recent years the human potential movement has had increasing impact upon laymen and clergy. Many advocates of group interaction have found in certain house church forms a natural environment for expressing their disenchantment with the established church and their desire for an experiential life-style. At the Louisville consultation on the house church a spokesman said that the human potential movement has a set of methodologies which complement the house church form. Such methods promise to assist the small group in moving beyond its tendency toward a plateau.

For some time now the behavioral scientists have sought a more lasting environment than that afforded by the short-term human relations laboratory or summer institute. At the same time much of the church has longed for that expertise which would enable congregations to be truly supportive and change-making communities. Thus, the meeting of behavioral sciences and the Christian faith within the house church offers a great deal of promise.

The human potential movement provides a means of experiencing self-affirmation. It opens the group to become a true caring community, revealing a spirit that can enable each participant to perceive his Lord in a new and vital way. Those experiences through a house church community which are a result of encounter group training may bring forth a more authentic personal claim of discipleship. This would be especially true for those persons who see themselves as a part of the counter-culture.

Present leaders working toward the merger of house church context and encounter group methods are quick to point out that the two are not synonymous. Their precautionary statement is needed. The joyful and often overpowering experiences developed through encounter group techniques cause some people to regard this focus as their sole reason for gathering as a house church. It is then that we need to be reminded that the human potential movement is only one set of tools among many by which the Christian community may find its renewed life and purpose as the body of Christ.

Although the house church needs, as aids to its life, the three disciplines of psychology, sociology, and theology, it is important to keep them in proper perspective. The house church is a support group, so it needs psychological insights to enable members to get in touch with themselves and with each other. The house church is a gathering of households influencing and being influenced by society, so it needs sociological insights to understand its response to that society. The house church is the church, so it needs theological insights to enable it to know the purpose for which it exists. The first two are supportive to the last. Theology, or the awareness of God, his will, and our response, must remain the basis for the existence of the house church.

✝ A major effort within the house churches at Trinity has been the concentration upon the family, for the purpose of supporting and aiding families as well as becoming a family unit itself. Through the many printed resources focusing upon the modern family, the house churches have been able to share their concerns and react to the challenges posed in these study sessions. Although we have few examples of extreme change by this means, there has been a constant response from one or two who say, "These sessions have made a significant difference in what goes on in our home." Whether or not studies about the family are being used, the house church, by its entrance into the homes of all of its members, provides a confrontation to the households that has at times been the source of their own decision-making, thus their wholeness.

Another relation our house churches have had to family units is in becoming a new type of family in and of itself. More than once when a house church is asked for an evaluation at the end of a year, members have expressed themselves by saying, "This is my family," or "This is like another family to me." This is especially true with the people who live alone, young or old. They find in this house meeting that feedback to their own personalities so vital to us all. To work through arguments with adults other than those in their immediate households, to express the tensions of the work or lack of work to different ears, to hear someone say in loving concern, "You're acting more distant than usual, what's wrong?" all illustrate the extension of a family type of gift giving. The house church as an extended family brings a unique type of caring community that adds perspective and support to the demands of lifelong interpersonal relationships.

When we look at the total influence of the homes on the house church and vice versa, it is obvious that all is not well. Much has been said recently about fortress-like, closed-in churches. When one looks closely enough, it is apparent that fortress churches come, in great measure, from fortress families. Our fearful, latched-in households make it next to impossible to be open to a broader reconciling community that dares to break down barriers. Obviously, current pressures upon families call for many types of outside support. In a unique way the house church can offer strength amid existing family turmoil.

This does not excuse us from including in our ministry, however, a clear confrontation with the prevalence of family idolatry, an idolatry openly asserting that the family unit, symbolized today as Mom, Pop, and three kids, is obviously the arena in life where one owes his highest loyalty. From childhood on, we are winged on the idea that to grow up to have a family of our own is the supreme goal of life. Institutions are created to serve the family, so that even the church is seen as that institution designed to fill the needs of families as their priority for existence. Dr. Roy Fairchild, Professor of Christian Education at the San Francisco Theological Seminary in San Anselmo, California, has written on the nature of the Christian family. Even though much of his work speaks to the need for support of such families, he feels that the Christian family needs to hear of its own idolatry. He wrote in *Christians in Families:*

"The modern American says, 'Marriage is the most important

thing in life. It is the reason for existence.' Popular songs proclaim this creed *ad nauseum.* At this point the New Testament brings us up short by declaring that the family is not the ultimate. If the family becomes the center of our existence, it will not stand.''[2] After discussing the selfishness evidenced in some marriages that do not want the "burden" of children, Fairchild goes on to say:

> However, a family with children can also be self-centered. As Luther put it so picturesquely, it may be "curved in upon itself." Jesus would shock us out of our idolatry: "If anyone comes to me and does not hate his own father and mother and wife and children and brothers and sisters, yes, and even his own life, he cannot be my disciple" (Luke 14:26). These searing words jar our sensibilities. They are harsh words designed to repel and to shock and not to win followers to him. . . .
>
> The gods that compete most for our loyalty, time, and energy are those which we see as good, not evil. . . . He stuns us who think that in being nice to our families we are satisfactorily serving Christ and his Kingdom. He is sounding an alarm bell to alert those of us who think that human affections and loyalty are enough. . . .
>
> Natural love enslaves; the love which is of Christ frees. . . .
>
> Jesus is saying that if you do not seek first my kind of love and the meaning of each individual life within the family, you'll not be fit to love. When you love your family in your own natural, possessive, or neglectful way, you move further from me. Your love must be screened through my love.[3]

In the face of Jesus' teachings we turn to the modern Western family today and realize that an appeal to family duty or a lessening of commitment made "for the sake of my family" is unquestionably proper in the minds of the majority of churchgoers. Families do come first, as our choice of priorities makes clear. The congregations today are clearly organized to emphasize the supremacy of the family unit. Family night suppers assume that those not living in family units will receive a welfare-like invitation from some kind, benevolent family so that the single person can come and act as though he is one of the family. The church "thinks" family where possible in its election to positions of leadership, program planning, and building usage. The church that puts more of its energy into helping confront its surrounding community with problems of race relations, drugs, poverty, pollution, etc., thereby putting these missions above building up the church school equipment for its families' children, is in for a great deal of pressure from irate mothers who see no greater calling than in providing the best for their families. Indulgence of the family unit is often no more than self-indulgence with society's, and too often, the church's blessing.

What is needed is a new kind of community enabling a family to reach out beyond itself in sacrificial concern for others. This type of community frees the family to extend its own supportive relationships and loyalties. Such a community frees the family to put loyalty to God above itself, thereby saving itself as a worthwhile unit of society. Jesus was in a family and there are indications that their emphasis on family loyalty caused them to call him back from his work.

> He was still speaking to the crowds when his mother and his brothers appeared; they were standing outside and were anxious to have a word with him. But to the man who told him this Jesus replied, "Who is my mother? Who are my brothers?" And stretching out his hand towards his disciples he said, "Here are my mother and my brothers. Anyone who does the will of my Father in heaven, he is my brother and sister and mother." (Matthew 12:46–50)

Jesus' priorities are a needed challenge today.

One emerging dimension in the quest for community is the willingness of so many, particularly young adults, to change the narrow meaning of "family." In the past the term referred chiefly to the primary family tree, including all of the cousins and half-sisters for at least four generations. In our own day the "family" often means the single household across the street whom we see going to work and school each morning. Now the word "family" may mean the number of friends who make up our boundary of extreme openness, trust, and commitment to a common goal.

Many house churches being started across the States today have as one of their primary goals the establishment of a meaningful family unit larger than the common nuclear family and related on a different level from the blood ties of the inherited family. These movements give credibility to a need expressed in a recent popular magazine by the writer George B. Leonard who said:

"We need bigger, less well-defined 'families.' We need groups of friends and neighbors who are willing and able to share the strongest feelings, to share responsibility for the emotional needs of all the children in the group. Thus no one will be childless, no one will lack affection, and no one will be deprived of a rich and varied emotional and sensual life."[4]

We have opted for a no-touch culture. We fear to handle what we want in friendships for we are uncertain how to strike a healthy balance between intimate loyalty to spouse and intimate meaning to friends. So the mighty fortress of shielded homes continues to hide the hurts and screen the screaming of half-lives wanting to be whole. Is it any wonder that the simple handshake "kiss of peace" in the church at worship is so traumatic for many? We want to reach out but do not know how to love in the freedom Christ brought to love. The kiss of peace and all other alternate forms in the church will remain stumbling blocks until we deal realistically with this fear of self-disclosure.

This concern for intimate relating does not have to contain overtones of the latest hot paperback on sexual license in communal living. It can just as well connote a new determination to move more closely to the priorities exemplified by Jesus in the meaning of family. Indeed, religious organizations, orders, members of the so-called underground church, as well as middle class suburbanites are finding in their ranks those who think it important to experience a new type of family more open than those from which they have come.

† One approach to a new type of Christian community can be found at Reba Place. Reba Place sounds more like a restaurant than a church. In fact it is neither. Reba Place is a street in Evanston, Illinois. On this street live members of the Reba Place Christian Community. Mr. Virgil Vogt, whose 1958 article on the house church shall be referred to later on, was one of the early members

of this community. He still feels "that this is a much more promising form for congregational life than the traditional type congregation."[5]

The group to which he referred began in 1957 when a few young families, including single men and women, moved into available housing on Reba Place. They were searching for an expression of the Christian community that would take seriously Jesus' words: "By this love you have for one another, everyone will know that you are my disciples" (John 13:35). So strongly do these new family groups feel about this command that they have made it the final purpose of the church. In a brochure used to communicate their style of life we find these words: ". . . the Christian church has no other purpose in this world than to extend the mission of Jesus by establishing communities of love."[6] Although one may want to quibble over some implications of this statement, it nonetheless stresses their determination to avoid the pitfalls of so much congregational pretense concerning true community. They are concerned to be a congregation, but one that avoids the stereotypes.

> One such stereotype connects the Christian church with a certain kind of building. Another links it to worship assemblies involving a set pattern of hymns, prayers, rituals and sermons. Still another stereotype associates the Christian church with a particular kind of clergyman leader. The great majority of people, when they see these three things: a "churchy" building, people assembling there for Sunday morning worship and a clergyman leading them, automatically suppose this is a Christian church. It is almost as if Jesus had said, "By *this* shall all men know that you are my disciples, by your buildings, by your worship services, by your clergymen."
>
> But Jesus had little or nothing to say about any of these three most prominent characteristics of the church in our time. He spoke instead of disciples loving one another.[7]

In searching for a life-style lived in radical obedience to the way of love for one another, the members of Reba Place have found that obedience affects most aspects of their lives. They point to four areas in particular: (1) loving obedience affects the choice of a place to live; (2) loving obedience affects one's economic life; (3) loving obedience affects personal relationships; and (4) loving obedience affects personal decision-making.

The members of the Reba community work to overcome the growing tendencies in our society toward urban isolation between persons. To counter this trend they attempt to find housing within the same neighborhood. The desire for Christian community dictates their choice of a place to live rather than letting the decision be made solely on a single family's taste or the dictates of the surrounding culture. The members have a common treasury, not just for their church offerings, but for the common distribution of all their economic assets and earnings. This is, of course, patterned after those earliest Christian communities recorded in the book of Acts.

The community seeks to live in a personal relationship of such openness that they can carry out in a practical way the biblical admonitions to confess to one another and to correct one another in the spirit of truth and love. Such open honesty, they feel, is the only way to create an authentic personal relationship where the group's guilts and judgments can be handled in the health of Christ's love.

And finally, the members feel the need to let the search for community affect their decision-making. They gather weekly to bring to the group those individual and group decisions that are presently confronting them. A number of the members have changed their jobs as an outgrowth of discussions concerning Christian vocations. They changed jobs in an effort to place service above the more worldly motives for job procurement. They regard group decision-making as the way to seek first the will of God—a way to call families out of themselves while supporting them. It is also seen as the way to overcome the tragic feeling of helplessness that overtakes great numbers of isolated family units in our cities today.

> The crucial point is that the individual or the individual family, once nurtured in a stable larger family or community, is making more and more decisions alone, unsupported or unchallenged by any one else. There is no one else. Small wonder that urban life has had to spawn a network of institutional counseling services unknown before. . . . The individual family was never meant to carry the load it is now trying to carry. The small family of mother, father, and children needs a larger supportive context. It thrives best in the give and take of a closely knit community of families. Where this is not present and husband and wife

try to face all the questions and problems of human existence by themselves, they either become more and more frustrated or simply ride with the tide of an ever changing mass opinion. This in part accounts for the breakdown of marriages in our cities, as many sociologists have pointed out. Jesus in his call to love suggests another way.[8]

The other way, to which this group referred and which is becoming attractive to a surprisingly growing number of people today, is the way of acting upon the Lord's claim that those who do the will of God are his family, and thus family to one another.

† **A**nother unique type of religious organization which makes reference to the house church, though casually, is the Ecumenical Institute operating with headquarters in Chicago but seeking to become global in membership and influence. The Institute emphasizes communal living and a high degree of commitment. At the headquarters campus situated in Chicago's West Side ghetto area as well as in their many religious houses scattered in cities around the country, these families pool their financial resources and share many common household chores. This in turn frees a number of the adults to work full-time on their chosen mission while others are employed as school teachers, engineers, nurses, and the like. Salaried workers contribute their pay in its entirety to the common treasury from which the material needs of the whole community are met and the mission work is financed. The missions vary, including work in the black community surrounding the Institute's headquarters. Their primary mission seems to be the spreading of the movement itself through an intricate pattern of training courses. Respondents to these courses may become a part of a cadre, or small group, in a local congregation; move into a nearby "religious house" to become a member of the community's extended teaching arm; or move to the campus headquarters to live and work with the dozens of others who call the Ecumenical Institute home. The espoused purpose of the Ecumenical Institute, which is not organizationally connected to

the World Council of Churches' institute similarly named, is the renewal of the church through the local congregation. The local cadre groups that are established in willing congregations are the means to this renewal, and their strictly taught theological position becomes the content of this renewal.

I attended one of their major seminars held at the Chicago headquarters for a week during the summer of 1970. While moving with the group through their day, which began at 4:30 A.M., I experienced a number of the modified monastic disciplines which provide for their spiritual growth. I was also introduced to two areas in which the term "house church" was used. One reference meant the large mass meetings held early on each Sunday morning where hundreds of persons gathered and went through a worship service unique in its chanting patterns of song and litany. The other reference appeared in one of the dozens of hand-out sheets describing in detail their plans for developing new models for local congregations. Program Unity Tactic 24 was entitled "House Church." It was described as follows: "A tactic pointing to the future form of the local congregation is indicated in the creation of the House Church, pioneering common mission, common study, common symbolic life, and common discipline." Following this introduction, the sheet listed a series of subject heads to be used at some future time in developing this particular model. From these experiences I realized that the teachers of this institute see the house church as a desirable model of congregational life, but one that must await their development of it.

Despite my reservations about the Ecumenical Institute's rather sectarian approach to renewal, I was gratified, nevertheless, by the evidenced enthusiasm and commitment of its members, who are mostly laymen. For in a day when the average congregation assumes that its members are "turned off" by studies weighted in theological doctrines and equally aloof to serious disciplines, the leaders of the Ecumenical Institute have captured the interest and depth commitment of hundreds of young adults with a rigid offering of doctrines and disciplines. For those not fearful of a rather authoritarian approach to faith and discipleship, this approach becomes an amazing example of the scope of mission that can be achieved by a serious dedication of will. It is to their credit that many of these young adults, who have tired of waiting for a challenge from their local congregations back home, count it as gain to leave their own homes to live as a family unit, sharing their financial resources as well as their lives, for the opportunity to make a contribution to the renewal of the universal church. Above all, they stand as further testimony to the institutional church that it has called forth far less from the laity than a great many of them are willing to provide if given a chance to uncover true meaning in the church.

† In a recent interview Dr. Roy Fairchild discussed a new dimension in communal sharing. Many of the seminary students with whom he is acquainted are sharing apartments communally. In this case, the purpose is not primarily for developing meaningful community relationships. These students believe that a person cannot share enough of himself to influence basic values unless he shares his economic life as well. If Christians have a true desire to grow together to the extent of affecting one another's lives, the economic life of each person cannot remain tucked away in its private corner. Dr. Fairchild said, "It is only the sharing of your economic life, whether it is the way you get your bread or the way you dispense it, that really determines your basic value structure. If 'house church' among other things means a grouping that is attempting to shape values, then perhaps there has to be more common life together."[9]

Communal life-styles are not without their own problems and shortcomings. They are not a utopia. In the resurgence of communes across the U.S. there is a great deal of searching through the trial-and-error method. Groups form with a great variety of purposes, living relationships, ethical and governing codes of conduct. At the present time communes are based primarily on the anarchistic, social contract or dictator style. The anarchistic does not appear to last as long and the dictator approach appeals to only a limited number in our society. The social contract structure, which appeals to many and has more consistency within it, calls for a responsible sharing of goal setting and task work. There is need for the church to take note and learn from the intensity with which so many are seeking meaningful community.

If an increase in mutual investment in one another's lives is vital to building true community, then any house church dedicated to share a few hours' discussion will have a limited relationship. The usual role of even the most challenging traditional church today asks us to share only our public selves—that benevolence which is tax-deductible, that extra time which can be freely given to church or civic involvements, that moral conviction which holds one in good standing as a citizen. In contrast to sharing these fringe facets of ourselves, communes have discovered that we grow and are liberated only as we share greater amounts of our private lives. We grow as we share our children's needs for other adult affection; as we share our own need to widen our personal relationships; as we share the dollar we use to buy food, recreation equipment, or even clothing; and as we share those family frustrations generally concealed from public view. This is not to suggest that man can do without a private sphere or that family units do not need their own private time. It does imply that we have wedged an unnecessary divider between our public and private selves. One can readily see why a house church that is meeting in a home only until the planned sanctuary is built or merely as a delightful change of pace in locating church study groups is really no closer to building meaningful community than is the traditional church. When nothing new is shared, nothing more committed, our lives are seldom affected.

We should not expect the average congregation today to be able, much less willing, to suddenly re-form itself into a cluster of communes. But is one expecting too much to assume that a congregation may discover those first signs of community which may evolve into communal life for those who feel so called? Certainly the organized church cannot dictate a plan of this type, although it can be more sensitive to the hunger for belonging evidenced by the recent development of more than eighty thousand communes in this country.

From group support to individual family units to communal life, we hear a common word: that people in today's world desire some form of true community.

The ability and the opportunity to experience a community, a personal belonging relationship, is alien to most persons in the United States. The organized church has followed the path of urbanized family units and has failed to pierce the facade of isolated living. With more than a decade behind us calling for a renewal of the organized church, the typical congregation still reflects that veneer which polishes over the real vibrating spirit and agony of those within. The difficulty perpetuating this glass wall is our fear of exposure. When the church does occasionally experiment in a deeper sharing experience, the fearful cry out against the move with an appeal for a return to the protection of the lacquered liturgies. We resist getting down to earth with one another in true community and are therefore kept from getting down to the Christ who is buried beneath the rubble of our religious routines.

House churches have a remarkable way of making clear, even to the novice, just how pitiful are our normal pretentions at worship, or at prayer, or in compassion toward one another, or in trust, or in our concern for the needs of the world. Through the confrontations inevitable in such an experience, the house church can serve congregations well today by cutting through forms, exposing where we are in community, thus exposing the Lord at the heart of his body.

GROUNDING

† I suppose the question about the real implications inherent in the house church was raised at Trinity in a serious way after the first round of house church communion services. The house churches had been in existence for over a year. Members had become accustomed to the weeknight gatherings. This innovation of communion in the home still came as something of a shock for many. Each Sunday they had been reading in the bulletin the location of the next gathering place for their group. One Sunday, the bulletin varied slightly. There was the usual heading which read, "All those seeking service, honesty, and Christian meaning to their lives are invited Wednesday to any of the following house church groups to share with others so concerned." Following this notice were the customary names and addresses of the homes where they would meet. The new dimension in their house church lives came as casually as the asterisk

which noted an additional comment about the meeting to be held in the home of Mr. and Mrs. Hueston. It said simply: "The Sacrament of Communion will be observed." The Eucharist was to follow soon in the homes of the other elders and later into many more households. Its presence became a *part of* the confrontation of what it means to be the church in the house.

It is one thing to *say* that these groups of approximately a dozen, who slouch in their chairs and kick off their shoes or who now and then gather with sudden formality are the church; it is quite another matter to act on that saying. For the first time the question of what this group really was became acute. It was an unspoken question that was felt by the individuals as they passed hunks of bread to one another around a candlelit dining room table and awkwardly spoke words that said this was the body and blood of Christ who forgives and frees. After that first introduction into several homes of what was clearly a church ritual, the intended significance of the group was becoming apparent. I know because some criticized this act as inappropriate for a home. They were innocently reflecting the time-honored image that "church" could only take place in a sanctuary set apart for that purpose. The fact that even our modified sanctuary where we come together each Sunday is itself a remodeled kitchen, dining room, and living room combined did not seem to alter the point. Others, not necessarily resisting the innovation, simply began to consider more seriously what their own involvement should be. "Now, tell me again just how it is that we are so different from a committee or a task group that happens to meet in a home?" The groups were different by their self-directing ability and their growing involvement toward one another as family. However, most had not seen these subtle changes coming. The theological understanding of their living room meeting was a new dimension.

If the total meaning of a house church was raised conceptually through the introduction of the Sacrament of the Lord's Supper, it was raised as a practical consideration when the house churches began to move toward their respective mission activities. With each new dimension, choices of priority and time allocations had to be made. The groups were faced with those who wanted to spend most of their time on their new-found projects. Others were finding the study of issues and the Christian understanding of their lives too valuable to overlook. Many wanted to meet for mutual fellowship and support, while a few hoped that they would not forget to worship as a group. Therefore the question: "What are the things that should comprise a house church?" was born out of varying desires and experiences. The question has become a living part of the struggles and growing pains at Trinity. This is not to say that most group meetings dwell on their own image or identity. This constant introspection would seem as out of place to them as focusing upon the automobile in which they are traveling instead of experiencing the trip itself.

† To avoid the so-called paralysis of analysis, we have kept the bulk of formal investigations of the meaning of house church limited to the new members' training class in which it is assumed that a "trip" or adventure in a new type of fellowship is being considered. This explorers' class is required for potential members. The class also serves as a personal search and growth experience for any interested persons who desire to participate. It explores the areas of traditional church developments and beliefs, the renewal movement, and the possible role of the house church as a current instrument for that renewal.

It is not feasible to present here an overview of the explorers' class with its great variety of subject matter. However, there is value in experiencing, in condensed form, a mock class which can reveal attitudes, insights, and concepts typical of those found in such explorations. Thus, while the time element and exact conversation are unreal, the following class description is a fairly accurate account of the spirit of an actual group as it wrestles with theological aspects of the house church.

Before the beginning of this class evening, we are able to see Ralph and Chris enter from the crib room of the church house where they have hopefully settled Julie—for at least a part of the meeting time. The family has been involved in the life of Trinity for over six months now and are clearly joining the group as their preparation for membership. In the room, already sitting on the couch are Richard and Nancy, newcomers to town who are out to see what this is all about. They became interested through conversations with some of the waiters at the coffee house. (Nancy and Richard will decide not to become members or to participate in the various house churches as associates.) Across the room in the only other soft chair is Susan, a young college girl who has come as Ginger's guest. Ginger, a teacher at the college, is also present as a member retaking the course for her own additional growth and for companionship to Susan. Mary, Bill, and Juanita complete the list. They will remain involved at various levels of the house churches' activities for awhile, but only Mary will take the step of joining Trinity. Don, teacher of the class, decides the group has been together for enough nights now to venture opening with a prayer.

DON: Lord God, we are grateful for this chance to share together again. We confess our fears and doubts, but ask that you grant to us the experiences that will free us to overcome them. As we search for your will in the midst of our own hectic and often confusing days, show us the opportunities that are before us to know and to make known your presence in this city. Keep us open to new things as we seek to know the fullest meaning in belonging to your body, the church. Open us up to know our own talents and to hear your call to use them. In Jesus' name. Amen.

Since Richard wasn't here last week I'll reiterate our thoughts of that meeting which moved us from talking about renewal in general to the house church contribution in particular. Dick, most of the group felt they knew a bit of what a house church is through their visits to some of them, but we also decided to get the ideas of those who have written on the subject of house churches. Hopefully, this will add to our perspective inasmuch as our brief visits will necessarily give a limited picture of the house church potential.

RICHARD: Well, that will be helpful because I have been to only one house church meeting and that night I couldn't see anything to it. Maybe I'll understand more if we look at what was supposed to happen at least.

MARY: I'm with you, Dick. Sometimes I can't see anything happening and I've been going to these groups off and on for years now.

BILL: Now wait a minute. I can't speak about what they ought to be, and this book you gave to me, Don, about that group in England, doesn't sound like anything I see going on around here, but I will say this: I don't know any other groups like these house churches. I mean, I've been in a number of churches and professional groups, social and issue-oriented, and none of them have had the openness, or frankness, call it what you will—none of them have had the trust that I've seen in these groups I've attended.

DON: OK. It is obvious that we recognize the vast difference between theory and practice. And we will intend to introduce more of what we have seen actually taking place through your house church visits. But our task for the next couple of sessions is to hear what others have said about the meaning of any house church so that such information might become a part of our growth, along with the observations. We don't have to buy it, of course, but it can provide us with greater criteria for comparisons and possibly for the improvement of those experiences now going on here by adding the experiences of house church groups elsewhere.

CHRIS: I think it does help. At least the material you gave to me to read enabled me to see a great deal more in what our house church has been doing all along.

GINGER: How about telling us about those things that helped, Chris, because I think we could all see a lot more actually going on as well as greater possibilities if we really looked at the potential that is there. Is it all right if Chris tells us what helped?

DON: Sure. There's no particular order here. Let's just throw your reactions or comments from your reading into the middle of the group and when anyone wants to react, butt in. Would you like to start us off, Chris?

CHRIS: Well, I had the chapter by Bishop Robinson—you know, the one who wrote *Honest to God*—only this one called *On Being the Church in the World* was written much earlier. Even so it seems up-to-date with what we have been arguing over in our house church. Some of the group think we might just as well do away with studying because it isn't a part of our purpose. Anyway, here are the parts I underlined in his book. He talks about the relation of the parish church to the house church and he sees one as a cell within the other. He says that because of untheological attitudes we make two mistakes in our concept of the house church. Listen:

> The first is to think of the house Church as a purely temporary expedient: a makeshift arrangement characteristic of the earliest Church in Jerusalem or in any other mission area, an organization which serves until the parish Church can be constituted. . . . And the second error is to think of the house Church simply as an evangelistic weapon, a technique for getting at those on the frontier not yet ready to accept the full Christianity of the parish Church. . . .
>
> But both these conceptions are inadequate in the light of the New Testament. For it, the Church in the house is not an *ad hoc* expedient: it is a theologically necessary part of the life of the body.[1]

RALPH: Wait a minute, Chris—when I read that part I couldn't help thinking of all the people I work with. They either think we are nuts, or they think, as he said, that the house church is just a new gimmick to do something different until we attract enough attention to recruit enough people to have a regular church—and do away with these house meetings and get on with building a great big church.

CHRIS: OK, but let me finish. He really says something over here you all can argue about if you want—and somehow I think you might want. Let's see, "I believe that . . ." No, wait. Just before that he is talking about the positive value of house church and he says that most of our parishes today are a collection of individuals or a collection of organizations. They seldom get people together except in sectional groupings by age, interest, or sex. The house church, in contrast, brings them together as the body of Christ and therefore it can legitimately celebrate the Eucharist. Then he says:

> I believe that the theological recovery of this idea of 'the Church in the house' is one of the most important tasks of our

generation. Whereas the organization is an optional extra . . . I believe that the cellular structure of the Church will be rediscovered as a necessity of its life.[2]

MARY: When did he say that?

CHRIS: This was written in 1960.

MARY: Well, to be possibly the most or one of the most important tasks of our generation certainly makes it look like a whole generation is going by ignoring it.

DON: Maybe it's a concept waiting for its time.

MARY: Some idea had better find its time. The way the church is today it will be too late if we wait much longer. Go ahead, Chris, I just wanted us to see that here are some more words with hardly anybody acting on them.

CHRIS: There's a lot more I underlined, but let me move to the part that I think can help us a great deal when we seem to get off the track. He says:

> The house Church, if it is really the whole Church in microcosm, *must* [my italics] reproduce in its life all the 'marks' of catholicity—the Apostles' teaching and fellowship, the breaking of bread, and the prayers.[3]

Of these marks he emphasizes communion as the one we are less familiar with in any unit other than the parish or congregation. And after saying what changes in understanding the celebrating of the Lord's Supper in the house would bring about, he concludes the chapter with a summary. The summary mentions three things in the house "which look to be emerging of permanent significance for the Church as a whole. . . .

"1. The first is a living experience of a *form* of the Church different from that which most people in this country have ever actually known. And it is a form which compels those who find themselves within it to face questions which other levels of Christian living still allow them to evade. . . .

"2. The second thing that is being discovered is the meaning of holiness."[4] And here he brings out the fact that what is holy is being seen as a regular part of our lives and not relegated to a religious place or exercise.

"The third question that is being thrown up is the nature and future of the ministry." Here there is mention of the need for what he calls "a supplemental nonprofessional ministry."[5]

RALPH: Looks like we can soon get rid of the minister, that is in the way we have had him, if this idea catches on.

GINGER: His role may change; in fact, it seems to me that it is already changing quite a bit, but I think there will always be a real need for persons with special training who are able to guide us. Our house church is always running up against some problem question where we need someone professionally trained to turn to—to whom we may turn.

JUANITA: I agree, but I don't think we use ministers properly. "Use" isn't the right word, but you know what I mean.

DON: I agree that the role of the minister is changing and will have to change more—out of sheer necessity if for no other reason, due to the changing and increasing demands, as well as the unwillingness of more and more clergymen to accept the traditional role of a sermon each Sunday and pumping up a reluctant organization the remainder of the time. But the real point of the quote seems to be that the presence of a house church makes obvious a newer and more vital role for laymen as ministers. It eliminates the sharp distinction between clergy and laity and creates, by its nature, more of a team approach.

At this point there is a break for coffee with illustrations of the way "ministry" is being seen and changed in the local house churches. As this idea runs its course, Chris takes advantage of the lull in conversation, upon her return from checking on Julie in the crib room.

CHRIS: There is another point I don't want us to lose before we go on. I think that statement about the house church having all the marks of catholicity is important to remember. Sometimes we tend to get a little "clubbish" or stuck in a rut. To be reminded that we are a little church is to be confronted again with what we are all about. It keeps us from getting small is what I'm trying to say.

RICHARD: But who is to say what that means—all the marks of catholicity? Why can't you call any little group a house church? What difference does a name make?

GINGER: It's not the name that makes so much difference, Richard; it's the ability of the group to meet all of the basic needs for the continuation of a Christian community.

RICHARD: Which are?

GINGER: Well—the ones we have talked about—and here they are spoken of in much the same way in the material I read by Dr. Hans-Ruedi Weber. He said:

> If the house-Church is Church in the full sense of this word, the constituent elements for the house-Church are the same as for the Church in general. There is no universally agreed list of constituent elements of the Church, but the four elements mentioned in Acts 2:42—fellowship, apostolic teaching, prayer and the breaking of the bread—would certainly constitute the bulk of such a list.[6]

I think it is interesting that he didn't limit or specify exactly, and it looks like anyone could have his own understanding of the basic elements.

SUSAN: But is he not saying, Don, that you have to accept as basic for the house church whatever you accept as basic for the church universal—and for the same reasons?

DON: As a matter of fact, the house church has even more reason to insure that all of the basic elements are there. The way I see it, the average congregation fragments the life of the members by putting them in slots that involve only a fraction of these basic elements or experiences. A person can, for example, serve faithfully for years as a church school teacher and never once be in a situation where she is confronted with her own ability to discover what worship is all about as a part of her life. Or another could volunteer to work in most of the projects planned by the congregation and yet never once be confronted with his own beliefs and the source of them. If each part of the church's life is important, then each part is important for every person. We have been so concerned about a well-rounded church organization and program that we have not considered the need for the well-rounded member. The house church, if you stay in one over a period of months, will bring you to a confrontation with all of the basic aspects of meaningful discipleship.

BILL: Is that list of Weber's what we say is basic to being the church?

DON: Would you say our house churches agree with his statement, Ginger?

GINGER: I think we do have all of these elements at times, but we refer to them differently and perhaps add some. I know from our own curriculum that we have pretty well accepted four basic elements as the marks of each house church. They are worship, mission, study, and community, or fellowship. Isn't that right?

DON: Yes, but again you can arrive at those same essential experiences using different breakdowns and approaches. They do help us to keep in mind a total challenge in our house church life. Others might have different ways of arriving at a similar total challenge.

Ginger, since you have shared something from Dr. Weber, did you have any other reactions that we have not touched on?

GINGER: Oh he has a great deal more to say which I think we would do well to look at. Here is a point that has been touched on but I think moves into some real basic stuff. To me it shows how revolutionary a group of house churches could be. He says:

> The house-Church is definitely *not* just another evangelistic weapon, a technique for getting at those who could not be reached otherwise. T. Ralph Morton is right in fighting against the conception of the house-Church as merely "the next step" after visitation-evangelism and evangelistic mass meetings. He writes, "The house-Church represents a first step in finding a new direction for the life of the Church. The danger is that we welcome it as a next step on quite a different journey and dismiss it because it is so slow."[7]

I liked that about the slow part because I sometimes think we can't really see the basic shifts we are making because it seems so slow. Mr. Weber adds: The house-Church is in fact a way of building up a missionary church, a spontaneously evangelistic community.[8] I think he is telling us that this is not just a revision of circle meetings, but that it is a whole new direction for the church today. It fits what we have so often said about reversing directions within the organized church. To me, he definitely places an emphasis on mission and one that comes spontaneously from the people.

BILL: By golly, all of a sudden something has come through loud and clear to me. I don't know if it's what you just said, Ginger, or what we've all been saying, but I see the house church purpose now—instead of getting people into the church through a step in between door knocking and joining up—that it is actually a first step in getting the church going the other way—outside itself, toward the hurts in the world. You know, I haven't believed that really. I've been suspicious from the first that this was merely a different approach to the same old churchy concern to build themselves up and get you tangled up in the machinery.

RICHARD: Bill, you have just helped me a great deal, and I accept what you said. But there seems to me to be a need for something more than reversing the direction, the flow, of the church's energies. If what we are taking to the world is the same understanding of religion we have had, then we're not going to do much for the world once we get there.

DON: That's a good point, Dick, and I think these writers would include a number of new understandings to the faith as well as a new direction for it. They speak, for instance, of the need for the church to rediscover its spontaneity and inner call to act as opposed to the usual adherence to planned emphases set up for the year by the administration. Also they speak of the Eucharist moving out not only in direction away from the church building, but taking into the world a new awareness of the fact that what is holy can be found in the common things with which they deal every day. It is this awareness of the holy in the midst of the common that is new. These thoughts represent just a few of the many radical implications of this concept. The most important fact about this movement, however, is that it is all based upon the essence of the church, so that newness does not leave behind what is vital to the gospel in every age.

GINGER: As a matter of fact, I was just rereading a paragraph where one of these new concerns has caused quite a bit of disagreement around here. Weber says:

> Recent developments in mission and Younger Church areas—especially the group movements in India and elsewhere —have shown us that we must recover this group approach and free our traditional mission work from Western individualism. The same plea is made also by those who stand on the evangelistic frontier of industrial society in the West. The 'house-Church' is an answer to this plea.[9]

This speaks to the need for corporate mission work and yet we still have a great deal of difficulty in thinking in terms other than that all Christian responses to the Word should be carried out on an individual basis.

MARY: I'm glad you brought that in, Ginger, because that is one of the main points emphasized by the writer I was assigned to report on. I agree wholeheartedly with the fact that we should get out of this hang-up that says being a better housewife or worker on the job on Monday morning is the *only* legitimate way a Christian can respond to the needs of society. In this day and age there just isn't any way to meet most of the massive needs through the limited individual approach. We worship as a group; why can't we protest injustice as a group, or help improve housing conditions as a group?

Listen to what my man says about this. I'm reading from an article by a Mr. Virgil Vogt who says:

> What we have sometimes overlooked . . . is that both "hearing" and "doing" are church tasks. These are matters which need to be worked out by the whole congregation, as Christ exercises His lordship through the functioning of various gifts. Members of the body of Christ are dependent upon the Head *and* [italics added] upon one another, for a proper fulfillment of either the "hearing" or the "doing" of God's Word.
> The general tendency has been to neglect "doing" and give the bulk of our attention to "hearing" God's Word. We have built-in provisions for teaching and the proclamation of the Word. The whole church works together to make sure there is a "hearing" of the Word.
> No matter how poor the congregation, if you go there on Sunday morning there will usually be a sermon. No matter how

impoverished the spiritual life of the congregation they usually work *together* [italics added] for a "hearing" of the Word through the Sunday school instruction.

But in contrast to this, we have made little regular provision for the congregation to work together with equal diligence to effect a contemporary response which is worthy, consistent and in rapport with redemptive history. . . . While "hearing" is understood as the task of the whole church, what should happen in respect to "doing" is left almost entirely up to the individual.[10]

NANCY: Would you mind repeating that please?

MARY: He says we need corporate mission also.

NANCY: Oh!

DON: Juanita, you look like you are bursting to come in and say something about now.

JUANITA: Well, I am and then again I'm not. I hate to always be the one to disagree, but you all haven't made me feel unwanted yet so here goes. I just can't see the necessity for all of this talk insisting that everyone in a house church be a part of a team mission. It looks to me like you're forcing a lot of people to either do something they don't want to do, or not be in that house church.

RICHARD: That does begin to sound like my nine-to-five routine, fitting the company mold.

JUANITA: I thought we were trying to get away from putting people into boxes. Why are you so against the good the individual person can do on his own, Don?

DON: Anyone want to speak to that—while I pick myself up off the floor?

BILL: I don't want to speak to the question because I don't agree with Juanita basically here. I'm not sure I know why. It just seems to be an argument that jumps from logic to emotions. But, I do agree with her on wanting to hear why corporate mission work is such an issue.

DON: OK. Let me throw out what this means to me and then see what reactions or ideas this puts into the rest of you. To begin with, the church is a corporate body, the body of Christ. So, corporateness doesn't seem to be a sin to me; it seems to describe the Christian community better than calling it an unrelated coming together of loosely knit individuals. The Holy Spirit was given at Pentecost as a gift of God for the church as a body. The Holy Spirit is not the property of or private tool of even concerned Christians. I feel it is in and through the body that the Holy Spirit, and thus its fruits of love and mercy, work best. I can pray alone, but if I want to grow in my prayer life and be stretched beyond my own present ability, I need the corporate prayer opportunities of the body, the church. For the same reason I feel I can respond in the town as a Christian, as an individual, but I am limited by ability and my own individual maturity as a disciple. Whereas, if I respond in the town with the body, I am able to be stretched beyond my present ability and the task needed to be done is approached with the power of the body, not just of an individual.

But there is one other response that comes quickly to mind about corporate needs for mission. When you look at the traditions of the church you find that we have without question accepted the necessity of a corporate approach to the other three marks of the church about which we were speaking—worship, study, and fellowship. It is obvious to me that the only plausible reason we have for restricting the fourth mark of the Christian's life to an individual basis is simply that it is the most difficult, the most confronting, the most hazardous, and the most likely to create sacrifice and maybe suffering. I guess I see us making arguments against any corporate mission with an appeal to staying closer to the Bible, when in fact we back away because the Bible message has come too close to us already.

At this point the explorers' class went into a lengthy debate over the pros and cons of corporate mission and the meaning of belonging to a given community. After another forty-five minutes the class adjourned until the next Wednesday evening. In addition to the three resources reported on, two other materials that dealt with the understanding of the house church were handed out.

On the following class night everyone was there except Susan, who had to study for an exam the next day. The class was opened with prayer and the teacher began with a summary of the study up to this point.

DON: Tonight we should have ample time to look at a couple of other writers who made reference to the meaning of house church. Because of our lengthy discussion last week on corporateness, let me remind you that we are, at present, simply looking at a number of suggestions on the subject. There is, of course, no authority here other than the experience of the church herself as she tries to act on the biblical understanding of the church for this time and place.

MARY: Have we left those references we looked at last week? There is a great deal there which we haven't begun to touch on.

DON: No, we weren't leaving them; we were hoping to get the gist of all five resources and then compare.

MARY: Well, OK. It's just that my fellow said something that we have been talking around, but he says it to the point and better than you did. Sorry!

DON: That's all right; it's to be expected. Let's hear what you have in mind.

MARY: Well, it's back on this definition idea. I'm beginning to see something here, I think. This Mr. Vogt is writing about the nature of these groups and he specifically says it is important to distinguish between a house church and the current move toward small groups in the church. He isn't knocking small groups, I don't think. He is saying they are short of the mark.

JUANITA: Why does he say that?

MARY: Well, let me read where he says it:

> It is on this point, more than any other, that we need to take issue with the prevailing interest in small groups. Even where these groups are operating within existent churches, the small groups seldom exist as "church" in the full sense. Often when the term "house-church" is used, the emphasis is more on "house" than on "church." . . . In the light of this prevailing

tendency, it is of utmost importance that the small groups we are talking about here be understood as *churches*. And as such they must be distinguished from all the other small groups already existent within our congregations and elsewhere.[11]

RICHARD: So, what's in a name? It's still a dozen people getting together to do what they want.

JUANITA: I agree with you, Dick. I think we're picking at straws now.

MARY: Now, wait a minute. Let me finish. There is a reason for this emphasis:

> Any group which is not a church may be defined as a special interest group, for it lays hold of only one aspect of man's existence. It is only the church which lays hold of all aspects of man's existence.[12]

He continues this point later on when he says:

> —to look for significant and continuing renewal through the work of a special interest group always represents a superficial analysis of the human situation. Only the church as the church is capable of undertaking such a great work as this. . . . Special interest groups tend to overemphasize or underemphasize their particular task, depending upon how faithful they are to the particular mandate upon which they are founded. The church, on the other hand, regardless of how small it is, stands for the whole cause of Christ—the total work.[13]

There! Now that makes sense to me.

BILL: I hate to disagree with Juanita, but I . . . I tend to agree wholeheartedly with what was just said. It's what I was trying to get at last week when I expressed the unique differences I felt in these house churches from my civic club or any former church committees. Here, you don't attend the meetings wearing just one or two of your several "hats" of life. You don't have to put on your business hat, or your pious face, or your benevolent contribution-time appearance. It's simply that you can be present totally, with all of your sides present and able to become a part of the group interaction.

JUANITA: But does the name or the people present do that?

BILL: Obviously the people, but I think the name, with all the self-understanding it can provide, determines a great deal of what the people present accept as a legitimate part of the group's reason for being. There is a difference between small groups and house churches.

This discussion concerning the small group or committee versus the house church continued for another half hour. After a coffee break, Chris left, taking her baby home with instructions for Ralph not to miss anything so he could report to her. At that point, Juanita was reviewing material by Mr. T. Ralph Morton.

JUANITA: And then after Mr. Morton relates the basic human needs that any pattern of church life should meet, he adds that the Western church has lost this ability to meet basic human needs, which have been forsaken for a set of rules and rituals. He seems to be saying to me that we don't start with a form and then see how effective it is; rather, we start with people's needs to be treated as whole persons and then see what form can best do this.

There are two lines I especially liked, and I suspect they are the reason I was given this man to review. They just go along with my nature. Mr. Morton says, "One experiment has attained a name —'The House Church.' This has its dangers. It can be regarded as a technique or patent medicine."[14]

But to be fair, I should read the next line, which adds, "But it has the advantage of suggesting consideration of general principles instead of peculiar circumstances."[15]

To me, his warning is well timed, so that we don't raise up new idols to replace those we are tearing down.

RALPH: It does seem to me, too, that we might be spending too much time talking about the definition of the house church and not enough time on the concerns with which it is supposed to deal, like family changes, racial changes, housing needs, drugs, sex, death, the poor and the rich—you know, the concerns we have.

GINGER: But those *are* the things we deal with in our house church. I don't think we have ever spent much time going through what this class is doing now.

RICHARD: Then why should we?

GINGER: I think it has been said why. If we don't get our self-definition in order, we limit ourselves on what we allow in the group. Also, I've seen us go overboard many times on a single track that didn't allow for all of our needs or didn't keep in balance our growth together with our reaching out to others. Individuals often try to make the group serve their own ends. Being a whole church, even as a small group, keeps us in balance and avoids becoming too narrow.

JUANITA: Just so that by balance you don't mean mediocre or middle of the road, because that sounds too much like where we have seen the church before.

RALPH: I think it is true that you can water down the full implications of the house church. Instead of being an effective reversal of many church patterns it could become just another place to get comfortable.

JUANITA: That's along the lines Mr. Morton said. He speaks here of the need to see its radical nature. Listen: "Unless we recognize the essentially radical nature of 'the House Church,' it will be seen as a possibly useful new device to keep the old pattern going and not as a threat to it."[16]

NANCY: Does this mean that house churches are supposed to threaten the church and therefore be a part of the underground?

RICHARD: It sounds like it.

JUANITA: I'm sure he doesn't mean that, although others might, because he also speaks of the importance of house church being a key part of the institutional church. When he writes about the house church in Scotland in particular, he seems to think our idea of having the elders as leaders in each house church is important, for he says:

> The linking of the "House Church" with the elder's district offers new responsibility to the lay leadership of the Church. It also provides the possibility of the "House Church" developing as an integral part of the organization of the Church and not as a fad, dependent upon a few keen people and likely to last only as long as their enthusiasm.

And the key line is, "No reform in the Church will be effective unless it affects the organization of the Church."[17]

MARY: Does that mean that for change you have to wait for the institution to initiate it? Because I don't think that will ever happen as drastically as it must be done.

DON: That is an essential question, Mary. It means the difference between determining whether or not the church should rise up in new situations on its own by a concerned laity, or whether it must wait for newness from existing organizational structures.

BILL: Well, can it?

DON: Can it what?

BILL: Can it simply rise up, as you say, on its own?

DON: Oh, it has, Bill, in many places. It certainly can. The question is: Should it just exist out there on its own as the true expression of the church or not? Should it somehow find the way to affect the organization of the existing church, as Mr. Morton suggests?

BILL: But that will never happen unless things such as house churches are planned by organizations, and then we're right back to Mary's belief that they will never allow it.

DON: I guess the answer hinges upon whether or not the present or future institutional church will admit that the church can rise up within its own framework as a happening and discover renewed life there, even when the movement in itself seems to be a threat to the religious establishment.

RICHARD: Sort of like putting its blessing on a questionable *ad hoc* group?

DON: I think, rather, that the renewal would depend on the institutional church sensing a stirring around and within itself and knowing that it is Christ's Spirit which has blessed the stirring. The parish church has no business passing judgment on what the Lord of tradition and renewal has approved. What right has the vase which the potter has finished to "allow and to bless" the vase the potter is now molding? Isn't it the potter himself who determines the shape and justification for both?

RALPH: Is this why this congregation has said that whenever two or three feel they have a purpose or calling not being spoken to by any other group, they can begin a new house church?

DON: That's the idea, so that the rise of the church is dependent upon any little group of laymen hearing a call or feeling a need not being met. This freedom should allow spontaneity to be brought into the central organizational life which, in turn, will insure a constant dynamic in the congregation.

NANCY: Now we're getting to the question that Mr. Hoekendijk writes about. In very strong terms he sees the house church as a crossing of the line out of denominational restrictions.

JUANITA: Great! That's what we need. All of this authority around here is stifling.

RALPH: But does that bring about new life in the church, just breaking away from authority? Because if it does, our answer is here. Many churches today, whole denominations, rest on a refusal of any external authority. But I don't see any more signs of renewal in them than in denominations where there are lines of authority.

NANCY: No, I think he is talking about much more than that. And this is what interested me so about this author. He spells out more clearly than the others you have reported on what is really radically new about the house church.

JUANITA: I thought you didn't see anything new or worthwhile in the idea.

NANCY: Well, I'm still not sure how much of it I accept, but I will say this—the more you ponder and learn about it, the more hope you see in it. Anyway, I liked what I think I understood. The whole book is about turning things inside out, and here he seems to be saying that the house church turns inside out what is normal. The abnormal becomes normal.

JUANITA: Now, that kind of group I could fit in with.

NANCY: I'm not so sure. The first abnormalcy, he says, is in the development within house churches of meaningful relationships.

JUANITA: Now see here! I can say that, but when you start in on me, it hurts.

There is a period of time during which this latest personality interaction is aired and clarified.

NANCY: What I was trying to say really speaks to the truth we have just experienced. This desire for a close community where we are so exposed to others is still abnormal in our day. Hoekendijk says, "We cry for the cathedral as 'a palace for undisturbed solitude.'"

This lays the groundwork for his point that the house church "certainly does not fit too well in our time. It does not run along the current trend, but rather counter to it."[18]

The other reversal here refers to what is seen as normal by people as the criteria for the real church. He says that we have kept the parish church—the congregation on the corner—as the norm for so long that we refuse to see any other expression of the Christian fellowship as equally real. He speaks of the typical attitude most churchgoers have toward a mission church or a student church or the church for the military person. They are all seen as temporary until those persons can be returned to the real church again: i.e. the congregation back on the corner.

RALPH: You know, I never thought of it just in that way, but to return to my old saw, that is what those guys at the office think when I tell them we are primarily a mission-oriented house church. They even said to me, "Oh, yeah—like that mission church out on the north side of town which is a branch of the mother church." And I couldn't make them see that by "mission-oriented" we didn't mean we needed the support of a mother figure, or that we would someday grow out of it. And of course when I added that our mission was that coffee house downtown, they gave up talking and walked away.

MARY: That's what I've been meaning! A genuine new concept is almost impossible to get across. Everything and everybody is judged by that same standard of what is normal. And what makes normal equal with what is right?

JUANITA: I'll buy that, but oh, are you in for it with ideas like that.

NANCY: Well, Dr. Hoekendijk says that is the feeling which brings some people to have to declare openly that they are nonconformists and act accordingly. He puts it very emphatically when he says:

> Where the loyal opposition is constantly frustrated and the nonconformists are isolated and ignored, only one road remains open: the crossing of the boundaries. . . . And it is precisely here that the house church comes into view again. . . .[19]

So it seems to me that he sees the house church as outside the denominations entirely, whereas these others have talked about it as an integral part of the congregational life.

GINGER: It depends upon whether it is allowed within the institution, it seems to me. And somehow I think we have been able to put the two together so that we are institutional *and* nonconforming.

RICHARD: How institutional or nonconforming the house churches are that I have been visiting seem to depend upon your own background. To the pillar of the church they might seem a bit radical, but to me there's a lot of traditional thinking going on.

GINGER: I agree, Dick, but I think you have to expect to see a little of renewal *and* tradition if you are trying to function within present denominational lines.

RICHARD: I guess you're right, but you are certainly causing yourself a lot of tension.

MARY: I agree, but I think our fear of tension has been our problem all along. Maybe we're supposed to see the church as always existing out there somewhere halfway between the old and the new. The alternative seems to be to get comfortable in society as it is or start your own new society and forget about those poor slobs that can't see any hope in change. I don't see how we can escape tension if we try to really be the church.

DON: That sounds great, Mary, and it is a good note to end on. At least I think we are now able to see that what determines a house church and where it is placed in the world is extremely varied. But I hope we have also seen that it is very important for each group to think seriously about their own answers to the questions concerning the marks and the stance of a house church in the church and in society.

The class concluded by summarizing characteristics of the house church according to the authors they had studied. Their list follows:

1) House churches are as legitimately the church as parish churches. (As such, they are distinguished from small groups per se.)
2) They have a right and an obligation to bear all the marks of the body of Christ deemed essential for a "whole" church.
3) These marks vary, but usually include fellowship, teaching, and worship through prayer and the sacraments (Acts 2:42).
4) The fourth and overriding mark is that the whole is for the purpose of becoming a spontaneous mission, a serving people of God.
5) The context of the house church is secular, "house" meaning where people live out their basic life-styles. It is holy in elevating the common. It need not be "religious."
6) The house church is the exercise of the ministry of the laity.
7) House churches exist as an integral part of a given denomination or local congregation, or as a part of the underground. Both locations serve to affect normal religious practices and open the way for the renewal of the church.
8) House churches reclaim the corporate body for growth together and mission for others.
9) House churches rise up wherever God's Spirit calls them into being. They are not limited by the definition of normalcy imposed by recent traditions of denominations.

While the above list is not conclusive, it does appear to cover many main concepts of the authors studied.

The class was dismissed to resume its exploration of other current trends and needs within the church.

The preceding explorers' class demonstrates something of the concern for a theological basis for the development of the house church.

To avoid continuing the deadening rules and oppressive restrictions might seem to call for ignoring such weighty matters as studying the marks of the church. In fact, the very opposite is true.

So thoroughly has the traditional church made its impact upon us that nothing short of a total reexamination of the image of the church will free us. There are those who say that to enable the church today to be free, we just have to hang loose and allow it to be. This does not take into account the tremendous hold which the customs of our immediate past have upon the majority. It is one thing to say to a chained prisoner, "Just hang loose." It is another thing to work equally hard in the opposite direction trying to pry him loose with the specifics that tied him there; the same tools that locked him in can very well loosen him.

There is no apology, therefore, for suggesting tools such as these marks as an effort to shift the theological focus and the structural direction of the church in terms as concrete as those that have held it down. Defining its essence does not shackle the church; indeed, it offers foundation stones for its new freedom, so that we are not soon captured by having gone out with only generalities, rather than a new footing as strong as the old.

† For example, there are few churches less bound than Berkeley Free Church, but this church knows that free styles are not enough. They realize the need to prepare themselves theologically for confrontation with society.

With its headquarters in a small house trafficked daily by street people and other dropouts, this ecumenical ministry in California is truly liberated from most forms of traditionalism. Its guerrilla liturgy confronts as it celebrates. It stands on the side of the counterculture in America. Its political defiance has caused Free Church headquarters to be gassed and its minister beaten by the police. Despite its liberated form, this group has a full-time resident theologian on its staff, who can give the full meaning of who Jesus is when asked, "What about this cat Jesus?"

Currently the Berkeley Free Church celebrates in small house church groups and with other communities on special occasions. The hub of their work is the Berkeley Switchboard—a telephone information, referral, and counseling service. They also serve growing numbers of cross-country hitchhikers by providing crash-pads and information on food and lodging. They are quick to confront the traveler by their hospitality sign which reads, "Two nights crashing —the Free Church is not your mother." Because of its counseling of the young, who have discovered here a group they can trust, Free Church is swamped with runaways, drug abusers, those contemplating suicide, and others seeking draft counseling. Berkeley Free Church has become a central clearing house for many liberated churches who wish to minister to these same areas of need. A directory of liberated churches is sent from Free Church to thousands of solicitors.

I asked the minister, Episcopalian Dick York, what they were discovering in the risky work of Free Church. He quickly replied, "Groovy or Gregorian, it doesn't matter if it doesn't get any closer to what the gospel is saying to issues and what we mean to each other."[20] In discussing the many trends toward innovations in worship, he went on to say, "The gospel is still too hard to take for most of us and we can still run away through our use of balloons and group encounter exercises."[21] These were not the utterances of a person turned sour by new forms. On the contrary, balloons and encounter groups would be quite acceptable at Free Church. Instead, he was expressing an awareness that, even with such free form, there is a gospel to be dealt with and discovered in the throbbing humanity they seek to serve.

As their statement of purpose says, "Free Church is an ecumenical community in Berkeley which is . . . working to strengthen and witness to the new thing that is happening: a renewed Church springing up in a thousand forms across the country; calling people out of the city of Babylon, and offering the reality of enlistment into the peaceable army of Jesus. . . ."[22]

The theological awareness which assures men of the presence of the body of Christ also frees them to labor with confidence without as well as within the traditional church as serious followers after the moving Holy Spirit in this age. Otherwise they will feel compelled to play church in a living room or else ignore the body of Christ as an important center in their lives in order to follow their own self-made organization. If such a group can be expected to be earnest in its goals, expectant in its gathering, and daring in its responses, then it must know it is the church—not an arm only, but the whole body.

If gaining confidence for one's tasks is one reason to emphasize the house church's identifying marks, remaining a bit humble is the other. There are those personalities who leap at the opportunity in a small group to set up their own kingdom in order to establish their own self-learned wisdom as the foundation, rock, and cornerstone for their fellowship. When one doesn't see that "great cloud of witnesses," it is easy to forget that we are bound to them by the same Lord and thus answerable to the same command. The house church can move freely and flexibly without much detailed organization, thus overcoming much of the stifling institutional routine, but it should not move without acknowledging that it exists through the power of God's act in Jesus Christ, thus creating a community which in its freedom is "bound" to live in the sign of the reign of God's kingdom.

REACHING

† **A** restless concern to reach out beyond the groups began in the second year of house church life at Trinity. Whereas those earlier moves toward developing into a real community were almost imperceptible, a growing interest for a common task was *overtly* expressed by a majority of house church members by fall of 1964. When new members and curious visitors, inquiring about life in these weekly home gatherings, made a comment such as, "The meeting was fine, but is sharing and studying all you do?" the common response was, "Well, yes, for right now. But we are searching for a mission that we can do together." It could have been otherwise. The answer could very well have been, "Well, yes, what else would you expect?" But, by now most members in house churches *expected* to be on a mission. The exact nature of their various activities was not immediately apparent, and members were to spend many uncer-

tain months wondering if they could ever hear a common call to mission. Thus the fact that they accepted as realistic the *principle* that they existed for the sake of a mission became the open door for that possibility to take place.

This assumed missionary stance came about as a result of several years of struggling and searching. The call came to Trinity via the church officers and through the preached word. The call came to them through their own background and through new visitors. The brochure "What Is God Saying to His Church?" played no small part in maintaining this emphasis upon reaching out. This statement, on pages 18–20, was that single effort by the session making public and specific a concern for a missionary approach to congregational life. We said more than we knew in that brochure, which has remained a healthy reminder of original goals.

Still other influences set the stage for our civic concern. For example, many of the members had come to Trinity concerned with social issues. The efforts of the congregational leadership to face such issues seriously enabled Trinity to see that worldly concerns must be the subject of their coming together. This recognition wasn't true for all, but such concerns were sufficiently present to keep each house church from being able to ignore community issues for long.

One of the first issues with which we grappled was race relations. Being an all-white congregation in the days before the Black Power movement questioned the value of integrating "white" churches, we invited several black ministers to lead the service of worship. At the same time individual members attempted to increase our contacts with members of the black community by visits to churches and homes as well as by participating in those community causes that sought to improve relations between the races. These attempts were minor in scope and tame in courage when compared with the stands taken by congregations elsewhere. Minor though they were, they began to cause rumors around town that Trinity was becoming known as that church "hell-bent" on integration. The emphasis was significant enough to open the eyes of several of our families to the call to "serve the Lord" elsewhere and also significant enough to cause a noticeable drop in the number of interested visitors. The actuality of our first integrated house church was years away, but this experience demonstrates that the public display of the desire of the heart to overcome racial barriers can become as great an affront to the citizenry as the ability to act decisively in these areas. In other words, it did not seem to be our progress that became an offense to so many since the progress was infinitesimal, but merely the direction we faced and the concerns we declared.

Since those initial steps toward a biracial ministry, we have remained aware of a continuing polite but constant exclusion from much of the community of a handful of our laymen who too overtly declare their concern for the black man. A number of the members have had to battle the social dictates of our small city. They have chosen to live under that constant pressure that only "small town U.S.A." can so effectively exert, but they have been able to hold their positions and risk their incomes because of their faith and the support felt within their congregation and house church family. Consequently, in this issue of racial concerns and in similar ways, the congregation was kept aware of their orientation toward the world outside the church house. But the actual sign of a congregation, the *laos,* making that all important outward shift in their corporate life appeared in small ways—ways that emerged occasionally within weekly house church gatherings.

In the monthly church paper, *The Nous,* an item appeared in April 1964, which read, "The Palmer House Church is placing a box on the library table for used greeting cards of any kind . . . to be used for people in Korea."[1] Food packages were also to be sent. Soon the specified table was overflowing with greeting cards creating a response far beyond the desire or intent of the house church. For weeks the congregation, on gathering at the church house, watched as the table piled high with birthday wishes from Aunt Sarah, Valentine cards from Susan to Frank, Easter greetings, get-well wishes, and of course scores of Christmas cards. Few members had any understanding of the purpose of these cards. The incident served mainly to point out the growing awareness that house churches desired to *do* something together that might fall within the broad category of mission. Their flood-like response to that simple and questionable mission was only a prelude to a tremendous outpouring of excitement released when a way opened for house churches to begin working on their respective outreach projects.

The pattern of growth within each house church was so amazingly similar that most house churches suggested mission possibilities simultaneously. By late summer of 1964 we were aware that there were, in fact, too many different options within each group ever to move out in a common thrust. Fortunately, these internal differences were not considered signs of weakness or division but a signal of a need to restructure the house church composition according to newly expressed areas of interest. Therefore, in October of that year the entire congregation gathered at the church house where a regrouping was proposed along lines of interest previously suggested. There was some early concern by a few as they looked to see *who* was changing to a new group but soon *what* these new groupings offered took precedence over the tendency to form cliques.

The new interest groups were formed temporarily to determine the potential for any serious ministry they might plan. Five categories of interest had been singled out as representative of possible projects to be developed. Surprisingly, the shuffling of members that evening brought about a reasonable redistribution of members in house churches. The evening's experiment was successful. That night the session had confirmed their belief that the house churches were ready for new experiences. They acted accordingly, beginning with a plan which asked the original family-oriented house churches to give up meeting on the second and fourth weeks to allow the new interest-oriented groups to discover their potential for mission.

After the restructuring, it took no expert to see immediately that the task-oriented groups were creating far more interest and excitement than the family-oriented house churches were maintaining. Soon expressions such as the following could be heard in the new interest groups, "We've only begun to cover the many plans scheduled for possible action tonight and it will be two weeks before we can meet together again. Why should we wait two weeks just to maintain our other house church? My former house church prepared me to find my mission but this is my group now and I just can't see belonging to two."

So it was that gradually, then suddenly, the growth together in community wasn't enough. The challenge to reach out beyond the groups became paramount. In less than six months from the launching of temporary interest groups, all of the older structures had given way to the contagious enthusiasm of the task groups. Without the need for any coordinating by the session this time, structures at Trinity evolved so that a new set of house churches replaced the old. They met weekly, keeping any family orientation and fellowship desired, but their single overriding purpose was now the mission.

Intense searching began. Some groups visited other churches to observe their ministry in the city. A number of carloads traveled to the Church of the Saviour in Washington, D.C., where they were introduced to a variety of urban ministries. Other groups asked representatives of the helping agencies in our city to attend their week-night house church meetings to acquaint them with existing services and areas of need.

Many months of excitement and disappointment followed as some concerns were sharpened into concrete planning and others were regretfully put aside as impossible for the moment. Disagreements, concern over dreams being too large or too small, eagerness to advance the pace of the work, and the inconsistency of commitment—all this and more made it abundantly clear that the call to mission is the most demanding yet exhilarating response a church can make to its life under the gospel.

The problems seemed to build faster than any possible move toward their solution. Then finally: "The session will come to order. Gentlemen, after the reading of the minutes the first item on the docket for tonight is to hear the request of the Coffee House House Church concerning their proposed mission." Members involved were invited in. With jovial talk they sat in the spaces provided in the circle of folding chairs interspersed among members of the session. There was excitement and apprehension in the air. Some of the associate members of the house church had been particularly upset and not a little shocked when the session had returned their request to them for further study a month before.[2] Their pastoral leader, a member of the session, had assured them that the delay was an effort to press them to think in more detail about some hard problems of staffing and financing. The procedure was not an effort to block their plans; but to those who had joined a house church for the freedom it offered, this action seemed a sudden jolt back into the "system" bottleneck against which they were rebelling. The fact that the opening of a coffee house would require interest, help, and financial support of other members of the church helped them acquiesce to the legal procedures necessary to achieve their goal. On this second attempt the coordinator responsible for spearheading the mission of the house church was abundantly prepared with answers to detailed questions. Where no answers were possible there was a firm challenge that we take the risk of failing. "Yes, we now have a fairly exact count of those committing themselves to work in the coffee house. Yes, we have decided on a night and the hours. Yes, we have gone through all of the legal procedures to become a licensed restaurant. No, there is no way of knowing at this time who will come or why. No, we know of no other examples where a coffee house has functioned in a city as small as ours. Yes, three thousand dollars is a lot to ask this congregation to borrow for a mission with no guarantees that it will 'succeed.' Yes, we do intend to require training for the coffee house workers."

The vote was taken, the congregational meeting called, and the house church that had been searching for a year now was commissioned to move onto Market Street in downtown Harrisonburg to develop a ministry through a coffee house. It would be called *The Marketplace,* a name chosen from those submitted by the entire congregation. It opened with standing room only, after six months of frenzied activity. To this day its ministry remains one of Trinity's most challenging and rewarding.

"The session will come to order. Gentlemen, after the reading of the minutes, the first item on the docket will be to entertain the request of the Clothes Closet House Church to be permitted to establish a used clothing outlet in the upstairs back room of our church house building—the purpose of said outlet to become a base of contact for a ministry to the impoverished."

"The session will come to order. Gentlemen, after the reading of the minutes, the first item on the docket tonight will be to hear the request of the Religious Drama House Church to be permitted to enter into a season of summer drama with members of the Lakeview Playhouse and to be funded sufficiently to carry their share of the financial burden."

"The session will come to order. *Ladies* and gentlemen of the session, after the reading of the minutes we will hear a request from the Community Service House Church to begin the operation of a summer day camp for retarded children."

Thus, in our third year now with mission-oriented house churches, the official board of the congregation learned well what a grass roots movement was all about. They experienced the reversal of the institution's usual flow from the top down and felt the full effect of a fresh new spirit that welled upward, challenging those in authority to yield to those with a vision.

Changes came more slowly after that first shift toward missions. Excitement gave way to the necessary commitment for the long haul. Most projects of those earlier years have been sustained. The purpose of existing missions is evaluated periodically but to date few have felt compelled to close down. The coffee house has had its seventh birthday and has for some time now been opening twice a week with calls for more nights if more volunteers come forward to staff it. A Sunday worship service conducted informally around the tables and developed very loosely according to its secular environment brought an additional outreach through the coffee house for several years. *The Marketplace* has also become the place where community issues are aired and groups such as the local council on human relations meet.

The retarded youth who have attended six summers of day camp can now be found in a year-round weekday program which provides for those beyond the age of public education and unable to enter into state-sponsored programs for the retarded or handicapped.

The Clothes Closet has entered into the struggles of more families than they could keep up with. The shop still opens faithfully every Saturday morning for any and all who will come to be outfitted, to talk, and to see if someone can help them at any one of the many entry points of their unending cycle of poverty problems.

Although most have displayed remarkable staying power, some house churches have lived out their apparent usefulness and no longer exist.

In the fall of 1968 a new house church was formed as a result of the growing awareness of some that there was no mission specifically addressing itself to social action, especially in the area of race relations. This group, consisting mostly of black Methodists and black and white Presbyterians, found its way slowly, realizing that a part of its mission was simply the ability to grow in full trust of one another. We said, only half facetiously, that being a mixed group of Methodists and Presbyterians was perhaps as great a challenge as being black and white. Yet even though they ran into a great many barriers to open housing, equal opportunity in employment, and social involvements, this tiny group continued to press, probe, and make its presence felt in a number of civic agencies. Through a lack of any precise mission opportunity, this house church has disbanded. Most of the members maintain a strong concern for work with the white problem in race relations so that a new group could form quickly given a new opportunity for a concrete mission.

For over five years one house church found excitement and challenge in a ministry through religious drama. Their weekly gatherings were more spontaneous than planned as they let the reading of plays lead them into moods and concerns for the evening. Sprawled across the floor or bunched under several table lamps, the members would read a play aloud. Such occasions brought frequent collapses into laughter or sudden high emotional involvement in the story being read. Now and then a play would be selected for production. When they were prepared, the group would present their story and engage in dialogue with the audience afterward concerning its meaning. Such dramas witnessed to an identification with mankind's many dilemmas. They were performed in our coffee house, retreat centers, and in neighboring churches.

In the fall of 1971 this group chose not to issue a call to this type of ministry for the following year. This meant that they decided to let their particular identity as a house church die. Later most of the members were a part of newly forming groups being called to quite different directions.

A major evaluation in the fall of 1971 led to the creation of two new house church groups with totally different emphases. Our house churches are created by the "calling" or expressed concern of any participant at Trinity to a particular mission, direction, or life-style. If enough others respond to such a call, a group is begun. They explore the possibilities of such a mission or community style, while examining their own willingness to become a house church. During the September 1971 evaluation time one member issued a call for a house church ministry to the internationals in our area. A participant in our fellowship, who is not a member, was responsible for issuing another call that began a house church ministry to a small prison nearby. These new house churches have revealed areas of critical need and have made a definite impact upon the total life of the congregation. Again, we are realizing how our total community awareness may shift in response to directions set by the inner call of one or two. It is only another example of the possibilities for the church once it is able to move quickly in different directions through the rise of flexible house churches.

It can now be seen that despite their many inadequacies, house churches have displayed a remarkable ability not just to remain in existence but to confront those points of life that promise meaning. This condition can seldom be observed in any one gathering or a month of meetings. It is discerned instead by the growth and changes that come over the years.

† The move outward through these mission-oriented house churches has brought us to a closer look at the meaning of _commitment_. It is one thing to speak of Christian commitment in general and quite another to determine how many workers will actually appear to "open the store" on bad days as well as on good ones. Each house church, out of its own unique ambitions, was forced to face squarely the meaning of group commitment. This was particularly difficult

when so much of the emphasis in developing house churches was directed away from regimentation toward a more spontaneous movement.

Commitment meant different things to different house churches. For some groups, commitment involved making out a schedule to see who would sign up for a turn at his particular task. This was the situation with the members of the Clothes Closet House Church, as their primary desire for discipline was to open their store to give clothing to the poor. Coffee House members had a desire for something a bit more all-encompassing. They actually came to a point where a commitment list had been drafted and a retreat planned to review it and begin the disciplines enumerated. The retreat did not accomplish its purpose; the disciplines became a source of tension, disagreement, and disappointment. The reason is that not all members had looked upon the purpose of discipline in the same light. There were those members who had been greatly influenced by the spiritual maturity and apparent closeness of other small groups they had visited and who felt that corporate discipline was the way to achieve this level of community. Others in the Coffee House Church were quite willing to work but not to take on what appeared to them to be discipline for discipline's sake. Underlying these differences one could detect a thirst for deep meaningful relations among those involved in a corporate task. This thirst, however, was accompanied by a lack of knowing how to bring such meaning about. Those who did not feel the need for deeper relations but desired to participate in the activity would of course not see the purpose of the efforts within such disciplines. A determination to sign up for certain nights per month at the coffee house was the only commitment attained—a disappointing compromise for many.

We have had other outstanding failures in searching for the most effective approach to a disciplined life. The session once adopted a paper calling for a commitment from every member of Trinity to attend worship services and their weekly house church meetings faithfully. This challenge was presented to new members through the explorers' class and distributed to all present members during several services of worship. Also, on two separate occasions a suggested checklist of possible disciplines was given the membership to use during the Lenten season. These disciplines were accepted graciously as nice things but few took them seriously.

Although a meaningful approach to the proper use of discipline has remained elusive, its need is seen time and time again. It seems that disciplines are hard to live with but more difficult to live without. We have known this from experiencing the agony and disappointment which exudes from a house church when no common specific discipline can be agreed upon. When a member says through spotty attendance that the mission means only so much, it is understandable that the group feels let down because caring about the mission communicates concern for each other. A minimum commitment decided upon by the group would clarify their expectations, thus unifying their purpose and concentrating the energy required to carry on the task. The house churches that have been able to make clear some unifying commitment are consistently more healthy. Those house churches that never wish to face such possibilities of specific commitments are forever struggling to discover why they cannot fulfill their own desires and expectations within the group.

The degree to which we have experienced any satisfactory response to this necessity of a disciplined corporate life has come from two factors. Commitment has been possible in Trinity's house churches when its purpose has been to accomplish a task rather than a mere exercise in group discipline. Secondly, commitment has been possible when its direction has been proposed by the grass roots members and devoid of any hints of being imposed.

Of course, there is also that beautiful commitment which occurs when no one is noticing. This seems to appear spontaneously when the sheer joy of the occasion sparks such an enthusiasm for the task that no one is asking how long it will take or when we must return. We have seen how commitment and joy go hand in hand. Observers have asked how it is that so many members, especially the teen-agers, are willing to devote so much of their summer to the day camp for the retarded. The only effective way to answer is to invite them to the camp itself, invite them to see joy in the faces of the retarded and the eagerness on the part of the helpers to make each day meaningful. Only then is it understood how the thrill of such a ministry takes care of the necessary demands of long hours, hot sun, rearranged schedules, and personality conflicts. We have seen how love insures the essence of the law; it does not replace it. In the same way, joy insures the disciplines necessary to do a task. Joy does not lessen the difficulty of carrying out the task.

† **A** number of Christian communities developing across the nation emphasize commitment in discipleship with a high expectation of performance from their members. One of these which I visited is the Sycamore Community in Kansas City, Missouri. It does not use the name house church but is nonetheless related to the concept. Sycamore Community is developing without a direct relation to any denomination and can therefore be called either ecumenical or underground depending upon their stance at the given moment. This small group was begun through the efforts of a layman, Mr. Don Campbell, who has been strongly influenced by the Church of the Saviour in Washington, D.C. Sycamore's beginning emphases are similar to those of the Church of the Saviour. Since a small group met to discuss the possibility of such a church emerging in Kansas City in 1968, preparation has been extensive while numerical growth remains consistently small. At present, there are only two full members, called journeymen. Not more than a dozen others are attending the weeknight meetings as potential apprentices.

In order to ensure sufficient training, an apprenticeship consists of at least a year of study, with the added requirement that an apprentice give evidence that he has attained personal growth as well as involvement in a corporate mission during this training period. Those who take the class which is designed to introduce a person to possible apprenticeship are expected to declare that they see nothing which could prevent them from becoming apprentices at the end of this course if they felt so called. In what may seem strange language to many, I was told that the class is limited to those with such a commitment "so that it may grow." Obviously the reference to growth means only one thing: depth in one's personal commitment.

Sycamore members will follow the same six points of commitment outlined for members of the Church of the Saviour. These are printed on wallet-sized cards by the Church of the Saviour for use by their members.

We covenant with Christ and one another to—
Meet God daily in a set time of prayer.
Let God confront us daily through the Scriptures.
Worship weekly—normally with our Church.
Be a vital contributing member of one of the confirmed groups, normally on corporate mission.
Grow in love for the brotherhood and all people, remembering the command, "Love one another as I have loved you."
Give proportionately, beginning at a tithe of our incomes.
Confess and ask the help of our fellowship should we fail in these expressions of devotion. We agree that continual failure on the part of any member will call for the restoring love of the whole Church.[3]

This group considers itself a full-fledged church with only two members and fewer than a dozen prospects. Yet their willingness to go slowly and remain small reflects the attitude of much of the renewal movement today as it turns away from those success marks of the world in an effort to recover a depth of commitment more consistent with the calling of the Christ. Although the members are temporarily working at a mission together by assisting other concerned groups in the city, they intend to develop missions of their own once the group is large enough and the proper use of the members' "gifts" or talents is determined.

On the evening I attended their love feast, I was escorted to a basement room in a residential home. There were approximately a dozen people present who could all fit into a stretched definition of young adults. I was impressed by the simplicity of the entire evening from the manner of dress to the expressions given to Eucharistic words. Everyone was made to feel at home. Yet one could not escape the awareness that here was a table where the quest for discipleship was being taken earnestly. It was that type of meeting which would make a person feel tremendously at home through the obvious unity and brotherhood of Christ's Spirit, or it could make one feel he had stepped in over his head if he had come with any casual thoughts about the meaning of Christian living.

The evening began with casual conversation and a simple meal of cheese, bread, and fruit. Members inquired genuinely about the well-being of one another during the preceding week. The meeting became orderly as Judy, who was sitting at one end of the long table, shared the reading of Scripture. Another read from Francis Thompson's "The Hound of Heaven" and discussion began on the readings. Later, following a prayer, each member of the group was given an opportunity to place an object of his own onto the table as a gift which symbolized some meaningful aspect of his life during the week. Communion simply consisted of passing the bread with each person expressing his own thoughts to the next person about the meaning of Christ's presence between them. After the wine had been similarly passed, prayers of petition were said with names of individuals tossed out at random from one end of the table to the other as such names entered into the thoughts of someone praying. No details were heard—just the staccato jabs of names now and then breaking into the stillness: ". . . for Frank . . . for Bertha . . . for Sam and his daughter . . ." until all joined together in the Lord's Prayer. Songs were sung, such as "Blowing in the Wind" and "They Will Know We Are Christians by Our Love," and the evening's worship was over.

When we left, the potential members prepared to move into an intense study session that was not open to visitors. The explanation was that the depth of sharing was such that it had become necessary to limit the study opportunity to those willing to make a commitment to the group, thus ensuring trust, frankness, and a meaningful search within the group.

As we who were visitors left, I could not help thinking back on the attitudes I had heard expressed so often from within the institutional church about such "break-away" groups. How frequently it is implied that such groups have left the organized church and have gone underground because they have drifted away from the true faith or seek a new license for immorality. Nothing could be farther from the truth. What if the elements of the Lord's Supper were unconventional and the bread was not diced? Or what does it matter if the leader who pronounced the words calling us to eat and drink in Christ's name was a laywoman? By their sincerity and commitment to Christ such groups make it clear that the institutional church has no corner on the market for the presence of the visible body of Christ.

It was that kind of evening when you knew that you were experiencing a moment which would extend into your own future. Some of the faces are forgotten, but some will never be. I left feeling not so much drawn to any particular method, style, or resource for my notebook as much as refreshed again by the same open, searching community I had left weeks before. The warm, free welcome indicated a spirit that bound Sycamore Community to the house churches I knew back home.

† If the vision of the Sycamore Community in Kansas City reflects spring love, the house church in Richmond, California conveys the impression of a mature marriage that has survived many winters. The Metropolitan Christian Mission, as this house church is called, had its origin in 1961. As members told me about their development, a confirming nod by one member to the other not only kept the story straight, it revealed how thoroughly they were bound in this experience as partners whose inner lives had been shared along the years. This depth of relationship does not come with age, for these are young adults. Their maturity as a house church is derived from the intensity of their commitment.

Assembled around the Reverend Josh Wilson, minister in the Disciples of Christ denomination, the first members were influenced from many directions. Emil Brunner's contacts with the non-church movement in Japan had intrigued them. Also, they, like so many others, had gone on a pilgrimage to the Washington, D.C. Church of the Saviour where they had spent days conversing with members and the minister, Gordon Cosby. Then they heard of a house church in New Jersey and sought out its members in hopes of broadening their vision of their own possibilities.

Josh Wilson said of this New Jersey group, "My evaluation

from one contact was that they were really on a live road towards the creative stand of the house church. They were regularly celebrating the Eucharist."[4]

As the visitor from the West Coast recalled, they were invited to a quickly put together potluck dinner. "There were about twenty or twenty-five members of this congregation. We gathered around the table and, I guess, the senior in the congregation at this point was a woman elder, who took the bread as we all stood around the table, broke it, and passed the loaf around. And wow! Just zap—we were off like this. It was like firing an Atlas missile to the moon."[5]

At the retelling of this early experience the California group relived the excitement of that event a decade ago when they had contacted a type of Christian life for which they had been searching.

Since those early days, this small house church has maintained weekly meetings, often on Wednesday mornings befitting the shift-work schedule of the men. A six-month intensive training period for new members begins only after present members have been in a special "mission posture" to a candidate for months or years. The house church is intentionally exclusive, for they believe in a servant role and a mutual encounter that requires a high commitment from each member. They feel this is necessary at a time when the church has again become a minority cult in society.

A typical mid-week meeting of the house church might center on an encounter with one person's situation and this concern might last for weeks. Or, an evening might move into several areas of concern with confessions, confrontations, and simple sharing of where they are in their ministry into the world. While communion is celebrated frequently, the group confessed that they would be uncomfortable with a regularly used study book.

Their mission is to take seriously the servant potential of each member, strengthening him in the gifts and tasks that are his. They do not carry on a corporate project as such. While in the early days their membership zoomed to eighteen, it has now leveled off in the neighborhood of a dozen. They stand firm in the conviction that they are as fully a church as other congregations within the Disciples of Christ denomination and have equal voting rights within the higher judicatories.

One outgrowth of the Metro Mission group has been the development and rise of a nonprofit enterprise called Eskaton, whose major areas are housing, health care, and education. Organized only six years ago by clergy and laymen, mostly members of this one house church, the corporation handles a ten-million dollar budget that includes four hospitals, two low-cost housing projects, and an educational-medical facility in Baja California, Mexico. The group attempts to mix the savvy of private enterprise, the resources of the federal government, and the Christian community's concern for all men. Their work draws nationwide attention and transforms the benefits actually received by needy people for whom the entire work is undertaken.

When I asked what has sustained their small house church over so long a time, the group slowly and deliberately listed three reasons. First, they stay together to abide by the covenant they took after a year's training. "We want to be a covenanting community," they said. Secondly, the group is unashamedly Christian in a very secular culture and they willingly undergo self-examination in light of the gospel. And thirdly, they each stay because their comrades are putting their whole lives into whatever they believe and whatever issues concern them.

When our evening discussion was over, everyone rose to form a circle. Without set form or fanfare, bread and wine was passed while expressions of Christ-centered love were shared, and wow—just zap—we were all off and running again.

† **A** realistic ministry of the laity has been developed through our house churches at Trinity. With their catalytic thrust of members into the lives of others by participating in the corporate missions, the house churches have enabled us to see the lay ministry at work in most meaningful ways. I have been privileged to hear of and to observe a greater amount of priestly care on the part of house church members than I dreamed possible. This, too, has changed the role of the clergyman in their midst so that he is called upon to

suggest resources, offer guidelines, or just share the concerns involving a layman's ministry rather than asking a layman to offer some assistance in a problem area which he is personally confronting. In other words, increasingly, when a member comes to the pastor's study and says, "I have a friend who has a problem," he means it.

Out of the contacts made through the Clothes Closet and the personalized services offered, there have come challenges to a lay ministry that have continued for years. A number of poor families have found to their surprise that the ladies who help them find suitable clothing are also willing to get involved in the rest of their home problems if the impoverished so desire it. The house church members not only dispense clothing, they go with it into the homes from time to time. One of our members, a schoolteacher, has become prophet and priest in the life of a particular family whose problems seem unending and center on the lack of husbandly support. Her lay ministry has extended from staying overnight with the children when the father was hospitalized to assisting the wife in placing him in jail until conditions could be improved at home. The strength this home has received has been graciously accepted even by the man of the house. After all, he has received employment through the initiative of this house church more than once, which ought to offset the fact that some members were involved in having him jailed. But in a more serious vein he *has* learned that their part in landing him in jail developed from the concern that the house church felt for him and his family.

Many examples of this ministry of the laity come from the mission of the coffee house. Through the long evenings when the crowds have slimmed down and the entertainers have put away their instruments, one can see this personal ministry at work by candlelight. On numerous occasions, glancing over to a corner table and observing her husband Jim sitting with a young boy, Emily has known to prepare herself for another series of long evening discussions or at least a strange new guest for dinner. She has learned to read quickly the signs of a father-son relationship developing as another boy, whose home is just a place to stay away from as much as possible, discovers his own worth upheld through what is to him the amazing companionship of this coffee house waiter.

In fact, once when Jim's easy openness to one and all caught the devotion of a teen-ager passing through, it led to a ministry of concern that involved people from California to New York City. The young man had left his anxious parents in California and was traveling across the country sleeping in his compact car. Somewhere along the road he had written them about meeting a man at a coffee house in Virginia. He gave Jim's name and address. This brief reference became the important link in a widening chain followed by the father as he later sought to track down his son to tell him of his mother's serious hospitalization. Through Jim they were able to learn of his next destination in New York and from that clue finally got word to him. These incidents are obviously small ones. Multiplied by the number of others who, by virtue of house church concerns, are given freedom to be involved in people's lives where they live, this reveals a real grass roots ministry—a ministry that we usually hear discussed only as the subject of yet another Sunday school class.

† The house church missionary stance requires a new awareness of what is deemed holy. Provost E. W. Southcott, whose book on the development of house churches in his parish in Halton, Leeds, London, speaks of the new movement of the church in the house. In an ecumenical meeting of about twenty-five persons interested in or working with house churches, which was held in Atlanta, Georgia in the fall of 1969, Provost Southcott had this to say about the subject of holiness:

> I think fundamentally that if I was pushed I would say that really one is asking what they mean by the word holy today. Where is the house of God? Where is the gate of heaven? Old Jacob did not find it in a church building primarily and I believe that the house of God, the gate of heaven, is wherever man is finding justice, truth, compassion, love, and concern, and there is no such thing as *Christian* truth, or *Christian* justice, or *Christian* compassion—there is just compassion, truth, mercy, and justice, and God can put his own tags on these things.[6]

Indeed a primary purpose of the house church through its outward thrust is the rediscovery of the location of what is holy. When Jesus' death was seen as the act that tore open the veil concealing the holy of holies in the temple, it was to reveal God's holiness in the midst of the everyday world, where it was observable by every man, woman, and child. The true religious act removes the brackets around God, unveiling his presence in the midst of Local #406 as well as tossing aside the strictly religious finery that has been used to lure man to keep God hidden behind our modern holy of holies. Indeed, there is no "religious" life that exists apart from a secular life. There is just life, period. And this life, out where man thinks he is frantically alone in his search, is where Christ said he would be and this life is what he said he would make abundant. The issues of our day that deny to man abundant life *where he is* become the only true religious issues we have. These issues—hunger, war, race, power—these things that dehumanize a man and make him a slave to that over which he was created to have dominion, is what the gospel is all about. As Provost Southcott once said, "The secular is the only thing that really exists . . . We have to elevate the sewer, we have to uplift politics, we have to uplift justice towards the have-nots rather than the haves."[7] This does not deny an inner awareness of the soul, for that is also a part of man's secular life. A person doesn't have to be religious to know the desire and difficulty of being put all together. He knows there is an inner dimension; he just doesn't believe the institutional church can show him how to tap it, and he is right too much of the time. His hope lies in the fact that he doesn't have to go to the temple to discover life; his God has made it clear that he *dwells* equally on Times Square.

The task of raising up signs of the Holy Spirit outside the narrow confines of religious institutions and within the marketplaces is a major purpose of the house church. In all house churches at Trinity, there is one constant expectation: that their ministry shall find them in the world, in a servant relationship. They are challenged to see the holiness of God's presence in that secular setting.

This new sphere of the holy is one way to begin differentiating between honest house churches and churches that happen to meet in a house. The house church is not "churchy" even though it draws the Christian community more and more into maturity of the faith in which becoming a loving human is increasingly understood. The house church is not evangelistic either in the traditional use of that word: that is, its aim is not primarily recruiting. It is, however, more evangelistic in that it enables a company of people to declare by secular terms and actions the good news that their Lord is still about his business in the midst of the school, factory, field, and business world.

† The words of renewal have been with the institutional church for quite some time whereas any real shift in congregational life remains, for the most part, indiscernable. The house church has been singled out as one real potential by which the institutional church may structure itself in keeping with its new-found direction and oft-repeated call to shift directions and face outward on mission. Any true renewal must be able to affect the core of congregational life to give validity to the existence of the people of God in a secular setting. The house church creates that possibility.

This concern for a structure to free the church for mission has been amply reflected in numerous writings from various departments within the World Council of Churches over the past fifteen years. The Department of the Laity in the World Council focused upon the house church in its spring edition of the periodical *Laity* in 1957. Much of what Mr. Hans-Ruedi Weber had to say there has been related earlier. The following remark speaks even more clearly concerning the potential within the house church.

> "He who has an ear, let him hear what the Spirit says to the Churches." This exhortation of St. John addresses not only the seven churches mentioned in the Book of Revelation but all the Churches at every time and place.
>
> What is the Spirit saying to the churches today? Some are convinced that one of the most important lessons of the Spirit today is the development of house-Churches and in general the

rediscovery of the primary significance of the living Christian community group.[8]

One of the primary advantages in this type of restructuring, according to Mr. Weber, is that "The house-Church is in fact a way of building up a missionary Church, a spontaneously evangelistic community."[9] To be spontaneous is to assume in part that the group composing this community gathers and operates within a secular setting. This enables it to respond immediately to the needs and expressions of the world. Spontaneity increases when the "world" is either in the meeting or the setting of the group's operations, or when the world is very much aware that the church is in its midst. As Christ did not preach to man from the outside but dwelt with man, so the church is seen as dwelling more fully with man where he lives in this structure of the church in the home.

In still another department of the World Council of Churches we find, eight years later in 1965, a growing concern for a congregational structure that is, at heart, mission-oriented. In the report from the World Council of Churches' Department on Studies in Evangelism entitled "The Quest for Structures of Missionary Congregations," reference is made to the house church as that type of structure which can play an important role in bringing about this desired goal. The report reminds us that a truly missionary congregation is a community for others. It goes on to explain how throughout the world, not in any one nation or region, the church is in dire need of discovering that form which will enable it to be authentically for others. After discussing this need in some detail, the report offers evidence of a beginning response.

"Little congregations" (as they have, not uncritically, been referred to in ecumenical discussion) have been forming everywhere—certain circles, cells and groups gathered for witness and service. In one way or another, these have arisen through earnest engagement with the growing number of new crises and needs of contemporary society. They have formed, for example, for the ministry of counseling the lonely and broken by telephone, or for service to refugees and to the racially oppressed, or for aid to migrant workers, or for the effort toward international understanding and attack on social problems. They have come to life among students, professional people, educators, legislators, and many others. They have formed themselves into house-churches, making possible a human community where it did not previously exist, or into brotherhoods, working parties, fellowships, and orders.[10]

What is clearly implied in the above reference is that the house church of today is rising up in direct response to contemporary needs. It is mission-minded from its origins. Because of the high degree of flexibility in such house churches, their workable shape is forming according to these worldly needs. This creates not only the mission-minded group but the mission-structured group as well. We should note in these references from the World Council the consistent referral to the *rise* of such house churches, as opposed to their being *instituted* or *programmed* by some organizational hierarchy. Since one is still hard pressed to uncover any official denominational calls for developing such structures within the system and since the concept is most certainly not found in any official church polity, it is increasingly clear that this is a genuine grass roots response to the needs of our world. To be grass roots in origin does not mean that the house church could never remain true to its purposes if it developed within the establishment. If the organized church is receptive to this form, it will be due to the same worldly pressures, therefore ensuring the same potential for the house church so long as it remains true to its original reason for being: responding to God's call to meet contemporary needs in a secular setting.

Given this reason for being, it is possible to discern a unique difference in the type of house church which is now emerging from house churches that have risen in times past. If the house church of the second and third centuries could be marked by its role as an underground, protective, and strengthening community to enable Christians to stand amid a hostile world; if the house church of the Wesleyan class-meeting type could be marked by its role as a developer of the truly pious in disciplined obedience; and if the house churches in Europe of recent decades could be marked by their attempts to reclaim the faithful, then I believe that the current rise of the house church, especially in America, may be marked by an increased concern for close community and a determination to meet the needs of society effectively. Of course the house church of the future may be motivated by additional forces not yet apparent. Depending upon the nature of present moves toward a complete secularization of society, the church may need to go underground or find new avenues simply to hold the faithful together. For the present, mission and community are the dominant forces calling for the rise of the house church.

The dominance of the mission concern as a chief force calling for restructuring congregations dictates a number of drastic changes that would under other circumstances be unnecessary. This is not to say that the church has not known a call to mission before. It has never experienced so great a missionary thrust as was seen in the nineteenth century. What is significantly unique about today's sense of a mission concern is that it threatens the existing institutional framework in a way the old response of "sending" representative missionaries could not have done. The World Council of Churches' study of the missionary *structure* of the congregation underlines this difference: "And now we realize, too, that for the most part our congregational structures are no longer appropriate for all those complex forms of human life within which Christ would have the Gospel made known through a servant Church."[11]

The implications are obvious. If a servant-mission in the world is what causes the church to experience rebirth in our day, then that orientation will inevitably be its central determining force. Thereby, the church will find the structure which allows for this dominance of mission orientation without losing its other reasons for being. If mission is dominant, then congregational worship is seen within its context. Again, if mission is dominant, then the quest for a meaningful community is carried out in its context. The house church provides a clear option for this new shift. The small group found within the house church can easily relate all they do—worship, study, fellowship—to the overriding environment in which they live—their corporate mission. This is as it should be.

This understanding of the radical results of seeing all church life under the influence of its mission was clearly stated in a subsequent preliminary report of the Ecumenical Working Group on Questions of Congregational Structure in the DDR (East Germany) drawn up in the spring of 1966. Their report to the World Council parent body pointed to the extreme changes incumbent upon the church if she is to take seriously the priority befitting her missionary purposes. The gist of this Ecumenical Working Group's theological basis for such a drastic shift in emphasis can be garnered from the following quotes: "The *gathering* of the congregation is not a primary event, followed by a second act of *sending* the church forth in mission; the assembled church is always the gathering of those who are sent." The Ecumenical Working Group emphasized a mission orientation even more by adding: "Only those who obey the sending required today have any capacity to know what forms of assembly are needed, and only they experience in depth how much they need to gather together. 'Precisely that congregation which has allowed itself to be drawn completely into the sending movement . . . will have the experience that now *really and in a new way* it has need to gather.' "[12]

In suggesting what this means in matters of form the report went on to say: "The congregation needs, as a form of assembly consistent with its mission, *small groups* which understand themselves as fellowships of life and service."[13]

The Council's preliminary report added, however, that although they were certain on this point that the sending movement must be dominant in the life of the church, they saw a definite hindrance to implementing the concept or even making it understood. This is due, in large measure, to the church's own heritage which has often declared that the church exists primarily in its gathered assembly "where the Word is preached and the sacraments are duly observed." Mission, according to this heritage, has generally been held aloft as a proper goal "over there" somewhere, or "in time" someday. Mission has not been upheld traditionally as the dominant experience that influences even the way in which the church should gather to worship.

A primary cause of the church's inability to consider this dominant thrust of mission is the relationship of the pastor to the congregation. The congregation typically sees their pastor as the one who serves and themselves as the ones who receive. Some pastors encourage this role. The hindrance to mission stems from the limitations inherent in this image of the shepherd to *his* flock: "Only in the

Pastoral Epistles is there a 'shepherd's office,' in the sense of an exclusive office to be performed by a single person in the congregation; otherwise the New Testament speaks of groups which exercise 'shepherd' functions in the congregation (Acts 20:28, Phil. 1:1, I Peter 5:2). There is no mention at all in the New Testament of the exclusive authorization of a single person in the congregation to proclaim the Word and administer the sacraments."[14]

If the congregations of today are to break through their traditional self-understanding which is one-sidedly determined by congregating, they must change their concept of why the church exists at all, how its pastor and people properly interrelate, and what forms and patterns are necessary to enable the people to respond to the distinct callings of our own time. The house church, by its nature, can expose these crucial questions and force congregations to wrestle with them. The house church can as well provide a flexible vehicle which can keep the church open for a yet unknown response.

STRENGTHENING

† There are many possibilities for exciting shifts in Christian education through a house church approach. The house church has much promise as an example of a setting where the totality of Christian experiences may be developed and Christian education has a chance of breaking out of its present compartmentalization. In such a setting Christian education more readily comes out of the experiences of the group's life. The house church makes obvious the importance of a program of nurture consistent with its life-style and mission. Since house church Christian education occurs in a secular atmosphere, its relevance to everyday living increases. Thus, the house church affords more effective growth possibilities in Christian living than the narrowly conceived church school.

Letty Russell writes out of her experiences with the East Harlem Protestant Parish, "Everything that happens in the witnessing community, be it faithful or unfaithful, is part of the educational process of Christian nurture of its members."[1] This awareness of the potential unfaithful witness to the gospel demands a context for teaching as responsible as the lessons taught. To lead a child year after year into the all-encompassing, breathtaking new expansion of life revealed in the Gospels and to confine this big-as-the-world lesson to a series of classroom experiences is a travesty of Christian education.

Although at Trinity we have continued to include study as one part of the life of each house church, the relationship between house churches and the total Christian education task has only recently evolved. Since their inception, our house churches have continued to provide their own brand of Christian nurture—a brand seldom found in more typical educational settings. Subtle in nature and not found by covering chapters in a book, this nurture has not been as obvious even to members as was the weekly rise and fall of church school attendance. It is the nurture which occurs through sharing in the life and mission of a visible Christian community. In this sharing lies our hope for the future: Christian growth through contextual education.

Contextual education enables growth or change to come about by participation in a learning experience at a point of need in a real life situation. For example, members of the Clothes Closet House Church confessed that they were becoming increasingly disturbed over some "customers" who seemed to constantly abuse the privileges offered. There was no small concern over the right way to handle the situation. Out of some differences of opinion yet unity in wanting to respond wisely, the group undertook a study of the Christian's helping role. They faced the problem as they worked with the poor on Saturday mornings. They faced the problem again as they met together each Wednesday evening. They looked at case situations, held discussions, and studied material dealing with common difficulties in such a helping role. The specific problem arose when some of the ladies discovered a small number of families regularly distorting the intentions of the gifts of clothing. The families were said to be returning too frequently for their obvious needs. The suspicion was that they were making the rounds of all such free clothing closets and selling the clothes or using them for rags. The question within the house church centered upon whether or not to make a list of rules designed to screen out those who abused the privileges, thus designating them as undesirables. While this step was being considered, the house church began to look searchingly into a handbook entitled *This Difficult Business of Helping.* The member in charge of the group's regular nurture diet seized this opportunity to relate their weeknight studies to the issue before them. It didn't matter that the booklet indicated an intended audience of senior highs. The fact that most of these house church members were well beyond young adulthood was immaterial, for they were not in a "class" where one thinks in terms of peer grouping; they were on a mission where any resource that could offer guidance was welcome.

During the weeks in which this problem was under study, a number of central Christian doctrines were seen as the pivotal points upon which their decisions hinged. No one said, "Let's look at the doctrine of grace to see what relevance it has for us in this case." Instead, as they read and wrestled, it became increasingly clear that beyond the specific questions about abuse was the deeper question: How does the realization that we are accepted by grace affect the way we relate to others? What did it mean to "act in grace" in issuing clothing to those who were often so ill-kept and whose children added so to the room's odors that merely staying on the job required a strong stomach and stronger will? What did it mean to continue trying to offer not only help but acceptance when often enough the father of the bedraggled gang was waiting outside in a car too ashamed to join them and too oppressed or lethargic to improve their situation so that they would not have to come? These questions caused many reflections. Did they serve differently those who were "worthy"? (Is that how "grace" comes to us?) Should they impose rules to control the use of these gifts before allowing them to be dispensed? (Do our own gifts come with strings attached?) How does one love such people when they do not seem to be "improving" or acting in any way appreciative? They don't accept these gifts in the name of the Lord or his church. Neither do they give us credit for it, nor do they even appear to see love going on here. "It's just another do-gooder handout place," they say. They aren't getting the point we intended. So, how and why do you go on serving and trying to love in such a situation? (Why does God go on loving us?)

These are only examples of the many doctrinal ideas the people of the house church wrestled with as they sought an answer to the dilemma arising from their mission. The willingness of some to rethink, to confess, and to rededicate themselves in light of God's will did not come about because these were healthy subjects for the church to study. The concern was there because the problem and its resultant confrontations were at hand. The learning which brought change occurred in context, where Christian truths were seen to make a difference in one's actions. In this case the action was a house church decision not to draft any set of rules to make the work easier or to screen out the most undesirable people. Instead, the ladies continued with renewed determination to be present to all who desired to visit the Clothes Closet to find a friend or take out a bundle of clothing—no strings attached.

Not many house church situations call for such a definite turn toward doctrinal studies to handle practical problems. Most of them do call for frequent discussions that involve them in debating the best approach to the many areas of interpersonal relations in which they are involved. Often the house churches are forced to ask, "But how should *we* approach the problem, not being restauranteurs or civic club representatives, but acting as the body of Christ?" This phenomenon illustrates how Christian education has often taken place through living in close association at the point of our mission. There is a continual unveiling in the house church of the meaning of the gospel in our lives. What is weekly revealed is our desire for acceptance and forgiveness coupled with our penchant for withdrawal and judgmental attitudes. When we live closely together in so many hours of family-like discussion and work, when we must face each other on so many of those days in which tardiness, headaches, and fatigue abound, we learn a lot about the teachings of sin and forgiveness.

Our coffee house is another area where Christian education occurs in the context of mission. On an individual basis the waiters and waitresses frequently become involved with a customer in brief table talk. Such opportunities in dialogue obviously run the gamut from silly chatter to an in-depth sharing which is often surprising in its quickness of exposure. In ways direct or subtle, such coffee house workers are challenged at times to the admonition in 1 Peter 3:15, "always have your answer ready for people who ask you the reason for the hope that you all have." Although the coffee house atmosphere is strictly secular and the workers are reminded that dialogue encounters do not have to be religious to speak to the truths of the faith, occasionally one can pick up echoes from a corner table where conversation has begun to sound like a tent revival by candlelight. More typically we hear in serious encounters a search for meaning, an expression of futility, a powerlessness to cope, or a despairing "to hell with it all."

It is obvious in such examples that we are observing a situation where the church's reaching out is occurring in a one-to-one relationship. It is a point of contact where one's sensitiveness is paramount. However, we should not overlook the fact that these confrontations involve the waiter's awareness of the teachings of the faith, for the truths he has assimilated determine just who he is in the particular encounter. If the waiter or waitress did not express a Christian perspective verbally, there is every likelihood that his honest beliefs were indirectly brought to mind as the dialogue continued. Such encounters press the worker to review or possibly to refine his own understandings of the faith. Under such circumstances, growth in Christian education becomes not what answers seem appropriate in a class, but what convictions make sense in this encounter where an honest leveling is the only way to stay with the conversation.

Christian education can be seen underlying the discussions at lamplighting time.[2] During such preparation periods a waitress may ask, "If Sam comes back tonight and wants to talk about his plan to change the world, how should I respond now?" No specific answers would be forthcoming from such a question, but the entire group would be challenged to think about their own Christian position under such circumstances.

The Coffee House House Church members have necessarily wrestled with problems of ethics and relationships. Often, in an argumentative mood, the body has agonized over doctrinal issues covering various responses possible according to the teachings of

Christ. When, for example, a small gang begins to frequent *The Marketplace* disrupting the conversations, destroying the property, and creating general disorder, there is a real context for some hard searching concerning the most Christian response to be made by that house church.

When differences of opinion over the best response to these issues bring about such broken relationships within the house church that some members cannot easily speak to one another, they are challenged to grow through a lesson from experience on the topic: "Being Reconciled to One's Fellowman."

In addition to such spontaneous opportunities for growth, there is an annual retreat for all coffee house workers where the meaning of evangelism for the contemporary scene is studied and discussed.

Because of their exposure to unique challenges, house churches have called for a type of Christian education suited to their life-style in corporate living and mission activity. For this reason the teachings encountered have a relevance seldom found in a sporadic coming together of a church school class, with its limited purpose. Most of Trinity's house churches have standard study materials as well, but these are selected or refused as the groups desire. Their specific study time is not unlike the average Sunday class. The significant difference is that such studies occur within the experience of the group's work and life together. In this context, education is more likely to reach that desired result where there is a change in behavior. It seldom settles for the questionable goal of reading a pamphlet a quarter or a book a year. If true Christian education is marked by growth experiences, then the distinct advantage of the house church as an improved context for experiential education is obvious.

The involvement of the youth with house churches is yet another story at Trinity. Although we have never had a youth program as such, the teen-agers continually come together in their own peer grouping through one approach or another. Such groups have met in homes or the church house, on Sundays or during the week, primarily for study or for food and fun. More importantly, through the years they have been included in the activities and missions of the congregation as equal participants with no classification due to their age. On a weekend when eight or ten workers appear at the coffee house for their brief preparation time to share, pray, and receive their assignments, the coordinator for the evening will ask each one to serve in a special capacity—as waiter, dishwasher, hostess, head waiter, or kitchen worker. If, by chance, two or three of the eight are teen-agers, there is no mention made of this, and no special treatment is given. The youth engage in mission alongside the adults within the group.

In similar fashion our youth have become an important part in the summer day camps for the retarded. Whereas the adults felt a certain hesitation concerning youth participation, they quickly recognized that the young people had gifts to share with the retarded as well as special rapport that the adults could not match.

Again, young people who have had little or no interest in the traditional programs of the church found new excitement and an acceptance surprising to themselves and the adults as they participated in the drama activities of one house church mission. Each learned that the other age group was "human" and that working on a mission together could not only be meaningful but fun. This is not to say that such activity is a substitute for growth in knowledge and a basic understanding of the Christian faith. It is to say that the relationships of the youth to the total life of the congregation, especially through the life of the house churches, creates that climate where the basic teachings can be desired and understood as relevant for oneself.

But what about the children's involvement in the house church? This is a question often asked. The effort to improve opportunities for nurture of children had for years been poor at Trinity although the congregation had an ample number of concerned, trained, and dedicated lay teachers. The problem was the system inherent in the traditional church school. We experienced tension between the expressed desire to discover vital ways to "raise up our children in the nurture and admonition of the Lord," and pressure to continue providing *all* of the traditional approaches to Christian education. This tension was not apparent during our first three or four years, since our church school received a great deal of the energy of the congregation. During this time house churches were slowly finding themselves. Gradually, dedicated teachers of children began to see as great if not greater ministry in their participation in the mission and study of the house church rather than in the routines of their Sunday morning class. At the same time the newer members, those who would ordinarily contribute the necessary new teacher reinforcements, displayed a tendency to be "turned off" from the traditional church school and found the approach to learning within the house church more to their liking. This trend obviously increased the difficulty of holding to past standards of teacher procurement and training. For example, how could a former teacher feel adequate for her traditional role on Sunday morning when she had been busily engaged in leading local retarded children into a more responsive life during two or more mornings during that same week? Or how could the teacher who had been up to his elbows in soapsuds in the coffee house kitchen until one o'clock Sunday morning bring his best to a children's class only eight hours later? Such tensions began a small change in emphasis concerning the relative importance of the church school within the total life of the congregation. Questions were raised challenging us in many different directions: If we have only so much time, what should receive our priorities? Shouldn't the mission get only that time left over after we have "taken care of our own"? Why do we need the church school anyway? Why can't we put it all together in each house church?

Although a number of experiences challenged the role of the church school in our lives, the main lesson learned during those years was how deeply rooted is the church school in the very lifeblood of the church itself. We were often reminded that many churchmen take comfort in the church school plant and program, accepting mere existence as proof that their intended purposes are being carried out. To merge, evolve, or eradicate the church school for the betterment of its own goals seemed foolhardy to most. Like many congregations, we continued to shore up a church school program in order to avoid facing the fact that little genuine Christian education was actually taking place.

A promising first step out of the church school dilemma was

taken at Trinity in the fall of 1971. We had tried weekday classes some years before as well as several other experimental approaches to Christian education. Out of those experiences and in the face of the obvious decline in interest in our church school, a search began for an effective way to carry out the biblical injunction to teach the faith.

Weeks of brainstorming and searching made us acutely aware that there is no easy road ahead. But we grew in our conviction that much of what we had been doing was not worth recovering. Clearly the way for Trinity was again ahead into the unknown. Our thinking was reinforced at this point by the inaugural address of Dr. Rachel Henderlite, Professor of Christian Education, Austin Theological Seminary. In her address entitled "We Can't Go Home Again," Dr. Henderlite recalled that in the nineteenth century, when the Sunday school was born, it ". . . was both an unofficial church and an unofficial school. It was not a part of the organized church. It was a separate institution organized and supported by laymen. It taught both the three R's and a popular Americanized Christianity. In this way it served on the frontier as forerunner of both the public school and the church."[3] The limitations inherent in the church school were further clarified as Dr. Henderlite went on to say: "The Sunday school was not designed as an agency through which the Protestant church might expect to equip men and women for life in the world. It was marginal to life from the beginning."[4]

We knew that the institutionalized church school had grave limitations by practice. Now we knew they were there by design. We also knew that our direction lay in the attempt to get Christian education away from its marginal stance and into the heart of life. For us that meant a movement away from the church building toward the pulse of the city, away from classrooms toward living experiences in family units, away from isolated subject matter toward learning in the context of a witnessing community. And that meant for us house church.

The result was the cessation of the church school as we knew it and the development of discovery periods, which occur mostly as inter-generational or family-cluster learning experiences. Now, for three Sunday mornings out of four, children and adults gather together, either as a total congregation, as house church units, or as household units to relate common Christian themes and concerns. Peer groupings occur once a month only. The prime time of eleven o'clock Sundays has been given over to this enterprise, thus shifting the worship hour and involving it in the process of change.

The discovery period brings to the house churches on the third Sunday of each month an opportunity to relate the theme of the total congregation's study to their particular life together. The groups seek to experience worship and nurture on such mornings in the manner most meaningful to them. At these informal discovery times most of the children and many adults sprawl on the living room floor. Often they act out learning games and share in yet smaller groupings what they have gained from this experience. By being placed with teen-agers and children in groups of eight or ten, the adults are now more aware how each person is a teacher of the faith and each participant a learner from the others.

Inter-generational education has added an exciting and confronting dimension to our house churches. The children and adults have a renewed interest in discovering the meaning of their life together now that they search in the freedom and joy of their extended family. They do not enter this educational experience in isolation. Each participant has had occasion to wrestle with the given theme on two previous Sundays as a part of a plenary experience and in a peer group setting. Participants are also aware that the discoveries of this day's house church event should be taken into individual households for direct confrontation and growth the following Sunday. The congregation is aware of a noticeable increase in the talk in their houses about the pilgrimage of God's people for our day and time.

Any attempt to evaluate the use of an inter-generational approach to formal Christian education is premature. There are, however, sufficient experiences for us to know that the experiment has possibilities.

The congregation of the First Baptist Church of Rochester, New York tried family cluster education with interesting results. In February 1970, they developed two clusters of four and five family units each. A typical group would have eight adults and ten children.

Meeting weekly, these clusters explored themes on communications and poverty, while their basic approach was through planned learning activities. Although their findings were tentative, the inter-generational approach obviously opened new dimensions of nurture which were highly appreciated by those participating. An evaluation paper following a twelve-week experiment revealed an overwhelming percentage of children and adults reacting positively to the experience and recommending family cluster education to others.

In Berkeley, California, Mr. Donald L. Griggs is pioneering new methods and a new curriculum as a result of his efforts toward inter-generational church school classes. While serving as the Associate Pastor of the First Presbyterian Church of Livermore, California, in 1967, Mr. Griggs developed what he called "The Junior Experiment." He applied unique methods to a fifth and sixth grade class of the church. Their parents participated as fellow class members. The objectives were fourfold: (a) to increase communication between parents and children, (b) to include children as a responsible part of the church, (c) to place Christian education in the context of the family's life, and (d) to enable children and parents to satisfy their curiosity by teaching inductively through learning experiences. Positive results of this experiment have led Mr. Griggs into a concentrated effort to provide curriculum aids to inter-generational education for the church at large. When asked about his current evaluation of such methods Mr. Griggs replied, "After a variety of experiences teaching adults and children in the same educational setting I am convinced this is one very valid model for teaching in the church. The occasions of my teaching adults and children together as co-learners are among the most meaningful experiences I have ever had as a teacher and learner. When we forsake the image of adults as having things to *tell* children that they should learn and instead see adults and children as persons who have much to give and receive from each other then perhaps we can discover what Jesus meant when he said, 'unless you become like a child. . . .' "5

By inter-generational education the church is saying in a new way that we are not merely in class learning. We are an ongoing community seeking to increase our understandings according to our varied relationships and missions. Our house church inter-generational discovery times are only a small step toward the tremendous challenge of effective Christian education in the church today. They are, however, pointing in a direction that holds new promise for equipping young and old to live responsibly in the world.

We have looked at one facet of Christian education which involves children: our discovery through inter-generational gatherings. But it has also been demonstrated that Christian education takes place in all that the members are and do, not just in their planned discovery times. For this reason the context of the total congregation with its shifts toward an outward ministry has also affected the children and youth of Trinity. They see the church differently, not just because of what is occurring on Sunday mornings, but because of what takes place around them as parents and friends engage in mission to the city and relate in extended family settings. For example, the children are present occasionally to see that the table where they have breakfast is now being used for a communion worship service. They are put to bed while house church is taking place downstairs. They know that they have often been left with a sitter because Dad and Mom were going out to see if they could help people in need. Twice now, Christmas has arrived on the eve or the day the coffee house is open. The workers' children have learned that their parents and others are willing to take a little from their own Christmas for the sake of those who are lonelier, and they have learned that children are thus denied expected conveniences in the name of love. What more effective training is possible for a child than to become a feeling participant in the sacrificial choices made by his parents for the sake of their efforts to respond to the gospel? Indeed, children have not responded well in our day to over-solicitous parents anymore than they have to neglectful parents. Perhaps they gain vision by looking through the window of their parents' concern for others, rather than noticing their parents' observing them and acting as mirrors which keep their children turned in upon themselves.

The fact that children learn in a fairly limited environment increases the urgency of insuring that their environment is consistent with the content being taught. I recall, for example, a spur-of-the-moment visit with the first-grade church school class under the old system. The material being used focused upon the church, and the children had been asked to draw pictures about the meaning of the church. As I looked over the drawings lined up against the backs of chairs, the children beamed. Here was their six-year-old version of church. I beamed too, for I saw that despite differences in subject matter in the foreground, all of them had clearly outlined, in the background, the antebellum house in which we were holding classes. Would it be too much to expect someday to see them include those missions that were carried on beyond the boundaries of their limited experiences, or to draw their family and friends at their breakfast table as the church? It was obvious that for this entire class their concept of the church, for better or for worse, had come to them, not from the curriculum and its nice pictures of traditional church buildings, but from their own immediate environment where for now church was a large house. Theoretically and perhaps practically, one can predict that their future understanding of the church and its purposes will come from the actual witness made by their parents as they engage in mission projects and gather in homes.

This same point was brought home to me when one of my four daughters asked why a number of people seemed to think our particular congregation is a little unusual. When I explained a few of the differences visitors might notice, she responded in genuine surprise, "I thought most churches ran coffee houses; they're not new." The awarenesses we wish to bring to our children will indeed come from that in which we are actually engaged rather than from that which we only preach or teach. In a day when so many youths have turned away from the church, it is obvious that our most important teaching will be to display a more authentically involved and concerned life-style within the faith.

The house church is not the ultimate context for Christian education; the world is. But it is one of the most dynamic at hand, for it can come the closest to breaking the vise-like hold the church school system has on Christian education. As long as the Sunday church school continues to assume the role of *the* guardian of proper Christian nurture, and it is likely to so assume as long as it exists, there is little chance of developing the necessary experiences so vital to discovering the exhilarating challenges within the life and teachings of Jesus.

† **A**nother approach to the task of Christian education in the church can be seen through the experiences of Christ Church, Presbyterian, Burlington, Vermont. This congregation has neither house churches per se nor an emphasis upon an educational program. They do function through a variety of small groups not unlike house churches at points. The interest in their approach to Christian education is due to this lack of an organized program. Their innovations here are worth noting.

Inasmuch as the members of Christ Church have been engaged in a number of challenging missions for over a decade, they have come to feel that the church must structure itself according to its priorities. This belief has led them to concentrate first on their ministry to the surrounding community (ministries involving them at the jail, a coffee house, and a halfway house for drug abusers are typical) and only then to consider the best way to further their own growth. The result is a number of corporate entities for reaching out and no organized structure for their personal education. There is no weekday or Sunday church school. There is no regular Sunday worship service at 11:00 A.M. or otherwise. Instead they gather monthly to celebrate the life of a community on mission and to carry out educational growth experiences as the opportunity presents itself. Adults do gather in small groups from time to time to study but only when the word has gotten around that a few of them have found a new area of interest or need and they invite others to join in such study for an indeterminate period. The education of the children is left primarily to the parents. This teaching takes place by the involvement of the children with their parents on special occasions they call festival days and at other times whenever the parents discover a teaching opportunity within the context of their home life. This free style of Christian education is deemed necessary by the members if they are to take seriously their primary call to be a missioning people and to seek ways to enhance their own growth and worship within that situation.

When talking with two of the young couples in Christ Church,

I was impressed with the seriousness with which they saw their responsibilities in Christian education while they rejoiced over their lack of a church school. They seemed confident that they could worship in each of their varied experiences without the necessity of organizing their praise weekly. They were equally confident that they could raise their children through a total reliance upon parental responsibility (which shouldn't sound as revolutionary as it does). This approach requires a sophisticated awareness of what experiences constitute opportunities for Christian education and an inner discipline to capitalize on these experiences. The people with whom I spoke seemed to have the necessary resources. Because of the natural concern of a people willing to be on mission, the natural demands upon learning impelling such a task, and the natural inquiries of their children living within this mission context, these couples felt assured that Christian education would not be lacking in such a climate.

The struggle over proper methods of Christian education is offered here as one of those factors which influence most heavily the effective rise of the house church, or similar renewal expressions. Resistance to meaningful breakthroughs in Christian education stem from at least three attitudes upholding the traditional church school plant and program. The first is the nostalgic imagery surrounding the church school which warmly reassures the congregation that something of true value undergirds them, even if it is a mortgaged building sitting empty for approximately one hundred and sixty of the one hundred sixty eight hours in the week. The second and more legitimate resistance is due to a concern for the marginal member who, it is feared, would not remain even marginal if a more challenging venture in Christian growth were prescribed. The third basis for resistance, and perhaps the greatest, stems from the pressure of society and its expectations of a "proper" church in the community. The marginal member and society combine to press the church into building an impressive edifice. Once the plant is oversized, it is a matter of corporate embarrassment to consider seriously any approach to Christian growth that does not presume to depend upon that confining space.

Constant pressures within the educational system cause one to look at the new possibilities in Christian education through the flexible house church. Because it has little appeal to the building-oriented or marginal church member who desires only to "use" the church, the house church can find itself free to consider the essence of the educational tasks it desires. If such a house church is oriented toward a mission, it will inevitably house its own nurture and experiments in new growth within that context. In such an environment Christian education can return to its rightful relationship as an integral part of the continuing preparation of members for their mission tasks. This would not deny doctrinal teachings; quite the contrary, it would enable them to come alive as a part of man's experiences calling him to his full humanity as a son of God.

CELEBRATING

† **I** arrived at the coffee house on the given evening trying to think on the run. The red swinging doors, squeaking loudly in response to my push, announced my arrival. In a matter of minutes I would be expected to initiate an experience worthy of the hopes of those waiting upstairs. What they hoped for was an opportunity to express whatever meaning existed in this remnant of a house church as it prepared to lose its particular identity. In a few weeks the two coffee house house churches would blend into one with a number of changes in the membership. On the occasion of the last meeting of one of these groups, a request had been made for the sacrament of the Lord's Supper. The need was obviously there for something special but I was totally unprepared. Old notes gave me a false security of having at least something to offer, but on the question of how I should approach the communion service itself I

drew a blank. Here again, I discovered how gifts of the moment are unveiled through the openness and presence of the participants in worship in a far grander way than any leader of worship can bring about.

Penny, Jean, Emily, and Bob patiently awaited my lead. The elements were quickly placed on a customers' table selected at random. Chairs were pushed back and all stood close around, within the light of the candle glowing in the center of the table. After some prayers and thoughts (my old notes were quickly put aside as inappropriate to the obvious mood of the moment), the words of the institution of the Lord's Supper were read and we were at the point of celebrating. I really don't recall exactly how it came about; I do know I hesitated in determining *how* and *whom* to serve. A hard loaf of bread was lifted; a piece was torn off and handed to someone with words about Christ's love. Suddenly, spontaneously, each person began to lift a part of the loaf or a glass and pass it random fashion across the table to another, all the while expressing from the depths of his heart his compassion for the life and gifts of the other. Like the rising wind the words moved toward a crescendo: "Emily, take this bread in evidence of Christ's love for you." "Bob, in Christ I shall always love you." "Penny, know your gifts." "Jean, receive the joy." "Don, receive Christ's presence." And then, over again, for one time was not enough to express all that desired to be poured out. More bread was torn off, arms reached again crisscrossing the flickering flame, and words began to meld into vibrant chords of grace, joy, love. We smiled, then had to laugh while tears were fought back. It was a time to dance. No one had to teach us that the sacrament of the Lord's Supper was a celebration. Celebrating could not be put down or denied, for this small community was worshiping out of all they had put into their years of working together, using their gifts in response to God's calling. Who would have dreamed that long nights of taking orders, filling glasses, carrying trays of dirty dishes, hauling ice, mixing coffee blends, and baking pastries could have been the source of such joy? This house church knew why it was so; thus they asked for communion.

If one could have his wish that the universal church could be present at a celebration of the Eucharist, it would be that all could have been around that coffee table where only a handful were gathered together in Christ's name.

Renewal in worship does not come about by liturgical innovations but through the emergence of a witnessing community. We celebrate joyfully, freely in worship because we have found common cause, not because the trend is in vogue.

The preceding experience of a coffee house worship service is not representative of any month or year in our house churches at Trinity. It is illustrative of the belief that significant corporate worship occurs primarily, if not exclusively, in those communities that have shared deeply together. Individuals who go to church at intervals and invariably come away wondering what worship is all about will not find out simply by returning for the evening service. They will discover its power by participating in a witnessing community as they attempt to take hold of God's admonition to be reconciled and to go out reconciling.

The effect of house church life upon Trinity has been to provide occasional discoveries through worship in homes which, in turn, have created a gradual exposure to more meaningful expressions in the Sunday worship of the congregation. For years, house church worship was limited to special occasions at infrequent intervals. A short devotional led by the pastoral leader usually took place during each meeting of a house church. Often the Scripture expounded to the entire congregation on the previous Sunday was used to bind each house church together under a common Word during that week. More often than not, this brief worship time was used by the members to gather themselves together, putting behind them for awhile the many diversions of their day.

The initial experiences of breaking bread and passing the glasses of wine around a dining room or kitchen table were highlights within most house churches. It was not uncommon in the freshness of that experience to see some members moved to tears while others were awed by the simple beauty these rites assumed in their secular setting. The intimacy between the participants brought them to see how the most meaningful worship center can be the radiant faces just across the candlelit table. The informality in the midst of such an atmosphere enabled them to learn that dialogue was a meaningful addition to one's praise to God. Often the conclusion of such an experience found the group wanting to linger awhile, creating in these few minutes of thoughtful silence their own postlude. Such encounters in worship can seldom be duplicated in a mass meeting.

We have seen how house church worship has demonstrated the dynamic created by a witnessing small group, thereby creating authentic praise and celebration. It has also been shown how house church worship develops a desire for the full participation of the body in dialogue and in a focus upon one another in praising God.

Another incident at Trinity revealed the growth in worship through house church as one group discovered how to praise God in the midst of a most ordinary setting. The Social Concerns House Church had requested a Eucharistic celebration in the midst of their regular Sunday dinner. This biracial group placed a great deal of importance in their house church family meals as an aid to the "social mixing" so difficult to achieve across the land. The dinner was to be held immediately after the morning worship hour. They selected the coffee house as the only place large enough to accommodate them as they were expecting invited guests from the all-black John Wesley Methodist Church. Heretofore we had experienced the type of home worship where the table was bare except for the communion elements and worship aids. On this occasion the sacramental bread and wine had no throne. They made their contribution to the table in competition with baked beans, fried chicken, salads, and pies. Like the Lord in the world, you had to know the mysterious presence was there to see it. Halfway through the meal, about when the young boys jumped up for seconds, the house church family was called to a corporate remembrance. Right in the middle of passing the salad they were asked to pass the "body" of their Lord. A brief statement reminding the group of the powerful significance of the holy in the midst of everyday events was uttered but the verbal lesson was unnecessary. Amid the occasional crying of a baby sitting on mother's lap and the restlessness of some children who had eyed the pie, we passed loaves of bread and poured out juice to drink, saying to young and old, "This is my body; do this in remembrance of me."

Frankly, I was concerned that this experience might have lost its intended confrontation so jovial and typically picnic-oriented was the group. There was no need for such concern as I learned that even the children wanted to talk, later in the week, about the meaning such a worship held for them. All of this is a reminder that we fear unduly and pompously that God might not be seen or understood if he is unaccompanied by *our* familiar religious trappings.

Maturity in worship also occurs through negative experiences in house churches. Now and then there is a concern to worship in a house church simply because of the span of time since such an event last occurred. At such times we frequently gather only to discover our inability to worship. What is uncovered is our strong dependency upon the forms and orders in worship. (Or is it our belief that following such forms and orders is itself the worship experience?) Such a house church experience, uncomfortable as it is, challenges us to penetrate the liturgies, the traditional and the renewed ones, in an effort to discover when worship is ever authentic. In a house church we cannot escape our occasional inability to worship. To believe we have worshiped in our customary fashion, all that need happen is to enter a given sanctuary and join others in the planned responses according to the minister's lead. Not so in a house gathering. If worship falls flat in the small group, there is no denying it. Yet this failure to worship can become a positive experience, for it is when we are exposed to our own emptiness that we are most open to a genuine search for that which fills.

† The continued existence of Trinity's house churches as the dominant structure within the congregation has brought about a sporadic questioning of many of the more traditional methods employed for the worship of our gathered congregation on Sunday mornings. In this way the house church has served not only as a catalyst for the outward move of the congregation, but as a constant source of evaluating its life within. This happens casually and indirectly the majority of the time. However, in 1969, a *confrontation* developed which centered on our congregational worship forms.

This event brought the struggles for renewal into sharp focus by an accident of enthusiasm.

It seems that enthusiasm can become an awesome thing as much to be feared as any movement afoot today. Becoming enthusiastic is confronting the nominal or well-worn Christian with his lukewarmness and placing in his midst that spark of light which is capable of flaring up, bonfire-like, to challenge all around with sheer cheer. Those who see the Christian life as one of upholding moral integrity instead of celebrating God's gifts are often uneasy around genuine, unadulterated joy. But joy's glimmering eyes are difficult to dull, so that whenever the spirit is within, a way will be found for it to be revealed. The truly celebrating life does not have to be pulled out of anyone. Indeed it quivers and shudders, pacing back and forth in its cage of rigid form until some daring release allows its sinews to stretch out in praise of its creator God.

The group of laymen who developed our controversial worship event had experienced house church worship a number of times. More significantly they had just returned from a week-long denominational conference which had released in them their true potential for expressing the celebration of God's gifts in a worshipful praise of his name. The awesome but breathtaking significance of our call to ". . . offer libations to my saviour, invoking the name of Yahweh" (Psalm 116:13) had broken through in a new dimension. After receiving permission from the session, this *ad hoc* group composed of members of several house churches, presented worship at the regular Sunday service.

The members had been prepared for a special presentation and, even though they had become accustomed to many variations, few were ready for the distinct new atmosphere with which they were confronted. When arriving members entered the "shoe-box" sanctuary, everything around them had a different air. Now in a semicircular arrangement the folding chairs faced a pulpit on the side of the room. Brightly colored banners jumped out from the walls. There was a blue and yellow one that read, "Rejoice, the Lord is King." The large brown one at the end of the room pronounced, "That which is heard in the holy places must be lived in the marketplaces." To the side was a multi-colored banner with sweeping lines declaring, "Joy! Joy! Joy!" The group which had composed the worship conducted it throughout. Members rose from all points of the room to lead the congregation in various contributions to this moment of celebration. The singing was contemporary folk music; the litany was modern; and the prayers pointedly confronted us with events of the day. Many members found a new source of strength, especially in the ability to worship through the faces all around rather than by looking at backs of heads. And so it was that outside experiences had finally brought into our most traditional hour an atmosphere that called for the celebration of God's gifts of life to be the dominant note and the participation of each member, the main staff upon which that note was carried.

Reactions to this particular service of worship and to the many similar ones that followed were in the extreme. Most members and visitors reacted positively toward the emphasis upon a joyful community, but many others were rigidly against it. The reasons for such tensions are manifold. Let it suffice for our purposes here to state that one pattern emerged from this experience which indicates the effect of house church life upon all approaches to worship. A definite pattern could be seen in this event relating to the participants' involvement or lack of involvement in a house church at the time. Without carrying out a scientific inquiry, it was possible to ascertain that those members who warmly received this new expression of worship, especially its call for total participation, were those who were most anxious for more open and meaningful relations within their respective house churches. *They responded positively if they had a strong desire for community.* Those most adamant against such an approach to worship were at that time not experiencing or had little meaningful fellowship in a house church. Most of the latter group were not members of a house church at the time.

This is not to say that renewal of the liturgy in our congregations today is inconsequential without the contribution of small groups or house churches, for the liturgical movement has its own momentum and source of direction irrespective of any presence or absence of house churches. It is to say, however, that growth in the ability to reach out to others through mission and in a close community causes house church participants to seek an experience of worship which reflects that desire for an authentic encounter with one another and with God.

The corporate services of worship at Trinity have undergone continual evolution. Our variety of approaches to congregational worship witnesses to the growing concern of the laity for genuine experiences of worship. Most changes in form have resulted from the increasing confidence of lay members about participating in worship services. It is not unusual for a house church or other *ad hoc* group to support their request for a special type of worship with a willingness to plan for and lead in the event.

Therefore, it was not the drastic step it could have been when the session suggested that each house church conduct its own worship service in homes once a month. This worship replaces the more structured orientation that prevails the other Sunday mornings of the month. The purpose has been to increase the children's experience in house church worship as well as to allow the creativity within each group to find expression on a regular basis. This experience has brought new interest to our celebration times for young and old.

These progressions in worship reveal how house churches, out of their corporate life and in their worldly orientation, become a determining influence in the call for the renewal of worship. What the house church creates is increased lay participation. If this is to be true in mission work, it should be expected in our approach to worship as well.

In their enthusiasm to experience meaningful worship, some stumbled over the barrier of others—a barrier which might well be indicative of the difficulty of worship in much of the church. Despite the centuries-old Protestant proclamation that worship belongs to the people, the man in the pew reacts traumatically to being asked to move from observer to full participant. To make such a move requires a growth in one's ability to find mutual encounter redemptive and in one's trust that such intimate sharing with brothers in Christ need not be feared. House church worship experiences develop this necessary ability and trust. They make it possible for us to see *Christ's* presence unveiled, not by observing a modern holy of holies replete with organ pipes and dossal cloths, but through looking into faces—other faces where he has promised to dwell, and by clasping hands—others' hands, through which he has promised to work. We praise God when we see him in others. We receive our calling when we observe others seeing him in us.

Our worship encounters have impressed me with how little most persons actually experience something akin to a community or corporate relationship in any facet of their lives. How many people spend their days moving in and out of a great variety of groups without touching or being touched by those groups? We are with our family community only a fraction of the day now, and even then we have learned to keep our compartmentalized selves partially hidden. Those who live alone are denied even that possibility. Our communities of work and play are likewise sporadic and press us to change "hats" of identification to take on the specific role now called for. Civic groups bring us shoulder to shoulder with yet another cluster of people, who ask of us only a portion of ourselves. Little wonder that so few understand the meaning of corporate worship, where the whole person is challenged to be present. Because we are compartmentalized, we are trained to hold back some of ourselves, keeping everyone else within his individual shell. We have a room full of wary individuals who would, under those circumstances, naturally resist a concerted effort to develop total community.

It should not be surprising, therefore, to expect drastic changes in approaches to worship once a sizeable number of the worshiping community have found themselves in a new trust relationship. When the barrier of individualism is broken, the church will discover ever new and ever exciting possibilities in praising God. The house church pushes against this barrier.

† Some house church developments in this country center primarily on the worship experience. In such situations the other aspects of church life which are dominant in many house churches —aspects such as mission, fellowship, or study—are either subordinated or encompassed by their chief purpose for gathering: to grow through offering praise to God.

One example of a worship-oriented renewal community is the Now Church in San Jose, California. Originally dubbed the "Edenvale United Presbyterian Church," this group quickly moved away from the name and the accompanying accouterments it suggested. The seventy-five members are not an organized church. They are a recognized renewal community within the Synod of the Golden Gate, of the UPUSA denomination. Theirs is a "now" congregation in spirit and in form. The fact that the first gathering was for the purpose of celebrating the present rather than organizing for the future attracted the existentially minded.

The minister, Pete Koopman, has said, "We are not going to sacrifice openness for unity."[1] This openness is illustrated by their definition of membership: simply those who participate during any particular week. In fact, a point is made of providing ways to identify quickly and "split" easily, enabling their membership to be freeing instead of binding.

The Now community is divided into four groups that meet weekly. Once each month they all gather in their small house situated in a new subdivision of San Jose. The heart of their corporate life is their Sunday morning celebration. The liturgy is developed by the members and each worship service is a happening which no individual can totally anticipate. An interesting feature of this house worship is the expanded significance of the offering. Instead of continuing the perfunctory collection of the offering, the members of Now Church have enlarged its meaning to include exhibiting a creation of their own making or sharing their personal concerns. In addition to this elaborate offering of themselves, the small group frequently engages in exercises which enable them to feel their aliveness. Discussion of some issue of immediate concern generally takes place with the group sitting in a circle on the floor. Pete Koopman brings ideas and resources at such times in order to facilitate the members' individual participation in community causes. He seldom preaches. Group singing and weekly celebration of the Lord's Supper round out the significant events in each worship service.

This gathering for building community extends in scope beyond the boundaries of typical worship in time and in content. For Now Church, worship becomes the source of their children's growth experiences, their calling into community tasks, their own development in sharing, as well as their praise to God.

While worship is the central visible sign of Now Church, they attempt to keep a balance between this inner growth and their concern for others. Utilizing a coordinating council and periodic task groups instead of a session and committees, the people are actively engaged in local projects on an individual basis. The migrant ministry, draft counseling, and the peace movement are representative of their interests.

The minister and members of Now Church are attempting to live out their belief that people need to be freed today to become the church on their own terms. They seek to challenge one another in all they do to make decisions in responsible freedom. Their worship life suggests these goals symbolically to the world and experientially for those who attend.

For the thirty-nine people squeezed into a modern suburban home in Richardson, Texas one Sunday morning, informal worship in the house church setting represented all the church they desired for the moment. Dissatisfied with customary approaches to worship, this new congregation is probing for a meaningful beginning. For the present, they are trying out their wings with cautious dialogue in the hope that the children and teen-agers will participate as well. The morning I visited with them, the seventeen children and six youth scattered across the floor indicated by their silence that this hope is not easily fulfilled. Even so, the members' anticipation that something exciting will evolve from their searching gives promise that a total family participation is possible.

The form for their worship combined a liturgical heritage and innovations contributed by the group. A printed liturgy was read and candles were lighted. Their pastor, Calvin Frisch, preached a brief sermon and people offered prayers. In addition, they worshiped through contemporary music, presentation of a book review by a layman, and lengthy discussion on the subject of what constitutes the true believer.

This fellowship, known as the Community Lutheran Church, has a shopping center bookstore as their chief point of contact with the surrounding region. Plans to utilize portions of this rented space for their worship may alter the present home orientation. For the moment, however, worship in the house constitutes the prime source for their search to be open to a new thing. It is obvious that the members of Community Lutheran Church are chiefly engaged in listening for the call to their own future as they praise God in their homes.

The First Presbyterian Church in Spartanburg, South Carolina, has worked with a worship-oriented house church concept for the past three years. Admittedly, their understanding of house church is somewhat limited at present, according to the associate minister Mr. Henry Keating. Intended initially to fill the gap left by the final demise of the traditional Sunday evening service of worship, a small group of approximately twenty-five persons has been meeting each Sunday evening. Only ten to fifteen of these are regular in their attendance while the rest represent the occasionally involved. In a congregation of eighteen hundred communicant members this obviously represents a fringe experience in the basic life of that congregation. The hope in such a group is still important to the church leadership, as they see within it a nucleus of people in a pattern worth expanding. The innovations in worship alone, which include an *agape* meal along with the regular diet of Bible study as well as openness to dialogue, express to them the possible advantages to be gained in reversing the trend of mass meetings and moving instead toward small-group experiences. Already their Sunday house church worship time has led to the rise of four brief mid-week sharing groups. These groups, in turn, have expressed a concern to look further into the possibilities of a small-group encounter. There has also been an emphasis upon the individual mission of the members with time allocated during the evening's worship for reports on the outreach activities of the various participants.

Filling the gap in the loss of meaning in the traditional Sunday morning religious routine has resulted in the rise of a nondenominational but Methodist-oriented house church in Atlanta. Organized and led by Mr. Ben Johnson, who is also director of the Atlanta-based

Institute of Church Renewal, this house church exists outside the institutional church. The fourteen family units who comprise the house church do not especially prefer their independent status but they do choose to develop their own brand of church school and worship. Until such time when they may be received as a legitimate church by some local church judicatory authorized and willing so to do, this group will continue to respond to God's calling essentially through their own house church.

This Atlanta fellowship of about forty persons, including children and grandmothers, rotates meetings among the homes of members. Their approach to study and worship is contemporary in expression and broad in its base. The host family is responsible for the form and content of the particular morning's experiences. This creates a great variety of styles, contributing to the breadth of their understanding of Christian education and worship. The two ordained ministers within the group lead the worship activities only when their normal turn as host comes up.

This house church meets routinely each Sunday morning but also gathers occasionally for special times of fellowship or business on a Sunday evening. Their time together is not without an emphasis upon mission. Each member is encouraged not only to improve his ministry in its day-to-day opportunities but to be alert to possibilities of service to which the entire house church may respond. One unique development of this group is the arrangement whereby any member of the house church is authorized to expend up to five hundred dollars of the corporate funds to help others whenever he believes the need exists. Such expenditures require no prior authorization and are merely reported to the group at their next business meeting. This indicates the seriousness with which they seek an outward ministry as well as a mutual trust relationship.

This worship-oriented house church has become especially appealing to those Christians who want a meaningful church life but have become disillusioned within their past congregational experiences.

Worshiping God is an elusive act seldom orchestrated with success. There is no simple manner by which the church can cause man to worship when a group of people gather. It is even more difficult to provide a regular worship opportunity relevant to secular life. Because worship in a house church challenges our understanding of offering praise to God and is clearly related to our group life, there is a greater potential for maturing in our appreciation of this act. As we grow in our understanding, we may be enabled through the benefits of the house church to return worship to its rightful place as the highest expression of an obedient people in the midst of their mission journey.

ESTABLISHING

† **A** realistic approach to the house church, regardless of any spontaneity which may have brought it into existence, must face the relationship of house church to the institutional church.

Seeking a renewal of life within the organized church has been a blessing, and at the same time, a curse at Trinity. It has provided that familiar base without which some members would never have considered affiliation. Because such people still see hope in the institutional church, although admittedly frail, they are not inclined to add to the splintering of the church with numerous off-shoots which have no connectional ties to their fellow churchmen. On the other hand, there are those who have watched the institutional church stifle innovation for so long that they are reluctant to believe in any group still under that umbrella. Inability to believe that the desired openness is possible keeps the skeptic from exercising the freedom he has. He just can't believe that somewhere there is not a big daddy ready to stop him if his eagerness gets too far out of line.

The fact that Trinity's house churches exist within a congregation continues to elicit a positive and a negative reaction. For example, Trinity has been a welcome witness to many interested congregations who see our efforts to renew within the institution as evidence of denominational loyalty. In contrast, many other congregations view our desire to express a unique style as a judgment upon all who prefer to follow the customary congregational patterns. "Why are you calling yourselves Presbyterians?" an elder from another state once asked. "If you aren't going to follow our committee structure and keep our men's work and women's work, then what makes you Presbyterians?" The institutional patterns have a larger hold upon the thinking of the average churchman than the church dares to acknowledge.

In the revolving influence between renewal concerns and congregational customs, Trinity has been influential in its minute way in reversing or at least altering institutional patterns. The first and most obvious alteration has been the congregation's willingness *not* to build a regular church edifice. The normal congregational tendency to emphasize the physical plant was not easily overcome, nor is it ever buried permanently. With our numbers remaining small (the average membership over these eight years ranges between ninety and one hundred ten communicants), the large antebellum house has proven quite satisfactory in keeping us warm and dry for any gathering purposes which have entailed the entire cluster of house church and non-house church members. On the few occasions when we have desired larger crowds, we have either rented a school auditorium or have gone out of doors. Although members have become accustomed to meeting each Sunday in a remodeled house, this fact continues to influence visitors who are well aware of the pressures upon congregations to build. Without the existence of its house churches, I feel certain that Trinity would have felt the absence of purpose by now and exerted pressure for a building program in order to establish some sign of progress. As it is, each week's house church gatherings have so many other concerns that building a church edifice is never seen as relevant to the problems at hand.

The financial bind which tightens around a congregation through its own church plant hardly needs expression, so obvious is it to most church officers. Recent statistics from my own denomination show a continuing high requirement for church maintenance for years following any building fund campaign. In fact, building receipts have remained relatively steady over the past fifteen years along with the almost casual rise and fall of benevolent giving. During this same fifteen year period, however, the current expenses of congregations have skyrocketed. Congregations are keeping their money at home, if not for the cost of new building extensions, then for the increased cost of maintaining them. Most church plants are built through vital contributions of nominal members who understand such material needs more clearly than the intangible ones. Unfortunately, their contributions generally return to an occasional gift after the three-year building debt is paid. Consequently an even greater financial burden is placed upon those committed members who must now undergird the increased cost of current expenses. When one considers what new potential for ministry the congregations would have once their own buildings no longer strangled them with indebtedness nor sapped their stewardship of time with maintenance demands, it is clear that the church in the house could redirect tremendous amounts of energy to the pressing needs of body and soul in our day.

† **A**nother congregational custom altered by virtue of the house church is the relationship of the clergyman. The release of the laity for ministry was described in chapter five which discussed the mission work of house churches. In addition to such lay breakthroughs, the clergy role also changes. There was a time when Trinity house church members were implicitly asking, concerning their minister, "What does *he* want us to do?" This concept of pastoral relations has long been held even by the "pillars" of the church, so the attitude was not surprising. Somewhere through the early years of growth in house churches the majority of our small communities began developing their own personalities and purposes, as well as

their own highly individual needs. This reversed the relationship, so that the minister came to ask, "What do *they* want me to do?" This does not mean that the clergyman's role is without its own initiative. It does establish a new interdependence between professional ministers and lay ministers by recognizing the need for each to contribute to the other. There are no higher and lower echelons of ministries between clergy and laity. There are only various gifts and various opportunities and callings to exercise such gifts. The ministry belongs to the *laos,* the whole people of God, which includes the clergyman but does not center on him.

At Trinity the clergyman is seldom expected in a house church meeting; once a month is frequent and once a quarter is not uncommon. There are times when a particular house church interprets this absence as neglect; at other times they count it a blessing. When the pastor is there it is expected that he should feel free to bring in requested resources, give some perspective to the group's work, or otherwise join their activities. He is not expected to lead the group.

This lay resourcefulness has been one of the most hopeful signs of the house church's potential to affect the institutional church. Due to the lay initiative inherent in house church life, commitments have been made and mutual involvement has developed that few clergymen would dare to expect in customary congregational structures. Openness to one another and innovative styles are hallmarks of the house church influence on the average layman. I have often returned from a trip aware that advances have been made in reconciling breaks within a group or in operating procedures for mission for which I had felt little hope. The Community Service House Church broke through the barriers hindering their development of a sheltered workshop in such an atmosphere. After months of explorations, their efforts to begin a workship were still meeting dead ends. Each suggested approach ultimately encountered a new rule or material limitation that thwarted their mission. In fact, as I prepared to take my vacation, I recall saying to them, "Well, it seems obvious that this idea must wait for another time, but at least you tried." With that I drove off with the family, putting all work behind temporarily and that particular concern behind forever. I returned to find a workshop off and running in our church house. The leaders were overjoyed with their ability to provide for the retarded young ladies the opportunities they so desperately needed. This is only one example of a number of ministries I had prematurely buried as I slipped back into institutional expectations of the laity. In our depersonalized society when much of the church fosters vicarious involvement, the house church promise of direct participation creates zest necessary to change radically the Christian's contribution within the church.

† Loyalty to the denomination is another question which inevitably arises relating to the house church within the institution. Does the presence of house churches within a congregation, accompanied by the absence of more typical programs, reduce the members' concern for the broader work of the church? Again, in the experience of Trinity, there has been little appreciable difference in this area in comparison with the more traditional congregations. The fact is that, aside from the absence of our women from the area Presbyterial meetings, numerous members of Trinity have served within the committees of presbytery, synod, and General Assembly. There is one difference in that members of our congregation hear less about program emphases and they attend fewer conferences stressing the work of the church. After all, is it better to keep attending programs designed to move the church outward or to be actually involved in that outward move, thus ignoring the program?

Members seldom discuss the issue of loyalties nor does it seem important to them. They do see the need to respond through traditional channels but they get impatient with those who consider it disloyal to move beyond prepared denominational programs. Like a reluctant parent who spends years preparing his child for adulthood yet hesitates to free him to contribute to society, some institutional parents only begrudgingly grant to the congregation that they are actually ready for mission and need not spend more time at meetings merely to discuss mission.

However, the real pressure against sustaining our basic convictions which bring changes in congregational life comes not from the official courts of the church but from acquaintances of the members. Such friends, by their continual assumption that traditional congregational patterns are the criteria of acceptability, plant seeds of doubt which undermine the congregation's openness to change. This pressure comes to members of Trinity frequently from friends and acquaintances at work and in other social groupings. It is a subtle force which appreciably hinders true renewal of the body of Christ. Unfortunately, the chief voices raised in objection to the house church, its existence, and its involvements come from within the church itself. The world seems to welcome the new look.

Many members are forced to contend with insinuations that they have left the fold of the true church and should return home. Such house church members have to live with the judgment of others in the town who accuse the house church of practicing a new kind of exclusiveness. Innovative approaches to church work are seldom interpreted as a genuine concern to bring new life and purpose to the membership. Here again we see how creative enthusiasm and genuine commitment within the church are more suspect than trustworthy as evidence of the power of the Holy Spirit at work. This persistent type of pressure has a decided effect. Some members seek more compromise with community standards concerning what churches should look like and do. Others fight against loss of hope for any real breakthrough where God alone leads. They move in ways which, if continued, would take them out of the institutional church.

Officially, Trinity's relations with the higher courts of the church have been open, mutually supportive, and encouraging. The Board of National Ministries and the local presbytery have invested large sums to provide staff members for two separate one-year periods. Officially, the congregation has not differed in its institutional relations from any churches in the presbytery. Consequently, the institutional church beyond the local level has shown itself more flexible and willing to encourage newfound directions than have many local churches.

† **W**hat would objective data show concerning the effect of belonging to a house church in contrast to membership in a church of traditional design? Realizing the limitations of studying only one congregation, our denominational Board of National Ministries nevertheless set about the difficult task of testing for demonstrable differences in house church participants. Trinity was their test group. Dr. Harry Lefever, a sociologist at Spelman College in Atlanta, was employed to create a suitable test instrument, administer it, and write an evaluation. The results of his work are now a part of the library of the Board of National Ministries.[1]

In his report Dr. Lefever disclosed that he had used as one part of his test instrument a questionnaire which would invite a valid comparison between the attitudes of Trinity members and those persons tested by Donald Metz in California. Mr. Metz' study is now the basis of a book which reveals important trends in new congregational growth.[2] He reveals that development is conditioned by the membership's approach to their security and to their mission.

In Part IV of his study Dr. Lefever writes:

> The commitment of Trinity members to sacrificial goals stands in sharp contrast to the findings of Donald L. Metz in his study of several United Presbyterian congregations, reported on in his book, *New Congregations.* He found that, although the official pronouncements of the denomination paid lip service to sacrificial goals (or what he termed formal goals), in the actual structuring of the congregations the survival goals tended to become predominant. Since Metz' study was used to formulate the questions on goals asked of Trinity members it should be helpful to review his study in some detail.
>
> After making a survey of the contemporary themes in theology and the official documents of the United Presbyterian Church, Metz concluded that the study of goals centers around four themes. These four are community, nurture, service, and sacrifice. The goal of community has to do with the quality of the internal life of the congregation, nurture with the intentions

of the congregation with regard to the individual, service with responsibility for society, and sacrifice with the manner in which the congregation assigns priorities to its goals.

The goal of community puts emphasis on a unity of belief, acceptance of the form of government which is practiced, participation in office and meetings, and fellowship of a quality that encourages candor and close personal ties. The goal of nurture emphasizes a program of education that includes all members, continual and widespread changing and sharing of the authority positions, and communication of the intentional activities of the members in their extra-congregational efforts. The goal of service emphasizes confronting the world with its beliefs and asking for direct response, and working to alter the social relations of men. The goal of sacrifice emphasizes the sacrificing of old forms of congregational life and work for new forms. It reduces to a secondary status efforts for organizational survival.

Metz designates these above four goals as the formal goals implicit in current theological themes. But he points out that often these formal goals are subverted into survival goals; that there is a tendency for the emphasis to shift from concern with mission and adventure to concern with survival. The survival goals put emphasis on recruiting and maintaining members, establishing physical facilities, and stabilizing a base of financial support. More specifically each of the four formal goals shifts emphasis in a direction away from those stated above. The goal of community is redirected and the result is a lack of tolerance for difference in doctrinal understanding, dissatisfaction with the leadership of the congregation, and lack of close personal relationships. The goal of nurture develops in the direction of survival when it focuses on a program limited to children, when it excludes laymen from participation in leadership, and when there is no means provided for lay members to share their extra-congregational efforts of mission with the rest of the congregation. In the case of service goals, they are subverted when attention focuses only on the internal life of the congregation, when the emphasis is on only the explicitly religious aspects of its service, and when there is a lack of any significant wrestling with the real social conditions of the world outside its walls. The goal of sacrifice is lost when survival goals become ends in themselves instead of being secondary to the formal goals.[3]

After a quote from Donald Metz concerning the proper relationship between formal goals and survival goals, Dr. Lefever adds:

"Perhaps Trinity will eventually be tempted to emphasize survival goals at the expense of sacrificial goals. But for the moment, as reflected in the findings of this study, it seems fair to say that Trinity members are quite conscious of the difference between sacrificial goals and survival goals and are quite consistently committed to the former."[4]

Dr. Lefever also reported upon the relationship between house church life and one's openness to change.

> It was found that over two-thirds (69.8%) of the total congregation is characterized by openness to change. . . .
>
> In summary of the study of change, it is clear that Trinity as a total congregation is characterized more by openness to change than they are by resistance to change. In comparing the house church group with the non-house church group, there seems to be evidence of a slightly higher percent among the house church group whose concept of the church has changed since joining Trinity and who are characterized by openness to change. The difference is slight and without applying statistical tests it is not known whether the difference is significant. All that can be said is that there is consistent evidence all pointing in the same direction.[5]

Concerning general commitment, the Lefever study shows that the church tends to be more important for house church members than for non-house church members within Trinity. The house church has become a greater source of meaning for their lives in individual and community identity. It becomes a major avenue for their civic concerns. This increased sense of meaningfulness on the part of house church members has at times suggested the existence of two distinct groups at Trinity: house church members and non-house church members. Dr. Lefever pointed out quite accurately the presence of such differences and added that this could be a healthy source for dialogue and the expansion of concepts, or it could become a source of the breakdown of the community desired. Inasmuch as the test instrument was designed to discover differences between the two categories of members at Trinity, it is not surprising that such lines can be drawn. It is clear that house church participation makes a measurable difference in a number of significant areas, only a few of which have been shared here. Without attempting to weigh too heavily the indications of this one small example, it yet seems evident that *the house church does have an effect upon the institutional church while remaining a part of it.*

† **A**ny discussion of the effect of the house church upon the institutional church must include the dangers, real or imaginary, which its presence might pose. One danger of the house church is that it might well add to the mounting sense of frustration and the feeling of inadequacy so prevalent in much of the church today. Clergymen, laymen, priests, and nuns all feel the turmoil within the church. To suggest a personal involvement in such a little-known tenuous path as the house church within the parish can appear like asking the man already standing on cracking ice to move closer to the thinner layers. Fear of taking one more step when it appears we've walked too far already leads many to search for reasons why the house church concept will not work.

The belief that the small group in the house church will destroy the congregation by divided loyalties is another danger often voiced. There are those who do not understand how commitment to the corporate life of one small group can avoid destructive competition with the larger congregation's similar family life. Such is the mind-set of congregational loyalties in most churchmen that they are incapable of maintaining a true sense of identity with the church in two spheres. This is, of course, just as difficult with those circles of the body of Christ that are drawn wider than the single congregation as it is with any smaller circles drawn within it. The result is a feeling of danger in that expression of the church which is any other than congregational. Thus, the house church and the World Council of Churches pose the same "danger": the fear that those spheres of the church in which an individual does not personally belong cannot be trusted to be as truly the church as is the congregation. Most problems of divisiveness seemingly created by the house church can more accurately be understood as growing out of the membership's attitude toward the church universal. This is not to say that any group cannot by its own peculiarities become exclusive and cause divided loyalties, but it does mean there is no basis for assuming that the house church is inherently divisive. With proper guidance and the awareness of such a risk, the house church can avoid this danger. It can, as well, bring about a higher degree of loyalty to the entire church by experiencing community on at least two levels of church life simultaneously. Mr. Canon Lloyd, in writing about the cell movement within the Church of England called "The Servants of Christ the King," said of the fear of divided loyalties:

"The essential feature of all cellular discipleship is that a small number of people are called out of a large number for special training, and this, far from separating them from the larger group—the Church or the congregation—actually deepens and intensifies their membership of it and loyalty to it."[6] The house church is not suggested within the congregation as a means to destroy it, but as a means to enable that parent body to come alive. There should be no competition in concept. There can be none in loyalties if properly understood.

This is not to say that one should approach the house church possibility unaware of the true risks. It is indeed a dangerous endeavor to move the congregation from its well-set pegs. Nonetheless, with all of its risks, the house church movement can assist in the drastic shifts necessary in the life of the church. It can, therefore, help to bring the church to a rediscovery of its essence in the calling of the Spirit of God through the Christ.

It is right to consider house churches a protest as well as a risk today, but a healthy one. They are a protest against the pressure of society upon citizens to become functional things rather than related persons. They are a protest against the church's being an immovable idol rather than a dynamic living organism. J. C. Hoekendijk writes, "We have canonized the parish church; from an incidental pattern it became a normative model; from a historically conditioned phenomenon it became an unchangeable divine institution."[7] House churches protest this canonization. House churches are a protest against the system and the loss of confidence in the ability of the individual to effectively influence that system.

As a protest, the house church could damage much that the institutional church holds dear. But this is not necessarily bad. Some upheavals within the church that have appeared to be destructive have been blessings in disguise. Dr. Roland H. Bainton of Yale lent perspective to such protests when he said, "The cleavage of the Protestant Reformation was lamentable but out of it good did come. Luther saved the Papacy."[8] Dr. Bainton reasoned that whereas the Papacy was about to become totally secularized, Luther's protest revived the religious consciousness of the Roman Catholic Church and of the Papacy itself. In something of the same way the house church, as a protest, might well bring energy to the staid institutional church by rekindling its determination to be effective.

Because of these dangers, real and imaginary, the house church cannot be assimilated into congregational life with business going on as usual. Where there are true house churches, there will be new counter forces at work bringing shifts in direction and changes that will confront and disturb. But one could say the same about the presence of the Spirit of God.

† The relation of the house church to the institutional church raises the question of form. What form does the church rightly take? There are many concerned Christians today who see all questions of form as restrictive in the renewal of the church. Such persons see any attempt to define the house church, for example, as an indication of a return to a deadening order inconsistent with the free spirit associated with church renewal. There are, however, an increasing number of freely structured groups who are recognizing that a complete lack of form is just as paralyzing as too rigid a form. We are more aware, of course, of that other view that considers traditionally prescribed forms essential to the life of the church, so that any change in form is a move away from the true church.

One of the great hindrances to the renewal of life possible in the house church, then, is the continuing ambiguity in relating form and essence.

Is the church really present when a certain ritual takes place? If so, where is the church if this ritual changes or is stopped altogether? To answer by pointing to the church invisible will not suffice. Moving into the styles necessary for the close of this century while committing ourselves to those truths of the church that have come down to us through the centuries necessitates a rediscovery of the essential forms of the *visible* church. Many forms and rituals perpetuate cultural, national, or denominational customs. These are not only unnecessary; they are conveyors of false teachings. They lead, by such customs, to a national church that will not comprehend a faith broader than national boundaries nor deeper than the national will. If the church is to regain the self-understanding necessary to speak meaningfully to a new day, then it must strip away those forms, rituals, and customs that limit its ability to challenge people and nations beyond their present condition of humanness. Only in knowing more accurately what is our essential nature together will the church be free to release the old and accept the new. By the same process, we will also be able to give answer to those who are so disestablished that they care little for any form, assuming that all forms alike are peripheral and suffocating.

The necessity of concreting the new was brought home to me in the development of our church in the coffee house. Once the coffee house began, we were aware of the almost impossible task of communicating what it was. The most solid community churchmen could not see there anything more than a novel way to provide for the youth of the church. For them the church remained on the corner. In saying, through a variety of methods, that the church was totally present in that coffee house on any given Friday or Saturday evening we discovered how completely incomprehensible this was even to dedicated laymen and clergymen. Because the customary forms were not present, people could find no way of accepting the proposition that the church was wholly present. The fact that the waiters and waitresses going from table to table in their midst were gathered as a believing community who based their common life in worship, growth, and service did not certify to others that here is the church outside the traditional form. The churchman might agree that the church is present as an extension of the congregation but not on the basis of those elements in the coffee house alone. How strange, when such a coffee house group bore more of the identifying marks of the body of Christ in their serving moments than most church members do on any given Sunday during the one hour in which they worship with others.

This repeated experience summons the renewal church to address itself to the problem of form. When the limitations by form are so apparent, then other new forms must be held equally high as examples of the location of the true and *visible* church. The house church is the church and needs no parent organization to give it legitimacy. Thus the house church in coffee houses, in halfway houses, in high-rise apartments should be recognized as though it had been baptized with all of the official formulas and pronouncements with which any congregation is organized in order to proclaim that in this form as well lives the body of Christ. It is frightening to know that so many churchmen cannot discern the essentials of the body of Christ unless they are wrapped in familiar trappings: a gathering of people on Sunday morning carrying out a prescribed routine of worship in a specially built sanctuary. Therefore, we need to unveil the essential nature of the church, not for the sake of a new idol but to break us loose from that single form for the sake of whatever new molds God would make of us as his instruments.

This is why it is vital that the remaining churchgoers get out of the church building to gather in units small enough for each to know of his worth and, bearing the name "church," begin the pilgrimage of discerning the purpose of life together out there away from that building which, as a nailed-down form, has closed them in. Only so will we be able to maintain the essence while adapting to new forms necessary to meet the changing demands for effective ministry in our day.

The importance of wrestling with the relation of form to essence in developing new structures of the church was underlined by Professor Hans Küng in his book *The Church.* In this work, Dr. Küng emphasized the fact that we must deal with the church in its historical form rather than in the abstract.

There are two important points here:

1. Essence and form *cannot be separated.* The essence and the form of the Church should not be divorced from one another, but must be seen as whole. . . . There is not and never was, in fact, an essence of the Church by itself, separate, chemically pure, distilled from the stream of historical forms. What is changing and what is unchanging cannot be neatly divided up. . . .

2. Essence and form *are not identical.* The essence and the form of the Church should not be equated, but must be recognized and distinguished. . . . How else can we decide what is permanent in the changing form of the Church?[9]

Although we may take comfort in knowing that the search for the essentials within the church must not be sought in some ". . . unchanging Platonic heaven of ideas, but only in the *history* of the Church,"[10] the author throws us back to the real difficulty of such a search by his reminder that, "The inner nature within the outer structure can only be seen by the eye of the believing Christian."[11]

What now becomes vital for the much needed fresh search for the locale of the church today is this dependency upon belief. The important thing in admiring or criticizing the church is the *belief* of the admirer or critic, not merely the act itself. In the same way the important ingredient for which we search in determining proper form and essence is the presence of a *believing* community. "Neither admiration of the Church nor criticism of the Church really matters. What matters is the faith of the Church: that the Church, the communion of the faithful, itself believes. . . ."[12]

The directions toward which we must move if we are to separate the superfluous from the necessary in renewal movements today are further amplified when Dr. Küng states, "A community that does not believe is not the church."[13] The absolute centrality of this statement can be seen by the following excerpt:

Jesus' proclamation of the "reign of God" does not involve a demand for men to follow a new, improved moral code. It demands rather a *radical decision for God.* The choice is clear: either God and his reign or the world and its reign. Nothing must prevent man from making this radical decision between God and the world. Jesus himself left behind family and career, house and home. And he summoned other men to leave their family and social settings and accompany him as his disciples. He did not call all to leave family, career and home; he was not a social revolutionary. But each one individually he confronted with a radical decision: where in the last analysis did his heart lie—with God or with the goods of this world? . . . Man must accept radical obedience towards the will of God, while remaining in the world and working for his fellow man."[14]

By putting in close proximity Dr. Küng's thoughts on the relation between form and essence in the church and his thoughts on radical obedience, one must conclude that the proper form of the church will emerge with its proper essence when the community of people exists in radical obedience. When the rule of God is the source of the joy and life of such a community, then its most relevant and creative form for a response in contemporary society will develop without questioning its "religious" propriety and without fear of losing its essence. When the rule of God is its core and the reign of God its call, form and essence are caught up mutually in a spontaneity of movement that will free the church from all former boundaries to reveal the church in new dimensions.

The urgency of unveiling the presence of the very real and very visible church in drastically new dimensions stems from the inescapable fact that the present dimensions and structures of the church are rapidly changing. How can we expect Christians to act when they see institutional churches closing and then interpret these closings as the cessation of a creative spirit within the church? Again Professor Hans Küng suggests a wholesome response to such crises. In an interview recorded for the U.S. Navy Chaplaincy work he said:

Things are changing very rapidly . . . I think (in 1980) the institution as such will become less important. The Church is not primarily the institution but the community. . . . The big organization will be considered only a secondary help for the community. . . . A lot of the institution will probably die out and we are not to be upset too much. . . . This is not a sign that the faith will disappear, but much . . . will disappear in order to have a greater concentration on the essentials. . . . Maybe we will have less people . . . I think the church will not ask less but more, but hopefully it will ask more reasonable things.[15]

Prophecies of drastic change in the church are not rare today; nonetheless, the average church member has yet to see many visible transformations. Except for the growing indications of unrest in the church and discontent with its ability to achieve the former results with the former methods, there is little that is appreciably different about the average participants' involvement in church work. Yet it is important to prepare, so that when the drastic changes do come about we have learned through experience where the faith continues to find authentic expressions. It is for this reason that we need the benefits derived not only from experimental ministries and the underground movement, but from strikingly modern approaches within institutional life as well. This straining after signs of renewal provides the necessary catalyst for the institutional church to discover its own possibilities in tomorrow's style of Christian community.

† In the previous chapters, an effort has already been made to describe the emerging types of house church developments as they have related to areas of interest under discussion. The following examples of Christian communities have been selected particularly to give additional insight into the ways in which the house church may relate to the institutional church in the near future.

The Kairos United Methodist Church in Kansas City, Missouri, is an example of a recent development where the house church is the fundamental structure within the congregation. It is therefore another test of the ability of the house church to exist within the institution without being totally engulfed by that institution's stance.

The congregation had its beginnings in the spring of 1970. At that time approximately twenty-eight families began to meet together in search of a new form for the church. Most of them had belonged to the same congregation previously; most were under forty years of age. The group reflects all of the exuberance and freedom that one expects from a new beginning; yet, they are quite aware of the probable difficulties in their attempt to break new ground.

My first introduction to this group was at an evening meeting of their newly elected coordinating council composed of representatives of their various house churches. On that particular evening they were drawing slips of paper out of a hat to determine their new name. The name drawn was Kairos. The explanation was given that Kairos, the Greek word for "time," indicates the "now" time as opposed to any given length of time in the past or future. Although it was a random choice made by casting lots, the new name seems to fit the group well. They are determined to speak to the "now" issues and function in ways that speak to the "now" generation. They chose the house church style as that which will enable them to carry out their desires.

Their desires have already led them to unique development in a number of ways. Guided by two ordained ministers, Mrs. Susan Halverstadt and Mr. Russ Hawkins, the congregation has departed from many customs that tend to hold churches to set patterns. Their only weekly gathering time thus far, when all house churches come together, is at 5:30 each Sunday evening. They have no church school; instead they have placed the responsibility of teaching in the hands of the individual family units and the house church units. The emphasis is on an experience-oriented approach to learning more than content teaching alone. They do not plan to have a church building of their own. They are presently renting the basement of a nearby Methodist church for their Sunday evening meeting.

At this point in their life the training program does not emphasize any given pattern within a house church except that it is to be free flowing yet remaining as totally the church as possible. The elements of worship, study, and mission will complement their community but these are not set forth in any specific plan. Mission or projects on a local level will be an ever present possibility within each house church but such mission emphasis is not a prerequisite for the establishment of a house church. The emphasis is upon a minimum of structure with a maximum awareness of the issues and problems of the day.

An interesting comment which may speak to a growing new role for the clergyman came during that meeting. In considering future specific plans a young lady suggested that the male minister of the church might even preach a sermon at one of their forthcoming gatherings. This proposal was not made with tongue in cheek bu was to be considered seriously along with a variety of other possibil ties. The incident clearly suggests that here is a place where the rol of the clergyman and the use of his time and talents does not pre sume a set traditional course. This reliance upon the Kairos staff fc possible contributions frees the clergymen and allows them to cor centrate on opening new avenues for the entire group. No doubt thi is one reason why they are able to become heavily involved i community service areas such as their "Project Equality." The cler gymen have the ability to open such avenues of ministry for th entire group because they are not held too close to the confinemen of the traditional clerical role.

The Sunday evening gathering does center upon worship bu in a free style. As described by Mr. Hawkins, the introduction of Hol Communion takes place casually wherein at some point during th evening, basic remarks about the meaning of the Eucharist are ex pressed and some bread and wine are passed around.

The weekly house meetings include children throughout mos of the evening. They emphasize fellowship and close communit relations. A few members of one particular house church have al ready moved in the direction of a communal style of living althoug this is more a coincidence of concerns than an expression of purpos for the house church.

This new development is an example of the wide variety o approaches possible through the same essential ingredient of th church in the house. It will be a noteworthy test of the new grou to see if the forces of tradition overpower them even as they see new responses to their free stance. It will also be a test of th institutional church in that vicinity to see if it will allow new form to rise up within it and know them as the church.

† The house church functions as a part of the undergroun church in a number of places. I will not attempt to discuss the broac aspects of the underground church, as others have written of suc groups with more detail than is possible here.[16] It is important to note

the many similarities as well as the broad differences that exist in style and in attitude between the house church within the institutional framework of the church and those communities which have gone underground. "Underground," as here used, refers to those Christian groups which have separated themselves connectionally to some degree and ideologically almost totally from the path of established churches. Following are two examples of communities that exist somewhere in this outer circle known as the underground church.

The Ecstatic Umbrella is a community house in Kansas City. It maintains only the most remote connections with the institutional church although some sponsoring and financial support tenuously remain. Ideologically it is still farther out and is certainly in all of its characteristics more a part of the anti-religious movement of our day. It was begun as a specialized ministry within the United Methodist Church which accounts for the presence of a young Methodist clergyman who coordinates the life of the community and its mission along with a few others whose services are volunteered.

The purpose of the Ecstatic Umbrella is to function as a referral and aid center for those with no place else to go. It serves the dropout, the disestablished, the turned-off youths, as well as any who need counseling or just a friendly place to spend some time. Problems such as transient housing, welfare, general medical care, and abortion referrals come to these workers. By far their most constant work centers on the drug user. In this area of drug referral the Ecstatic Umbrella has broken barriers which enable the members to work with those on "both sides" of the drug problem. Their four telephone "hot" lines, frequently busy twenty-four hours a day, keep the lines of communication open between several establishment services in the city and those who have lost trust in them.

Their own community is small, varied, and flexible. The house in which the small group of approximately six to eight persons live is situated in a residential district of Kansas City. Two to three families comprise the core, and an occasional intern period by interested students make their "family" swell. During my brief visit, which included the evening meal served cafeteria style, we sat around on the floor in the upstairs living room. While the children moved from one lap to another, the adult talk moved from one subject to another. Terry commented on how seldom they sat down to discuss the state of the church or to reflect upon their own community life. As another member put it, "Most of us are up against the wall with our day's work right here in this building with the telephone ringing itself off the hook. So it is often eleven o'clock at night before we get a chance to sit down to consider how the other person is doing." But each one's consideration for the other person is obvious; the concern for how he is making it through the day has little need of verbalization.

I was particularly interested in this group's attitude toward those types of church life they had left, for most of them had recently been associated with the traditional church. The responses to my probes in this area were surprising. The atmosphere in which this particular community felt most at home was obviously loose, congenial, easy, and without fanfare. When the conversation moved around to the relative values of free form and strict form, and to no discipline versus a covenant of set disciplines, I expected to hear a decided attitude favoring free form exclusively. Yet in discussing the attitudes toward worship, for example, the common opinion was that they saw equal validity within both forms—strict and free. They said they could worship through the ancient liturgies just as easily as through the contemporary styles, complete with guitar, dialogue, and a loose order for the progression of worship. The same reaction was found regarding any group's concern for self-discipline. Instead of questioning whether all such disciplined groups had gotten more "uptight" than the traditions they had left, there was again a common expression of approval of that particular style of Christian community if it was what a group thought would be helpful. "If the strong disciplinarians want rigid rules, and if it suits them, then it is fine," was the general response. Somewhat puzzled I asked, "If ancient worship seems as acceptable to you as modern, and if ordered disciplines seem as appropriate a Christian response as where everyone is 'doing his own thing,' then what, to you, makes the institutional church an anathema?" The answer came quickly and without a second thought from them all, "Lack of authenticity! Falseness! Insincerity!" What the established church had communicated to these young adults was that the institutional church, even in its desperate attempts to reach the youth through an occasional folk mass of their own, was plagued with its overriding lack of an authentic life-style in the faith it claimed to uphold. I was hearing what was to be confirmed again and again in my visits: that those who are earnestly seeking a renewal of the meaning of discipleship today recognize a great flexibility of approaches but insist upon one common denominator—a total embodiment of whatever style that community claims.

During our discussion a Volkswagen bus pulled up in front of the house and about eight transient young people piled out looking for a place to stay. One of the men at dinner left us for awhile, then returned, indicating to the others that the new arrivals were making themselves at home downstairs using the bath, rest, and referral facilities that are available on the first floor.

The particular joy I felt about this group came from observing their ability to flow so smoothly from the language and relationships expected of them by their "establishment" visitors to the language and relationships that fit in with the traveling hippie, entangled drug addict, or searching student. A sadness about this group was their obvious awareness that the institutional church was at best lukewarm if not suspicious of their efforts to minister in a nontraditional, innovative way. They were not so much bothered by the risks involved, nor by the insecurity in having their few remaining support funds cut off. What bothered them was that the thin thread of hope might soon be cut by the institutional church's failure to understand what discipleship meant to them. There was a strong feeling within this group that their present mission could not long count on the understanding or the support of the organized church. Nor did they see any way for their task and concern to achieve any strong success accounts. They were left therefore to a commitment based upon their present belief in the rightness of their task with no expectations for the future except to remain true to their ministry as they saw it until someone stopped them.

This final sober accounting of their future prospects did not bring with it any dismal outlook, however. Soon there was laughter, a move to clean up the dishes, talk of a few other people who might soon join their "family" and its mission, and preparation for the needs expressed as the evening phone calls began coming in.

† Even a visitor can detect that Sunday in New York has a number of sounds not heard the rest of the week. Most of them come from the city's new found silence—which enables one to hear and see in a different way. Gone is the roar of dozens of machines, thousands of cars and trucks, millions of voices—all competing for a frequency by which they establish their presence and determination to play a part in moving the city through its hectic week. On Sunday the empty buildings appear strangely out of place. I was made especially aware of this new perspective one hot summer Sunday by the intruding crow of a rooster. The day began early with the fog settling down on Broadway. With the tops of the tallest buildings now extinguished by the haze, and the empty street disappearing into a mist only a block away, one got the impression that this place called Broadway could lead one to a country road instead of to lower Manhattan and Times Square. Only the sporadic and distant sirens reminded one of the noisy reality that would return to such streets on other days. On this day, the machines seemed to give way to the humans who ran them. There was the sound and sight of a waiter and waitress arguing behind the breakfast counter, carrying on as if they were man and wife. The fuss was not hidden from those of us who sat there feeling like the quiet members of the family. I left wondering which one would win the raging battle to decide who would mix the batter of cream next time. There was the deadening sound of the phone box as a bearded and ragged man tried to force it to release some of its tightly gripped coins; the same old man had been seen earlier peering in the restaurant window. Walking toward 116th Street, I observed a young delivery boy yelling up to the eighth floor where a bulky woman leaned out of the window. He asked whether he could bring his bike up the stairs to keep it from being stolen while he delivered his package. Sunday did not reduce the threats of a hostile world. A little girl turned her coloring book for her smaller sister while they half-crouched, half-stood on the

steps just a quick leap away from their basement apartment sanctuary.

A few blocks along 116th Street there was a door with a familiar name blended in with all of the other windows and storefront signs along the way. A person would miss it if he went by with his thoughts elsewhere. I entered and looked around for a few minutes in the small bookstore and the back room office. After awhile I was invited upstairs for a cup of coffee. I had had no lunch, so I gladly accepted. The upstairs kitchen was like any other might have been in East Harlem except perhaps for the large table which was painted purple. I was unaware of what was to follow but was overjoyed to discover that I had chanced that hour to drop in on the people of Emmaus House. Soon eight or so young men and women were seated around the table. No questions were asked but first names were offered. Strong coffee was served in mugs painted in flower designs. A man in a sweat shirt produced a pulpit-sized Bible and began to read. A young woman read some poetry. Reactions to the readings were invited; all of us were brought into the conversation. Prayers were offered spontaneously around the table. Dry bread was broken and passed with the familiar words, ''Take, eat, this is my body.'' Some homemade wine was hastily concocted out of a mixture of random juices found in the refrigerator. It too was passed; ''this is my blood poured out for the forgiveness of sins.'' It was then that we all became aware of those sounds in the back courtyard. During the prayers of celebration of life a jazz combo had struck up some Dixieland music outside the window, unaware that they were becoming the choral accompaniment to the holy Eucharist just a few yards away. As if to accompany them, a rooster crowed. (I will resist the obvious scriptural allusions that could be offered at this point except to say that a jazz combo and a rooster crowing do not make a bad accompaniment for the various frames of heart needed to really appreciate Holy Communion.) Needless to say, I learned quickly that no one is a stranger at the table as it is spread at Emmaus House.

Since 1966, when it was begun by three Catholic priests, Fathers Kirk, Young, and Mann, Emmaus House has existed as one sign of the underground church. The vision for this interdenominational community began in Rome where Father Kirk and Father Young dreamed of a community patterned after the house churches of early Christendom. Emmaus House is patterned after that early house church style. The association here of Emmaus House to early house church life is not one of form but of the stance taken toward the establishment. As with the early Christian community, Father Kirk sees the true role of the Christian community as revolutionary in its implications for life, in contrast to the present culture, as a necessary move to bring about such a life. He means by revolutionary, a stance whereby today's value systems are rejected, and those of the gospel are seen in their true radically new nature. He does not seem to mean by revolutionary the violent overthrow of existing structures, although it is understood that such structures should be confronted at every possible opportunity.

In the book, *The Underground Church,* Father Kirk writes:

> This process of faith implies a rejection of those forms of religion which are an occasion of idolatry, which become a cave where one escapes from the presence of the living and free God. For our God is not a temple dweller. He advances through time. Again and again he lets the new conquer the old. He is not the God of the status quo, but rather is the Lord of the future, history, and the world. Living a life of faith for Emmaus means exposing ourselves to the endless new doings of God in the secular world.[17]

The new doings of God as seen by the Emmaus members have led them into a community life that includes residential members who move into Emmaus House or close by for a year's commitment. There are also nonresidential members who meet with them each Sunday for their corporate worship and fellowship. Unstructured prayer, simple Eucharistic celebrations, and serious Bible study mark a part of their life together.

Serving others is implicit in their new birth. They have found themselves responding to needs that come from the simple but highly effective ministry of presence—being there in the midst of those persons for whom you care. Some of the calls for services have led to a remedial reading program, a hospitality house, service in local political and social organizations, and meetings organized by Emmaus to deal with pertinent issues of the day. At the present time one of their concerns is to bring the issue of nonviolence before the various organized groups that are seeking to bring about radical change in East Harlem.

No one is paid a salary at Emmaus House. The members volunteer all of the services performed, from cooking for the rest of the "family" to providing a guest speaker service for those who want to hear more about their type of ministry. Father Kirk further describes their unique life as they understand themselves.

> Together, we seek to *be* the Church of Jesus Christ, which is "where two or three are gathered together in his name." We feel that the Church can no longer witness corporately as a community. So we must think more in terms of the Church in small *koinonia* groups. Faced with a Church which so often is building-centered—our money, time, and life are sometimes centered around Church buildings and organizations, and the "good layman" is one who is linked with this kind of institutionalism—we are saying that a return to the cellular structure of the Church is a necessity for its life. As exemplified by the early Church, which was lived and spread by house-communities, any community which comes together with the basic elements for "Church" (Acts 2:42)—fellowship, teaching, prayer, the Breaking of the Bread—*is* the Church in its fullness.[18]

Although Father Kirk has written that the members of Emmaus House are uncertain about their future forms and directions (preferring to maintain an emphasis upon that Abrahamic style of venturing into an uncertain future knowing that it is God's), he has offered some thoughts about the church that may emerge tomorrow.

> In the Church of the future, the worshipping community will be structured around house churches like Emmaus, and the big, geographically determined parish will become obsolete. The worship groups must remain small—no more than sixty— because there is a leavening action in small groups. Only small groups can offer a liturgy that relates to *your* intimate life problems, that increases *your* sense of social action, *your* sense of responsibility toward others. The large parish is a pre-industrial concept. Let the churches crumble! We must de-propertize, renounce the matériel of power. The Church as a corporate structure will always remain reactionary—she has too much to protect. She must divest herself of property to return to the spiritual roots of the Gospel.[19]

The members of Emmaus House validate in their corporate life the words they say. They work toward the visions they see.

Later on the same Sunday of my visit, I found myself wandering along Riverside Drive by the Hudson. A mighty temple of a church there that occupied one entire block was closed. The janitor seemed genuinely sorry that he could not allow me to view the interior which was apparently the customary reason for which passersby desired entry. We talked awhile between the bars of the tall black gate. In coming upon this mighty edifice that dominated the skyline like the temples of old, I could not help feeling the strong contrast between the two approaches and situations of discipleship that existed in Emmaus House and here.

It was third-century Dura rediscovered; in going to the market, one would take the usual route past the temple of Zeus and thence to the center of the city's marketplace and the great temple of Artemis. It was to sense again in awesome wonder how tenuous is the relationship of the small Christian cult in the house to the life and power of the city.

The huge stones piled high in their stateliness seemed to symbolize a religion in our day that everywhere stands impervious to the cries of so many locked within its form—cries to know the gifts that God has turned loose in the world and offers freely to those who can also turn loose to take them. It was enough to make one wonder which place embodied God's unique type of power, which place would be able to stand. I remembered Jesus' words of rebuke to the Pharisees when they did not appreciate the crowds proclaiming that they had seen God at work in a new place and in a new way. They said to Jesus, " 'Master, check your disciples,' but he answered, 'I tell you, if these keep silence the stones will cry out.' As he drew near and came in sight of the city he shed tears over it." (Luke 19:39–41) Surely it is within the precedence our Lord has set to shake the foundations of our mighty fortresses, rip the veil, and cause an unrelenting voice to make it known once again that his Spirit is released and moves from our temples down into the masses of people in our Times Square.

PROJECTING

† We have seen the unveiling of God's Spirit calling the church to rise up as an authentic presence in the world. We have seen the house church emerging in a variety of patterns, developing new approaches as a means of responding to that calling. We have had some feeling of the pulsations of a number of house churches as they strive to move toward the city in mission and toward one another in community, acknowledging God in both spheres.

We have seen that we can be the church when there is no building; we can hear the call to mission in the world when there is no church program directing us; and we can dance to the joys in God when there is no music.

We have seen the charismatic outbreak of many house church groups as a new dynamic peppered across states and continents. Dozens of house church communities are offering variety, freshness, and hope to the disillusioned who are not in the institutional church and to those desperately seeking new life from within.

We have seen this phenomenon and it is enough. We do not need additional signs to lift our hopes. If we experience such breakthroughs of the creative Spirit once in awhile, we know that our lives shall never again be without anticipation.

What projections could now be offered regarding the contribution of the house church as a viable form of Christian community? In making such an evaluation, it cannot be overstated that the necessity for our day is to view all movements as tentative. We must maintain an openness to allow for directions yet undreamed of.

We should never forget that, while men dare to work with, evaluate, and improve their life together in the church, the body of Christ is not man's. No organization of man should be equated with what God is doing and has done throughout history in calling to himself a peculiar people who, through faith, constitute his church. This pilgrim people moves through the centuries in and out of man's organizations so that God's church is never limited to what man sees as the church either in new birth or old traditions.

Even so, while I am not at all tempted to make messianic claims about the house church, I do believe that the messianic spirit can be seen there more clearly than in most expressions of the church today. I do believe man can gather in community in ways that more closely reflect God's moving Spirit than our customary organizations have allowed. It is presumptuous and risky to point to any specific movement, such as the house church, and to say here is where God is revealing his renewing Spirit today. That cloud formation in the sky which we think is the sign of a new wind just might be the vapor trail of a much swifter movement we did not look up in time to see. Whether the house church phenomenon is hailing the future or saying a last farewell to the past can be known only in time. What is clear is that it is here.

Whatever else must remain conjecture, one thing is certain: the house church is a present reality. Interest in it is growing. It is exciting. The people who have entered into this new style of Christian community are, for the most part, open-minded in their search for new meaning. They are positive about life's joys and challenges and are dedicated in their desire to be a part of needed change. The house church is here in many variations within a broad range of denominations. It is not here at the request of an organizational hierarchy but as the result of a grass roots concern. The house church seeks to be a sign of things to come, not a schismatic movement calling for a return to the past. It is here and, therefore, must be taken into account by those who hail it and those who are suspicious of its unorthodox rise.

The rise of the house church cannot be understood in isolation. It is occurring in a cultural context which will affect it for good and for bad. A brief look at the forces within society which will be detrimental to the emerging house church life-style will be helpful. Four elements stand out: secularization, fear of change, mounting suspicion of the unorthodox, and insulated living.

If the house church is to survive effectively, it must deal with the growth of secularization. In such a setting those who wish to communicate a sophisticated understanding of the church in the world will have to contend with an audience that knows less and less of the meaning of church in any form—traditional, historical, or renewed. The decline in serious faith which demands church renewal is the same weakness which makes that renewal almost impossible to achieve. As secularization adds to a religiously illiterate society, there will be fewer people open to a call to a new form of the church where only the essence is given and the style must be developed.

The fear of change that remains in every generation but increases in times of national unrest will no doubt hinder this movement. It is unfortunate that the institutional church today is composed of that level of comfortable society which resists taking risks. Those Christians in the grandstand are not as anxious to change the rules of the game as are those Christians in the arena contending with lions. If the house church rises authentically it will find less acceptance by the church-dominated middle class than it will in the subcultures that are anxious for change.

Natural suspicion of the unorthodox by the various power blocks within any given community will be another force working against the success of the church in the house. If one could imagine how the city fathers would react to an underground civic club, one might come close to the incomprehension to be expected by the community at large regarding the house church. This lack of understanding will place innumerable barriers in the way of the effectiveness of the house church.

The detached American is still a major hindrance to any move toward meaningful community despite a hopeful new segment that seeks to overcome our neurotic fear of involvement with one another. We are a land of joiners as indicated by any obituary, but we resist like the plague an organization that reveals our true nature. Since the house church is not an organization or church that might enhance our image but one that reveals our true nature, this no-touch culture will not warmly receive the house church challenge.

Along with those cultural forces that are seen as detrimental to the house church, we may observe other developments in society which should contribute to the growth of the church in the house. These more positive facets of society are found within the sociological, psychological, and even theological realms.

Sociologically, we see a tremendous new interest today in being a part of a genuine community. Paradoxically, this desire for close community exists in the midst of the continuing detached style of living mentioned earlier. In other words, secularization makes new birth more difficult to achieve, but more authentic once it has occurred. We seek detachment out of fear and despair. We seek community out of hope and love. The paradox is not new. What is different is the increased need today to act on our hopes. This desire is leading many suburbanites into close community groupings. The necessity for rapid assimilation into a community, brought about by the mobility of modern families, lends itself to the quest for a house church type of fellowship. Also, the growing social breakdown of traditional lines of family identity is a force that will invite attention to the house church and its potential for becoming an extended family.

The increased availability of psychological resources which contribute to group sensitivity provides an improved center for house church development. We are now able to take more risks in being open to one another for we know how to work through our difficulties in close interpersonal relationships. It is increasingly evident, especially among young adults, that people desire a deeper level of communicating than that provided at an afternoon tea. Increased understanding of group dynamics provides this opportunity.

Although there is less interest in religion today, the man on the street assumes that wherever God is, he is not confined to the institutional or liturgical restrictions of his past. While there is a reported decline in institutional religion there is a comparable attraction to that religious approach which sees God at work in the secular world. The house church can offer an embodiment of this contemporary theological awareness. Each of these forces at work outside the church will play an important role in determining which paths the church in the house may follow.

Let us now turn our attention to a current evaluation of the house church itself to observe what factors within are contributing to its present strengths and weaknesses. Present weaknesses consist primarily of the untried aspects of the house church style which one must assume will become a test in the near future.

One test has to do with its ability to function as a self-sufficient community. Heretofore most church experimental ministries have been dependent upon the parent congregation or higher church agencies for the resources necessary to serve and survive. Although the house church need not cut all ties with the institutional church, it should strive for a self-sustaining interdependence similar to that maintained by most congregations. Inasmuch as most house churches are quite limited in material strength, there is a need to experiment with ways to cluster for determining goals that will allow the group to move according to its own resources without undue dependency upon a parent body.

Another area of the house church development which has yet to be tested adequately has to do with the relative distance of the house church from the more traditional congregational forms. How closely can a group seeking to be a living organism align itself with those structures that are already fixed organizations? It is apparent that most house churches are considerably removed from the domain of any particular congregation. The poles of the problem can be seen by recalling statements by two house church authors. Dr. T.

Ralph Morton of The Church of Scotland has said, "No reform in the Church will be effective unless it affects the organization of the Church."[1] Taking this cue we can recognize the value in developing those clustered styles of house churches which exist as an integral part of a congregation. In this way the catalytic effect of the house church will directly influence the core of the institutional church. At present, there are few congregations which have successfully replaced their organizational charts to make room for such a network of house churches. Allowing the church to exist within the church in a visible cellular fashion releases the Spirit to influence the whole body.

There is, of course, a great danger in moving toward this institutional core. Bishop Robinson of The Church of England has written in personal correspondence of his view of the house church today. He said, "The house church seems to me now one of those innovations that has got thoroughly absorbed into the life of all our traditions and no longer really raises serious controversy."[2] He reminds us of the hazardous effect of the establishment upon the church and its penchant for draining the zeal of a group. It is true that we can easily run from our true purposes by getting caught up in the programs of an organization. Recognizing the great risk involved in developing house churches close to the core of congregational life, I believe such risks should be taken for the hope of the church.

Although a small number of congregations have house church clusters within their fellowships, there are practically no official statements from higher church courts recognizing the house church as a valid alternative to basic congregational life. A notable exception is the recent study within the Synod of the Golden Gate of the United Presbyterian Church. In a committee "think" paper adopted for study in 1971 this synod said, "Much happened in the time of the First Century Church—new groups are arising today. They are seeking to witness to new forms of the expression of the Spirit. There is a need for conversation between established congregations and newly arising groups so that both may hear the voice of the Spirit through the other." The paper went on to declare, "The committee [on Experimental Ministries] will seek, where appropriate, to *recognize such groups and encourage the total Church to respond to them as full participants in ministry along with other forms such as local congregations.''*[3] [Italics mine] This example constitutes a seldom observed effort on the part of the higher judicatories to recognize Christian communities outside the congregation. We would do well to support similar moves in other church courts.

Still another facet of house church life that needs to be explored lies in the development of new approaches to nurture in the faith. The absence of suitable guidelines for Christian education within a house church setting and the common tendency among house church members to resist traditional educational procedures leaves most house church groups without adequate approaches to the data of the faith. Their embodiment of the faith cannot last forever without a system of nurture that deals more deeply with a Christian's total education. Some groups are experimenting with variations of inter-generational education. This broadly graded resource available in some denominations is a first step in the necessary development of house church family education. The hope that the house church may contribute an innovative alternative to the Sunday school is as yet on the horizon.

A final area to be explored at length is the problem of new wine versus old wineskins, thus the classic question: Will we throw out the baby with the bathwater? Any reformation faces this danger. In reacting against deadening religious forms, the house church risks attracting persons who would just as well throw out the Lord of the church and feel creative in doing so. Many house churches are reluctant to consider any activities that smack of institutional staleness. The ones who are able to overcome this dilemma approach new styles openly while accepting boldly the presence of Christ as the heart of their house gatherings. Through kitchen Communion, they submit to the test of being in the world but not of the world, of standing in awe of the majesty of the Lord, but seeing that majesty present in the sweat and fears of society.

Can the church which meets in the commonness and simplicity of a kitchen or storefront maintain its awareness of the global existence of the body of which they are a part? The obvious answer is that where form and ritual and size and grandeur are taken away, a greater maturity of the living faith is needed to maintain that awareness. The house church, because it is small, need not lose its experience in the church universal.

The above areas of house church life reflect uncertainty. They are reviewed to confess incompleteness and to suggest specific directions for improvement. It is equally important to note those strengths of the house church which already stand out.

House church life most certainly increases the level of trust between participating members. When members, meeting weekly, deal with their basic needs and fears, their true identities soon surface. Each exposure increases the trust level, thereby inviting further openness. As we desperately need one another today, this experience of honest community becomes an effective instrument in the ministry of healing and reconciling love.

Another house church strength is its enhancement of participation in corporate decision-making. Caught as we are in the midst of so many systems where our own contribution seems impossible, the house church enables us to play a significant role in determining our own life-style. There is no chain of command, computer, or involved machinery making arbitrary decisions. It is not necessarily efficient this way, but each person knows that he makes a difference.

The house churches rising up today are bringing about a dramatic change in the area of outreach. By listening to their own communities' needs they are letting the world call them to their common tasks. This brings the mission of the church down to a grass roots effectiveness that can seldom if ever be effected on a denominational level. Because the house church feels the call to mission personally and locally, the resources and the commitment to sustain such a task are increased many times.

Also, house churches today are for the most part naturally ecumenical in outlook even though they may belong to a particular denomination. While church officials are still seeking ways to heal our many divisions, laymen within house churches are demonstrating how little denominationalism matters.

These observations of present strengths and weaknesses of the house church movement offer insight into at least four directions this trend of new church life may take.

First, house churches could become absorbed into the church

as another passing fad with the accompanying depreciation of its prime influence for renewal. This is a pattern that has been seen in many other renewal efforts within the church. It is a pattern that brought about the temporary halt of the growth of the house church concept in Britain. Institutionalization is the most likely end in store for the house church movement unless it does indeed represent a new breath of the Holy Spirit. If it is simply a new way of running from the confronting power of the gospel, it will soon pass.

Second, the house church could evolve in such a way that it has the true spirit, yet has no option but to go underground due to the fear of that spirit by the institutional church. We are prone to be suspicious of new forms rather than to rejoice in the possibility that the Spirit of God may be working in their midst. There is, of course, a need to test the spirit but often the verdict has been decided before the testing gets underway. An underground church could well be consistent with God's will in our day.

A third possibility, and one that continues to hinge upon the movement of the Holy Spirit, is that the house church could become the only true remnant of the church in a society that, through secularization, has brought about the death of the institutional church. In parts of Europe and the United States the non-Christian populace already so outnumbers the Christians that it is only a matter of time before the church's mighty edifices will be forced to break down into small communities to survive. In this case the house church style might become the dominant one for the Christian community in a totally secular age.

A fourth and final prospect for the future of the house church is that it would be allowed to remain a healthy catalyst for renewal and be welcomed by the institutional church. Without losing its unique power for renewal, the house church may well become an acceptable and primary substructure. Indeed it could become the most welcome style within the institutional church. This possibility is evidenced by the growing number of congregations showing interest in procedures for implementation within their congregations. It is my belief that this latter is the most desirable at the present time.

Recognizing its many inadequacies, the house church movement emerges as a realistic hope for the revolution of God's love. The community which follows the Way *is* capable of surviving, changing radically, and carrying a meaningful gospel into our new world. This is affirmed because the historic events that shaped and gave creative power to those first communities of house churches are events effectively present today. The love revealed then is here now. The Lord revealed then is here now. And the common man with all of his faults is still here with the same potential for renewal we saw then.

In our highly complex world the house church will seldom resemble its earlier form. There is, however, no reason to doubt that a small band of dedicated Christians cannot send out the same shock waves that turned the world upside down in the beginning of our Lord's revolution. This hope is realistic because the house church movement is not built upon an improvement in form or structure alone. It is based, rather, upon the style of life Christians maintain in the midst of their world. It moves the Christian into his secular world in the company of those with whom he has made a particular contract to be community. It becomes the gospel incarnate. The house church is a realisitc hope because it can move us from the temple to the heart of Times Square.

The hope is realistic because the house church can reveal the realities of faith and fear within the body of believers. By exposing who we are, we are freed to face the God exposed in our midst.

The house church is a realistic hope today because through it we can act. Hebrews 12:1 reminds us that we "should throw off everything that hinders us, especially the sin that clings so easily, and keep running steadily in the race we have started." Big church buildings and large gatherings are the world's criteria for effectiveness. If the race is to be run effectively we cannot maintain our encumbering robes of real estate with their accompanying self-deceptions regarding the fruits of the spirit.

In the church in the house many fears can be overcome that enable us to discard our security blankets. We fear the loss of an accepted community identity. But the house church challenges us to live without a known image, except as humans bound within the covenant and freed to live in a worldly insecurity. We fear unacceptability among ourselves without the proper dress and speech of the church. But the house church provides that setting in which we can relax in the assurance that we are recognized ultimately for our common hope in love even after we are known through and through. We fear the demise of the church without impressive structures. But the house church calls us to let the Lord build us up instead as living stones. By its life-style we are called to overcome the fear that says unless we build the house, our Lord labors in vain.

In other words, the church in the house keeps on reminding us that we are kept by God's grace and not by our own cunning or capabilities. Its way dares to believe that we can go through the revealing of our own failures and still come up smiling with an assurance that beneath the darkness there is a light that the darkness cannot overcome.

The house church movement promises to reveal anew how God is with man. It gives form to that trust which says that when all is explored, all is stripped bare, all is known, what is exposed is not our final despair but our ultimate joy: God is love, and man lives in the midst of good news.

From the cross, God's victory of love over hate brought about an unveiling of man's significance and life's purpose that had been hidden in the religious temples for centuries. "But Jesus gave a loud cry and breathed his last. And the veil of the Temple was torn in two from top to bottom. The centurion, who was standing in front of him, had seen how he had died, and he said, 'In truth this man was a son of God.' " (Mark 15: 37–39) Today there is need again to see this Son of God in the midst of the commonplace, to celebrate life through his kind of love, and to take off our shoes aware that man dwells in the presence of God.

NOTES

PROLOGUE

1. The Very Reverend E. W. Southcott, taped conversation, Atlanta, Georgia (November 1969). Used by permission.

BECOMING

1. "Harrisonburg's House Church: Hope of the Future?" Frances Furlow, *Presbyterian Survey,* John Allen Templeton, ed., LIX (June 1969), p. 27. Used by permission.
2. See Donald L. Metz' *New Congregations: Security and Mission in Conflict* (Philadelphia: The Westminster Press, 1967) for an excellent explanation of these forces at work in new congregations.

DISCOVERING

1. J. G. Davies, *Daily Life in the Early Church* (London: Lutterworth Press, 1952), p. 25. Used by permission.
2. *Ibid.,* citing M. Rostovtzeff, *Dura-Europos and Its Art* (Oxford: Clarendon Press, 1938), pp. 130–134.
3. Rostovtzeff, *op. cit.,* p. 100. Used by permission.
4. *Ibid.,* p. 130.
5. "The Church in the House," Hans-Ruedi Weber, *Concern,* No. 5 (CONCERN Pamphlet Series, 721 Walnut Avenue, Scottdale, Pa. 15683, June 1958), pp.9–10. Used by permission.
6. *Ibid.,* p. 13.
7. Edwin H. Robertson, "The House Church," *Basileia,* Jan Hermelink and Hans J. Margull, eds. (Stuttgart: Evang. Missionsverlag G.M.B.H., 1959), p. 366. Used by permission.
8. He is now Provost of Southwark Cathedral, London.
9. From *The Parish Comes Alive,* by E. W. Southcott, published by A. R. Mowbray & Co., Ltd. p. 69. Used by permission.
10. *Ibid.,* p. 72, citing Dr. John Robinson, *Theology* (August 1950).
11. See *Journey Inward, Journey Outward* by Elizabeth O'Connor (New York: Harper & Row, Publishers, 1968) and *Call to Commitment* by the same author and publisher for an excellent description of the life and contribution of the Church of the Saviour.
12. Father Dan Brown, Chaplain Claremont Colleges, Claremont, Cali-

fornia, taped conversation quoting Father Gerard Sloyan, Chairman of the Religious Studies Department, Temple University, Philadelphia (March 1971). Used by permission.
13. Ritschl, Dietrich, *"Mini-Churches" with Special Foci—A Suggestion Concerning the Spirit's Polymorphic Self-Expression,* Occasional Papers from the Division of Evangelism, No. VII (Board of National Missions, The United Presbyterian Church in the United States of America).

BELONGING

1. From *The Church Inside Out,* by J. C. Hoekendijk, pp. 91–92. Published in the U.S.A. by The Westminster Press, 1966. Copyright © by J. C. Hoekendijk, 1964. English translation copyright © 1966, by W. L. Jenkins. Used by permission.
2. Roy W. Fairchild, *Christians in Families* (Richmond: The CLC Press, 1964), p. 69.
3. *Ibid.,* pp. 69–71.
4. "Why We Need a New Sexuality," George B. Leonard, *Look,* Vol. XXXIV (January 13, 1970), p. 54.
5. Mr. Virgil Vogt, Reba Place Fellowship, Evanston, Illinois, personal correspondence (November 1970). Used by permission.
6. "The Way of Love" (Evanston, Illinois: Reba Place Fellowship, 1966), p. 1. Used by permission.
7. *Ibid.,* pp. 1–2.
8. *Ibid.,* pp. 7–8.
9. Dr. Roy Fairchild, San Francisco Theological Seminary, San Anselmo, California, taped conversation (March 1971). Used by permission.

GROUNDING

1. From *On Being the Church in the World,* by John A. T. Robinson, p. 84. Published by the Westminster Press, 1962. Copyright © J. A. T. Robinson, 1960. Used by permission.
2. *Ibid.,* p. 85.
3. *Ibid.,* p. 87.
4. *Ibid.,* pp. 93–94.
5. *Ibid.,* p. 94.
6. "The Church in the House," Hans-Ruedi Weber, *Laity* 3, World Council of Churches (April 1957), p. 8. Used by permission.
7. *Ibid.,* p. 12.
8. *Ibid.*
9. *Ibid.,* p. 13.
10. "Small Congregations," Virgil Vogt, *Concern,* No. 5 (CONCERN Pamphlet Series, 721 Walnut Avenue, Scottdale, Pa. 15683, June 1958), pp. 55–56. Used by permission.
11. *Ibid.,* p. 59.

12. *Ibid.*
13. *Ibid.,* p. 60.
14. "The House Church in Scotland," T. Ralph Morton, *Frontier,* Vol. V (157 Waterloo Road, London, England; Annual subscription rate in the United States $6.50: Spring 1962), p. 342. Used by permission.
15. *Ibid.*
16. *Ibid.,* p. 343.
17. *Ibid.*
18. Hoekendijk, *op. cit.,* p. 92.
19. *Ibid.,* p. 95.
20. The Reverend Dick York, Pastor, Berkeley Free Church, Berkeley, California, taped conversation (March 1971). Used by permission.
21. *Ibid.*
22. "Berkeley Free Church" (Berkeley, California: Free Church Publications, n.d.). Used by permission.

REACHING

1. House churches at this period in the life of Trinity were identified by the name of the ruling elder placed in charge by the session.
2. An associate member category was created to enable persons wishing to join a house church but not the Trinity congregation to participate as members and not perpetually as visitors.
3. Used by permission of Miss Elizabeth O'Connor.
4. The Reverend Josh Wilson, taped conversation about the Franklin Lakes Presbyterian house church, Franklin Lakes, New Jersey (March 1971). Used by permission.
5. *Ibid.*
6. The Very Reverend E. W. Southcott, taped conversation, Atlanta, Georgia (November 1969). Used by permission.
7. *Ibid.*
8. Weber, *Laity, op. cit.,* p. 1.
9. *Ibid.,* p. 12.
10. "The Quest for Structures of Missionary Congregations," (WCC [World Council of Churches] Study on the Missionary Structure of the Congregation, *Study Encounter,* I), p. 31. Used by permission.
11. *Ibid.,* p. 29.
12. "The Congregation for Others," (WCC [World Council of Churches] Study on the Missionary Structure of the Congregation, *Study Encounter,* III), p. 101. Used by permission.
13. *Ibid.*
14. *Ibid.,* p. 105.

STRENGTHENING

1. From *Christian Education in Mission*, by Letty M. Russell. Copyright © MCMLXVII, The Westminster Press. Used by permission.

2. Lamplighting refers to the brief gathering of workers prior to each coffee house opening. It is a time for devotionals and assignments for the evening.
3. "We Can't Go Home Again," Rachel Henderlite, *Austin Seminary Bulletin*, Vol. LXXXII, No. 7 (April 1967), p. 12. Used by permission.
4. *Ibid.*, p. 13.
5. The Reverend Donald L. Griggs, personal correspondence. Used by permission.

CELEBRATING

1. The Reverend Pete Koopman, II, taped conversation, San Jose, California (March 1971). Used by permission.

ESTABLISHING

1. Harry G. Lefever, "The House Church in the Twentieth Century: A Study of Trinity Presbyterian Church, Harrisonburg, Va." (Atlanta: Board of National Ministries, Presbyterian Church in the United States, 1969). Used by permission.
2. Donald Metz, *New Congregations: Security and Mission in Conflict* (Philadelphia: The Westminster Press, 1967).
3. Lefever, *op. cit.*, pp. 60–62.
4. *Ibid.*, p. 63.
5. *Ibid.*, pp. 53–55.
6. "The Servants of Christ the King," Canon Roger Lloyd, *Laity* 3 (April 1957), p. 29.
7. Hoekendijk, *op. cit.*, p. 98.
8. Dr. Roland H. Bainton, Yale Divinity School (Baccalaureate Sermon, Union Theological Seminary, Richmond, Virginia [May 1970]). Used by permission.
9. From *The Church* by Hans Küng, p. 5. © Verlag Herder KG Freiburg im Breisgau 1967, English translation © Burns & Oates Ltd. 1967, published by Sheed and Ward, Inc., New York.
10. *Ibid.*, p. 13.
11. *Ibid.*, p. 26.
12. *Ibid.*, p. 32.
13. *Ibid.*, p. 33.
14. *Ibid.*, p. 52.
15. Professor Hans Küng, taped interview, recorded by Navy Chaplain Jude Senieur (Princeton Theological Seminary [Fall 1970]). Used by permission of Prof. Küng.
16. For further information see "Emmaus: A Venture in Community and Communication" by David Kirk, in *The Underground Church* edited by Malcolm Boyd, © Sheed and Ward, Inc. 1968. Used by permission.
17. *Ibid.*, p. 139.

18. *Ibid.*, p. 142.
19. "The Bread Is Rising," Francine du Plessix Gray, quoting Father Kirk, *The New Yorker*, Vol. XLIV (January 25, 1969), p. 56.

PROJECTING

1. T. Ralph Morton, *op. cit.*, p. 343.
2. Dr. John A. T. Robinson, personal correspondence (August 6, 1970). Used by permission.
3. A Committee Think Paper, Draft #2 (Synod of the Golden Gate, Experimental Ministries Executive Committee of Mission Strategy Council), p. 2.